Learning Through Life 2

Adult Learners, Education and Training

Learning Through Life

The other volume in this series is:

Culture and Processes of Adult Learning
Edited by Mary Thorpe, Richard Edwards and Ann Hanson

This reader is one of two that have been prepared as part of the Open University Undergraduate course, *Learning Through Life: Education and Training Beyond School*.

It is one part of an integrated teaching system and the selection is therefore related to other material available to students. It is designed to evoke the critical understanding of students. Opinions expressed in it are not necessarily those of the course team or of the University.

If you would like to study this course, please write to the Central Enquiry Service, PO Box 200, The Open University, Walton Hall, Milton Keynes, MK7 6YZ. A copy of *Studying with the Open University* is available from the same address.

Learning Through Life 2

Adult Learners, Education and Training

A Reader

Edited by
Richard Edwards, Sandy Sieminski and
David Zeldin

London and New York
in association with
The Open University

First published 1993
by Routledge
11 New Fetter Lane
London EC4P 4EE

Simultaneously published in the USA and Canada
by Routledge
29 West 35th Street, New York, NY 10001

Reprinted 1995

Phototypeset in 10/12pt Garamond by Intype, London
Printed in Great Britain by Mackays of Chatham PLC, Chatham, Kent

British Library Cataloguing in Publication Data
A catalogue reference for this book is available from the British Library

Library of Congress Cataloguing in Publication Data
A catalogue record for this book is available from the Library of Congress

ISBN 0-415-08982-4

Contents

Figures

Tables

Acknowledgements

For permission to reproduce the materials in this volume, acknowledge-
ment is due to the following sources: Chapter 1, 'Participation and non-
participation: a review of the literature', edited version of Section 1, in
McGivney, V. (1990) *Education's for Other People: Access to Education
for Non-participant Adults*, (reproduced with permission of the National
Institute of Adult Continuing Education (NIACE)), © NIACE; Chapter
2, 'Self-planned learning and major personal change', Tough, A. in Smith,
R. M. (ed.) (1976) *Adult Learning: Issues and Innovations*, Clearing House
in Career Education, Northern Illinois University, pp. 58–73; Chapter 3,
'Adult education policy in Sweden 1969–91' (edited version), Rubenson,
K. (1992) in *Policy Studies Review* on 'Adult Education Policy'; Chapter
5, 'Adult literacy and basic education in Europe and North America: from
recognition to provision', Limage, L. (1990) in *Comparative Education*,
vol. 26, no. 1 (reproduced with permission of Carfax Publishing Company); Chapter 7, 'Vocational training and new production concepts in
Germany: some lessons for Britain', Lane, C. (1990) in *Industrial Relations
Journal*, vol. 21, no. 4, pp. 247–59 (reproduced with permission of
Blackwell Publishers); Chapter 8, 'Skills mismatch and policy response'
(edited version), Haughton, G. (1990) in *Policy and Politics*, vol. 18 no. 4
(reproduced with permission of the School for Advanced Urban Studies
(SAUS), University of Bristol); Chapter 9, 'The changing role of the in-
company trainer; an analysis of British trainers in the European Community context' (edited version), Evans, K., Dovaston, V. and Holland,
D. (1990) in *Comparative Education*, vol. 26, no. 1, (reproduced with
permission of Carfax Publishing Company); Chapter 10, 'From new
vocationalism to the culture of enterprise' (edited version), Coles, B. and
MacDonald, R. F. (1990) in Wallace, C. and Cross, M. (eds) *Youth in
Transition, The Sociology of Youth and Youth Policy*, London, Falmer
Press; Chapter 11, 'The inevitable future?: Post-Fordism in work and
learning' (reworked version), Edwards, R. (1991) in *Open Learning*, vol.
6, no. 2 (reproduced with permission of the Longman Group, UK);
Chapter 12, 'Community education: towards a theoretical analysis' (edited

version), Martin, I. (1990) in Allen, G., Bastiani, J. and Martin, I. (eds) *Community Education: An Agenda for Educational Reform*, London, Routledge; Chapter 13, 'Adult education and community action', Lovett, T. (1980) in Thompson, J. (ed.) *Adult Education for a Change*, London, Hutchinson, pp. 155–73; Chapter 14, 'Dangerous knowledge: Canadian workers education in the decades of discord' (edited version), Welton, M. (1991) in *Studies in the Education of Adults*, vol. 25, no. 1, (reproduced with permission of the National Institute of Adult Continuing Education (NIACE)), © NIACE; Chapter 16, ' "Drinking from one pot": Yemeni unity at home and overseas', Searle, C. and Shaif, A. (1991) in *Race & Class*, vol. 32, no. 4, Summer (*Race & Class* is the journal of the Institute of Race Relations); Chapter 17, 'Adult education, community development and older people', Pilley, C. (1990) (edited extract of the report by the author, London, reproduced with permission of Cassell).

Introduction

*Richard Edwards, Sandy Sieminski and
David Zeldin*

The organization of learning opportunities for adults has become a major area of policy debate, and has led to a steady stream of books, articles and newspaper reports. In contributing to this stream, we have focused on three major areas of debate: the issue of who has access to what forms of learning; the relationship between education, training and the economy; and the role of community-based adult learning in changing power relations and improving quality of life. Other topics have been excluded, such as health education and leisure pursuits. This is not to devalue their importance; we simply do not have the space to encompass the full depth and breadth of opportunities for adult learners.

Participation, that is who engages in what forms of learning, is one of the central issues in the education and training of adults. While initial schooling is compulsory, encompassing everyone up to a certain age, adult learners are overwhelmingly voluntary learners, *choosing* to participate. Participation in education and training generally contributes to social mobility, providing a ladder of opportunity for some, a snake for others. If it is established that certain groups participate more readily than others in various forms of learning, this is a comment on the distribution of life opportunities within a social formation. Whether such patterns of participation and non-participation are due to the individuals concerned because they lack motivation (i.e. blaming the victim), the system (it selects and excludes people), or a combination of situational (e.g. lack of money), institutional (e.g. middle-class ethos) or dispositional (hostile attitudes towards education) barriers, there is an argument that social justice and equality of opportunity demand that measures are taken to enable all adults to have access to opportunities.

However, as McGivney and Tough make clear, the very notion of participation is deeply problematic. We first need to define the boundaries of the learning within which we are exploring participation. Is it participation in publicly funded, formal providers of education and training, e.g. colleges of further education, universities and adult education centres? Do we include participation in private education and training organizations, e.g. secretarial schools and correspondence colleges? What about learning undertaken in the workplace, the home, in the local community centre, or a leisure complex? The more we think about the arenas in which adults learn, the more problematic the notion of participation becomes. And if we shift the emphasis on to adult learning, as Tough does, and away from the formal and non-formal provision of learning opportunities, participation encompasses everyone engaging in a learning project of at least seven hours duration. Thus, conclusions about who and how many do or do not participate depends primarily on the area of learning, provided or unprovided, which is being examined.

The focus of most studies of participation and non-participation has been on the public, formal arena. These have demonstrated a general trend for participants in education and training to be younger, better educated and from higher-income groups. The higher our attainment in initial education, the more likely we are to continue to engage in education/training activities. This is true for studies from a wide range of countries and for different levels of education/training. The corollary is that non-participant groups tend to be older adults, particularly males, those with least initial education and from lower socio-economic backgrounds. Thus, questions of participation and non-participation are not simply educational issues; they are tied up with economic and social factors and policies. Thus, as Limage points out, lack of literacy – a fundamental area of education – is usually only part of a wide range of 'disadvantage' in a person's life.

This profile of participants and non-participants tends to be reproduced by social practices. In so far as more middle- and upper-income groups participate in education and training, the more likely it is that they will be seen as having a middle-class ethos, which in turn is most attractive to middle-class people. A particular culture is engendered, a culture of non-participation, in which forms of provision are perceived to be part of a middle-class culture. As McGivney notes, for working-class people and particularly males, such opportunities are perceived as 'not being for them'. So complex reasons of status, culture and power are tied up in the questions surrounding who do and do not participate in particular forms of learning opportunity.

These issues have become a focus for public policy in many countries, as the importance of adult learning to the changing needs of modern, complex social formations have demonstrated the inadequacies of relying on initial education as sufficient for the rest of our lives. Non-participation systematically 'disadvantages' certain groups and has an impact on the economy, politics and culture of nations. This has become particularly apparent in the period of rapid economic and social change from the late 1970s.

However, the bases for policy discussion and initiatives can vary. The provision of learning opportunities can be developed as an instrument of social policy, part of an attempt to provide greater equality of living standards. It can also be an instrument to facilitate economic and technological change, to service the needs of the economy. Both provide the basis for a greater range of opportunities to learn being made available to adults. However, as Rubenson charts in his discussion of adult education policy and practice in Sweden, the different bases give rise to differing forms of provision. In the 1970s, Sweden invested heavily in selective measures to provide opportunities for previous non-participants to gain access to education and training. Adults with under nine years initial education were targeted, outreach activities were funded. There was an attempt to widen as well as increase access as part of an overall thrust towards the democratization of Swedish social life. However, as the economic situation deteriorated, there was a shift towards providing opportunities relevant to economic and technological change and a move away from the funding of selective measures.

Similar debates over access to education and training have been experienced in the UK. Creating opportunities for more adults to participate in education and training has been part of policy debate since the early 1980s. Not just more, but also different. In other words, access should be widened as well as increased to include those groups who have not previously engaged in formal learning. However, as Tight argues, much of the focus of the access debate and practice has tended to be on higher education and the provision of Access courses for people without the formal entry requirements to gain entry to degree courses. While valuable in themselves, Tight believes the radical agenda of those who argue for wider access has been undermined and that there has been a debasement of the concept. In other words, as the notion of access for adults has gained greater acceptance, with consequent government attention and funding, it has been narrowed to focus on a particular sector of education, higher education, and a particular type of provision, Access courses. The broad vision of access is, therefore, being lost.

A lot of this may have to do with the increasing focus on education and training as primarily or solely a servicer of the economy. As its role in relation to democracy, citizenship, personal development and culture has been marginalized, it is those areas which service the economy which have been emphasized and funded. This has resulted in the redefining of certain areas of learning. For example, in the area of literacy, Limage argues that it is a human right fundamental to democratic social formations. More recent tendencies to construct literacy as a set of skills necessary for employment makes it susceptible to cuts in funding if the economic imperative disappears, if literacy is shown not to be necessary for economic competitiveness.

As lack of initial education is a prime factor in non-participation, the need to provide for literacy among adults is basic to any attempt to provide access to learning opportunities for people across the socio-economic spectrum. However, whether provision, argued for solely on economic grounds, can result in that goal being achieved is open to question.

However, it is economic and training policy which has been the focus of most debate in recent years. The assumption is that advanced economies require highly educated and trained populations, and skilled and flexible work-forces. The debate is how to develop and maintain relevant and productive education and training systems. In the UK the urgency of this debate has been exacerbated by a balance of payment crisis, a falling share of world exports of manufactures, and an inability to sustain rates of economic growth equal to those of its European competitors, Germany, France and Italy.

Training, like participation, cannot be disassociated from its wider social and economic context, or institutional frameworks. It is closely linked to history, tradition, industrial and commercial development, the nature of product markets, managerial structures and education, labour markets, industrial relations and shop-floor organization. The development of the education and training systems is largely dependent on technological developments and the economic and political interests of dominant interest groups. Advanced technologies are readily available and can be used anywhere in the world. Hence the importance of an educated and trained work-force, to attract investment in high technology industries, although, as Edwards suggests, high-skilled secure employment may only be the experience of the minority in the future. We therefore need to be cautious about the calls for creating a highly skilled, flexible work-force and to examine what that means in practice.

In the UK, for more than a century there has been growing criticism of the education and training systems. First, the class bias and the inherent ethnic and gender discrimination within the systems have been challenged. Second, the weaknesses and shortcomings of the systems relative to that of its main competitors have been exposed. For example, staying-on rates in full-time education and training, school leavers' highest qualifications, the proportion of trained workers and managers in the work-force, and the provision of continuing training on and off the job are all behind that of the UK's main competitors, Germany, France, the USA and Japan.

In an overview of the UK's training policy, Keep uses international comparisons to detail the way in which its training performance is weak and the pace of change relatively slow. He highlights the widening gap to be bridged. Politicians of all parties accept the need for improvement in the UK's skills base, but profoundly disagree about the means of effecting improvement. Keep explores government efforts to change Vocational Education and Training (VET) policies and structures. Since 1979, the government has adopted a distinctive diagnosis of the situation and radically changed its approach to the development of VET. The government view was that the absence of a 'free' market created 'unnatural' obstacles and mitigated against the development of a relevant VET system. The proposed solution was simple and self-evident: the creation of a 'free' market in which VET would be employer-led and employer-controlled. Keep analyses the gradual way in which government turned its beliefs into implemented policies. The emerging system is one of central control, centrally formulated objectives, including standardized vocational qualifications (National Vocational Qualifications/Scottish Vocational Qualifications – NVQ/SVQs), and local delivery; a system where government is rapidly disengaging itself from responsibility for training provision and progressively reducing its financial support. Keep examines the emerging problems of the VET system – for example, short-termism and *ad hoc* methods of policy-making – and the shortcomings of a voluntarist approach where Conservative governments rely on exhortation and employers' self-interests rather than mandatory legislation.

By contrast, the German system of VET illustrates the generative effects of legislation and government regulation. But the German example also shows the support of societal institutions and culture in the development of innovative policies: the need to go with the grain. Lane discusses the effectiveness of vocational training in Germany and explains how the culture has steered managements into increasing investment in human resource development. She draws some formidable suggestions for UK governments, employers and trade unions.

However, barriers to employment innovation and economic growth are not only to do with education and training, industrial relations (perceived as trade union restrictive practices and strikes), and pay (perceived as high wages for young people and excessive demands for increased pay). Also important are social barriers to labour supply (for example, women re-entering the labour market) and 'imperfections' in labour demands (for example, employer stigmatization of workers by age, address, race, nationality and ethnic background). Haughton explores how these social factors have exacerbated skills shortages and skills mismatch in the UK. He argues for a shift from old attitudes of 'training for life' to one of 'training for change'. There is also a need for better training for quality and quantity, and an urgent need to broaden opportunity and access of talent into education and work from all social classes. Haughton questions whether training can be improved sufficiently without major legislation which also tackles social and racial discrimination.

The increased responsibilities of employers for training have focused attention on the changing role of in-company trainers. Evans and her associates report the efforts of industry to improve their training provision. More companies are seeing training as part of their human resource development and business planning. Evans *et al.* note an increasing role for first line supervisors, an increase in team or group learning, and the integration of in-company training and trainers within management strategies of the firm. Their conclusions include a demand for greater recognition of the needs of trainers, and for the development of practical means of providing trainers with pedagogical skills, including the improvement of their abilities to relate with learners.

High youth unemployment in the early 1980s resulted in an enormous expansion of youth training. Within this area there has been a dramatic shift from 'vocationalism for some' to 'enterprise for all'. Coles and MacDonald explore the assumptions and meanings that underpin the ideologies of the 'new vocationalism' and the 'enterprise culture'. They trace the effects of introducing them into the development of the Youth Training industry and increasingly in Higher Education institutions.

As we said earlier, not all learning is for economic purposes. 'Disadvantaged' communities, members of minority ethnic groups, workers' and women's organizations have often drawn upon forms of adult learning opportunity in attempts to enhance or transform the quality of life. Adult education has played an important role in enabling and shaping the understanding, aspirations and strategies that oppressed groups have pursued. In this respect an understanding of the ideological assumptions that underpin certain forms of community and popular education is crucial.

However, as Martin points out, no clear definition of community education exists. He identifies three major strands within the world of community education: 'universal', 'reformist', and 'radical'. It is unlikely that community educators will operate within the confines of any one of these 'ideal types'. In reality they are likely to adopt elements from different categories, which is consistent with the view that community education is about 'breaking down barriers' between learning and living, and must therefore remain relevant to people's experiences. To be able to achieve this, he argues, community educators must continually redefine and reconstruct the concept to reflect the changing reality of people's lives.

By contrast Lovett highlights two approaches to community education. First he describes a community development strategy, which creates social and economic institutions at a local level. Second, a community action strategy, which offers educational support to emerging social movements to help people effectively campaign to alter existing political and economic structures fundamentally. The two are not necessarily mutually exclusive, although the economic and political goals of the community action strategy may come into conflict with the interests of the state, local and national, which may support the goals of community development.

Lovett discusses how the strategy adopted by adult educators in Belfast, Northern Ireland, who are working with a divided community, has been influenced by their reflecting on the work of those who have adopted community development and community action approaches elsewhere, particularly in North America. He outlines the work undertaken to assist in the creation of a radical and social movement which will eradicate narrow republican and unionist stereotypes. The role of adult education in this development is to encourage a dialogue and analysis that is not only about community development, but which also focuses on wider social and political problems. Lovett believes that the creation of new relationships and new structures at a local level provides the community with a vision of what a new society might look like.

Other examples of community-based adult learning are offered by Pilley, Searle and Shaif. Pilley's case studies illustrate how the resources of adult education, combined with those of other agencies, have assisted older people in becoming agents of change. People have been able to improve their situation whilst making a contribution to the community at large. For example, he describes the Glasgow Pensioners Action Group in Scotland, which operates in a 'deprived' inner-city area. In this instance, community-based education was used to enable older people to acquire the necessary skills and knowledge to become competent committee members and assist them in organizing effective campaigns. The benefits derived from these efforts have been both social and personal. The group succeeded in obtaining urban aid for an advice and action centre for pensioners and, participants experienced a growth in self-confidence.

The basis for community development among the Yemeni community in Sheffield was provided by an Arabic literacy programme. Members of the community wanted to organize themselves to learn about the revolutions taking place in the north and south of their homeland. As they engaged in discussions and debate about the situation in Yemen a new confidence and consciousness was formed. In his interview with Searle, Shaif describes how the younger generation was able to reflect on the plight of their parents. They discussed and analysed the needs of the community and developed strategies to achieve the goals identified. Generally people felt more able to formulate responses to the difficulties that the community faced in relation to racism, redundancy and industrial injury.

Groups may form to improve the quality of life of their members and this may also result in attempts to change the power relations of a social formation. In the early part of the twentieth century, projects, such as the People's Forum in Canada, were critical of the effects of industrialization on the lives of working-class people and advocated community action strategies and increased political involvement. Welton describes how the Winnipeg Trades and Labour Council and other organizations provided opportunities for workers to reflect on their conditions which encouraged them to challenge the existing power relations in the social formation. Such organizations held that education was essential to the process of change and that socialism would arrive through voluntary action that derived from clear, methodical, rational argument. However, the defeat of the general strike in 1919 and the jailing of labour leaders resulted in one important lesson for the disillusioned Canadian workers: they learnt how dangerous their newly found knowledge was.

When one looks at the ways that the term 'community education' is used, it is apparent that there is a general consensus that it is a 'good' thing for educators to engage in and that it 'benefits' the communities. However, Welton argues that particular discursive practices regarding authentic adult educational practice are intimately connected with social power and control. To support this claim he identifies the ideological assumptions informing the approach adopted by academics and intellectuals responsible for the establishment of university extension and the Workers' Education Association (WEA) in Canada. The crisis in education in the early twentieth century reflected class polarization within Canadian society. This was manifest in the presence of two languages; the untutored and rebellious language of the street, and the cultivated legitimate language espoused by intellectuals. The task was one of promoting national unity by extending higher culture to the lower classes in order to create more like-minded people. Welton argues that it was one of the aims of university extension to curb the spread of working-class radicalism. Consequentially, it can be said that the educators' role in this instance was one of quelling insurrection rather than encouraging and participating in it. Similar arguments can be made of the university extra-mural practices and the WEA in the UK.

This may put too great an emphasis on the role of educators as outside agents of socialization and social control. Deem points out that even though self-organized women's popular education is based on the experiences, problems and social positions of the women involved, such education does not necessarily lead to the formation of oppositional or feminist groups. She shows how some of the groups she observed were able to challenge some aspects of their role, for instance, by asserting the right to an independent social life in civil society outside of the home. However, they may not always challenge gender stereotyping or indirect discrimination. There may thus be a graduation of scales of change engendered by community-based adult learning, and that it is not simply dependent on educators/trainers asserting control over the learning that does take place.

The range of learning opportunities organized by and for adult learners is therefore large and diverse, the aims and outcomes of which may be personal, social, economic, or political. In the following chapters you will encounter at least some of that diversity and the debates and issues which are integral to the field of adult learners, education and training. We hope you enjoy it.

Part I

Participation, non-participation and access

Chapter 1

Participation and non-participation
A review of the literature

Veronica McGivney

Source: Edited version of Section 1 in V. McGivney, *Education's for Other People: Access to Education for Non-participant Adults*, Leicester, NIACE, 1990.

Research on participation and non-participation has been prolific, particularly in the United States. However, participation is a complex field of enquiry and it is worth signalling from the outset some of the misgivings that have been expressed about this kind of research. First, the sheer size, diversity and complexity of post-school education makes the concept of participation impossible to pin down:

> The concept of participation may be a different species for different strata of society . . . 'Adequate' or 'successful' participation is a chameleon set aginst a background of quick-changing groups, courses, centres, areas and times. Lack of participation is an equally elusive reptile flitting across the same institutional neon.
>
> (Courtney 1981: 104–5)

Second, in view of the diversity and complexity of human beings and their circumstances, there is no single theory that can satisfactorily explain participation or non-participation:

> We are presented with a set of partial and overlapping existing explanations in which the different approaches each offer plausible suggestions for lines of enquiry – in effect they are investigative pointers rather than testable propositions.
>
> (Usher and Bryant 1989: 106)

For the purposes of this chapter, however, some of the main findings of existing research have been taken on trust in order to provide a general starting point.

WHO ARE THE PARTICIPANTS?

[. . .] Participation surveys inevitably vary enormously in methods and terms of reference. The definition of 'adult' can vary from anyone aged

17 or over to anyone aged over 20, and estimates of adult student numbers fluctuate widely, according to whether learning activities are defined as all voluntary learning efforts or institutionally-based activites and courses taken part-time. This divergence suggests that survey results should be treated with caution. Nevertheless, there is enough consistency in research findings to take them as a reasonably reliable guide. In Britain, for example, most of the larger-scale surveys suggest that, discounting school-leavers who go straight into further or higher education, adult participation in organised education usually lies somewhere between 10 per cent and 15 per cent at any given time, although this figure would be much higher – over 40 per cent – if *any* participation since leaving school is taken into account. A Further Education Unit (FEU) survey of participation in adult and continuing education in three different English locations suggested that 14 per cent of adults were currently participating and 32 per cent had done so at some time in the past (FEU 1987). Research in Scotland (1988) came up with a higher figure: approximately 42 per cent of a sample of 2000 had returned at least once after leaving school to organized education, defined here as courses or systematic programmes of learning lasting for seven hours or more within a three-month period (Munn and MacDonald 1988).

Participant typologies

'Mature students do not represent a cross-section of the adult population . . . adult education is largely the preserve of the middle classes' (Woodley *et al.* 1987: 85). This conclusion, based on the results of a survey of mature students attending qualifying and non-qualifying courses in England and Wales, confirms the findings of virtually all British national and regional surveys in the last 20 years. The 1970 National Institute of Adult Education study *Adequacy of Provision* showed that while the non-vocational adult education service had expanded, it had chiefly benefited younger, better-educated and higher-income groups. A decade later the ACACE survey showed little change:

> All the indications show that those with the longest initial education, those who are in the higher social classes, the young, men, and those seeking vocational education are consistently better able to take advantage of the existing opportunities for continuing education.
>
> (ACACE 1982: 58)

The 1987 FEU survey, also found participation skewed towards the young, higher social grades, owner-occupiers and those with access to a car, while the Munn and MacDonald survey in Scotland (1988) reported that adult 'returners' – people over 20 who had been out of full-time education for at least two years – were predominantly in socio-economic groups A and B. Unsurprisingly, an investigation into use of education information, advice and guidance services also found that people seeking advice and guidance about education, training or jobs were more likely to be young, male, from the higher socio-economic groups and in possession of some educational qualifications (Alloway and Nelson 1987). Smaller local surveys confirm this general picture.

Thus, despite their diversity, studies of participation in the UK reveal a striking consistency in the composite picture they yield of the typical participant body:

> The empirical evidence . . . consistently shows that adult education of all kinds recruits disproportionately from certain parts of the adult population: those of working age rather than the retired; those in non-manual rather than manual occupations; and those with more than minimal previous educational success.
>
> (Woodley *et al.* 1987: 5)

This phenomenon is not confined to the UK. Similar findings have been reported in OECD countries. [. . .] Moreover, the general profile of adult participants appears to be consistent across all levels of education. [. . .] Thus, in spite of developments such as comprehensive schools and polytechnics and repeated calls for improved access, inequalities in access to post-school education have not been eliminated.

It has been observed that, even in lower occupational groups, the same general characteristics distinguish participants from non-participants. This became evident in a French study of participation in targeted programmes in several mining communitites (Hedoux 1982). Confirming the findings of other French researchers, this enquiry demonstrated that participation in education within working-class groups is governed by exactly the same sociological factors that create inequalities in access between different classes and social levels. Jacques Hedoux, the author of the study, discovered that participants in the programmes comprised an 'active social minority' characterized by certain favourable attributes, namely: *good material circumstances* (higher income and occupational levels); *greater mobility* (ability to anticipate and instigate social change); *cultural familiarity* (higher level of schooling, extended social relationships and cultural practices).

Involvement in social, community and cultural activities

Hedoux observed that educational participation was strongly connected with the extent of an individual's integration into community life. Participants were generally leading a more diverse and intense social life than non-participants, and tended to be more involved in voluntary groups, political parties, unions, churches, and local cultural activities. In consequence they had more contact with key local figures (*notables*), such as teachers, religious leaders, council members and people in management positions.

He found that whereas participants and non-participants engaged equally in *mass culture* (newspapers, TV, holidays), participants and their families were significantly more engaged in cultural practices such as reading, and visiting cinemas, theatres, museums and exhibitions. For Hedoux this implied 'a dynamic of cultural development within families which reinforces the positive thrust towards education'. He concluded that participation in adult education arises from 'particularly tenacious social differentiations' and that voluntary participation in education in itself constitutes a strong discriminating variable in the working-class population. [. . .]

WHO ARE THE NON-PARTICIPANTS?

There are substantial numbers of people who have been defined as failures by the schooling system and who remain outside the world of adult education. The lower you go down the social hierarchy, the more there are.

(West 1987)

The ACACE national survey of 1982 estimated that 51 per cent of the adult population of England and Wales had not engaged in any kind of education or training since leaving school. The survey in Scotland (Munn and MacDonald 1988) found a slightly higher proportion – 58 per cent of the sample population – to be non-participants. An OECD conference report referred to non-participation as an international phenomenon: 'Irrespective of their political ideologies, technologically advanced and industrially backward countries alike testified at the Tokyo conference that the overwhelming majority of their populations were not participating in adult education' (OECD 1977).

Major characteristics

The characteristics that distinguish non-participants from participants are age, educational background, and socio-economic status.

Age

Older adults are less likely to participate than younger ones and most available research shows a fall-off at retirement age, particularly among men.

Educational background

Non-participation in education in adult life is closely linked with initial educational experience. Virtually all the British and non-British survey reports consulted for this chapter show that people who do not participate in any form of continuing education or training tend to be those with the least initial education. The ACACE national survey revealed that the majority of non-participants had left school at the minimum leaving age; in the 1988 Scottish survey, 80 per cent of non-returners had left school at age 16 or under.

Socio-economic status

Socio-economic status (which is often linked with experience of and atti- tudes to initial schooling) also contributes significantly to non-partici- pation. One of the 'most persistent' findings of a large-scale survey in the USA was 'the great disparity in involvement in continuing education of segments of the population situated at different levels of the social hier- archy' (Johnstone and Rivera 1965: 231). An OECD report referred to the striking under-representation of unskilled manual workers in learning activities in the USA, Denmark, France, Italy, The Netherlands, Spain and the UK (OECD 1979). In England and Wales, the low proportion of participants from working-class backgrounds and occupations in all levels of post-compulsory education frequently arouses comment. A study of post-initial education in the north-west of England (Percy 1983) found that only 18 per cent of participants were working class, and a wider national survey (Woodley *et al.* 1987) concluded that working-class people, particularly women, are 'massively under-represented' throughout post- school education. The close relationship between occupational status and participation is stressed in the Woodley survey, in the findings of the American researchers, Anderson and Darkenwald (1979), and in the work of de Montlibert (1973), whose study of paid educational leave in France highlights glaring disparities in access between different occupational groups.

Non-participant groups

Cumulatively, the evidence implies that irrespective of location or edu- cational setting, certain sections of the community tend not to engage in any form of educational activity after leaving school – older adults; less well-educated people in lower social, economic and occupational strata; women with dependent children; ethnic minority groups; and people living in rural areas. These groups, which were singled out in the large American survey in the 1960s (Johnstone and Rivera 1965) have remained virtually unchanged in two succeeding decades. The 1977 OECD report, for example, identified the following non-participant typologies:

- unemployed young adults (especially premature school leavers);
- some rural populations;
- immigrants;
- the aged;
- urban poverty groups;
- unemployed and underemployed workers with little education;
- unskilled and semi-skilled workers;
- some groups of women (housebound mothers, women from lower socio-economic groups);
- people with linguistic problems.

Taken together, these groups add up to a large majority, whose main characteristic, according to the OECD report, is social and economic deprivation. There is a certain amount of crossover betwen groups: the least educated are often unemployed or in unskilled occupations and have low incomes; people on the lowest incomes are likely to be found among the elderly, immigrant groups and women. However, each of the categories listed is a large and heterogeneous section of society and each contains many sub-groups, some of which are more likely than others to engage in voluntary learning.

Non-participant categories vary according to different geographical, demographic and cultural situations. In the US, research shows that women, especially young mothers, are particularly educationally disadvantaged. In France, a survey of participation in specially targeted programmes in mining communities revealed two sets of non-participants: a group mixed in age and gender who knew about the programmes and were favourably disposed to them but still chose not to participate, and a hard core of non-participants (*radical non-public*) made up of unwaged married women, older adults, non-qualified manual workers and people on the lowest incomes who claimed to have absolutely no knowledge of the programmes, even after ten years of intensive and widespread publicity (Hedoux 1981, 1982). In the Republic of Ireland, rural dwellers are likely to be non-participants, while in England and Wales, several groups have been identified as persistently under-represented in post-school education: ethnic minorities, women, physically and mentally handicapped adults, manual workers, and the elderly.

[. . .]

WHAT ARE THE REASONS FOR NON-PARTICIPATION?

Lack of information

A common finding in participation research is that non-participants have little or no knowledge of the educational opportunities available. A British review of research into disadvantaged adult groups (Osborn *et al.* 1980) estimated that up to two-thirds of non-participants simply did not know what learning opportunities exist. A reason for this was suggested by Hedoux (1981). He observed that the most striking feature separating the *radical non-public* from participants in the targeted learning programme *Action Collective de Formation* was their general lack of involvement in communal life. This led him to infer a probable link between social and communal involvement and people's knowledge of educational opportunities. People involved in social and cultural activities are in information networks, and are therefore more likely to be aware of existing educational opportunities. However, there is little evidence that simply knowing what is on offer leads to participation. The research carried out by Hedoux identified a second population of non-participants: people who knew about the targeted learning scheme and were favourably disposed towards it but still failed to participate. It is clear, then, that while a positive image of a learning programme and all the necessary information to enrol are essential prerequisites of participation, by themselves they are not sufficient to bring about enrolment.

The reasons for participation and non-participation are numerous, complex and much debated. [...] In her synthesis of American research, Cross (1981) divided deterrents to participation into three categories – situational, institutional and dispositional. Although they have been described as oversimplified, these categories provide a useful starting point for considering the problem of non-participation.

Situational barriers

Time

The obstacle most frequently mentioned by adults in American and British surveys is lack of time for participation in education, a constraint arising from family responsibilities and work schedules, with people working part-time or shift work at unsociable hours reporting the most difficulties. None the less, most research findings show that the majority of participants in part-time education programmes are in paid employment, and people without job-related obligations are less likely to take advantage of learning opportunities. Thus an increase in leisure time does not necessarily lead to a boom for adult education. A time budget study in the US revealed that a general increase in leisure hours was almost entirely absorbed by increased television viewing, mostly for non-educational purposes (Ruben-son 1986: 30).

Costs

A comparison of stated deterrents in Great Britain and the US (Darken-wald 1988) revealed that the financial costs of participation were rated of low importance by the American sample, but considered a significant deterrent by British respondents: a difference which undoubtedly reflects the income gap between the two populations. The ACACE survey (1982) found that cost was a major perceived barrier by both men and women, and there is some evidence that economic factors have had a negative impact on wider participation in Great Britain. National reports described how increased participation in adult education by people from the lower socio-economic groups was abruptly reversed as a result of 'frequent and steep' fee increases in the second half of the 1970s. Local surveys have confirmed this effect. One conducted in south-east Derbyshire revealed that sharp fee increases resulted in a 28 per cent fall in enrolments among those with relatively less disposable incomes (Daines *et al*. 1982). [...] However, while there is no doubt that increased fee levels affect the most economically disadvantaged groups, the evidence overall is inconclusive and contradictory. [...] Information received from local education authority (LEA) providers collectively suggests that costs may be less of a barrier than is generally supposed, although groups such as the elderly, those receiving Social Security benefits, and the unemployed clearly require some financial concessions or assistance. It has frequently been found that non-participants who cite expense as an obstacle have little idea of the actual cost of learning activities. This has led some researchers to suspect that cost, like lack of time, may serve as a socially acceptable or face-saving reason for not participating, camouflaging more complex and possibly unrecognized reasons.

Institutional barriers: the unresponsive system

One of the principal reasons for non-participation is the education system itself. The middle-class character of adult education is a well-documented, international phenomenon. Mee and Wiltshire (1978) estimated that only 5 per cent of education provision for adults was targeted at educationally or socially disadvantaged groups. Over a decade later, although there have been a variety of targeted initiatives supported by special funding, locally organized LEA, Workers Education Association (WEA) or university pro-grammes for adults have retained a strong middle-class ethos. [...]

Imbalances in the nature of participation are even more evident in the other post-school sectors. Further and higher education institutions have traditionally catered for a young, white, middle-class and predominantly male section of the population. 'Non-traditional' students who do succeed in gaining entry to such institutions often experience a range of problems. O'Shea and Corrigan (1979: 229) have given a graphic description of the tremendous cultural conflicts experienced by adults from working-class backgrounds who enrol in higher education. Moreover, there is widespread evidence that ethnic minority individuals feel even more alienated in white, middle-class learning environments where the curriculum, in some subject areas, is essentially ethnocentric (see Jones 1988). Until relatively recently, the system has done little to support non-traditional students in further and higher education. [. . .]

Paid educational leave (PEL) completes the picture of middle-class dominance. Traditionally, this has mainly benefited higher-status workers, and men in particular. Even when such opportunities are increased, the evidence in most industrial countries suggests that the chief beneficiaries are people in more advantaged circumstances. In France it was observed that the workers who took most advantage of the new opportunities offered by the 1971 law on PEL were those with most qualifications and 'cultural capital'. Indeed, de Montlibert (1973) asserts that increased PEL in France strengthened previously established inequalities and reinforced the gaps between participants and non-participants. This process is well documented and has been described as 'the phenomenon of second creaming: an increase in services principally benefits those who just failed to profit from what already existed, leaving others relatively worse off' (Schuller 1978: 25). But why is this the case?

O'Shea and Corrigan (1979) maintain that other groups hold back not because of low motivation, but because of powerful constraints arising from cultural and social class divisions. Many educationists and researchers have observed that adult participation in education is the continuation of a process which starts at school. School creates (or reinforces) sharp divisions in society, by conditioning children to accept different expectations and status patterns according to their academic 'success' or 'failure'. Through the use of imposed standards and selection, the education system traditionally rejects or excludes large numbers of the population, many of whom subsequently consider themselves as educational failures. To a significant degree, post-school education perpetuates the values and status patterns embedded in the school system. Many further and higher education institutions still retain the ethos and procedures of the compulsory school system, with people being ranked or excluded according to their ability to reach imposed sets of standards. Thus, post-school education can all too easily reinforce inequalities that commenced early in childhood. It is not surprising, therefore, that amid all the identified reasons for non-participation, one factor consistently stands out. People who have ostensibly 'failed' in the school system do not wish to repeat that failure. Many are consequently suspicious of education in any form, even informal learning opportunties specifically designed for them.

De Montlibert (1973) has described how a new centre offering educational opportunities to redundant steel workers in Lorraine attracted only ten enrolments. The same thing happened in the Vosges region when a textile factory was due to be closed. Enquiries revealed that the concept of education was perceived as totally alien and irrelevent by the workers threatened with redundancy: ' "Culture isn't for us", said one worker, to the approval of all his colleagues'. De Montlibert interpreted this reaction as a 'quasi-political revolt' against a situation of which people saw themselves as victims. However, it could also be viewed as a gesture of class solidarity. The process of 'social stratification' achieved, cumulatively, through the influences of family background, school and work, results in education becoming part of the value system of some groups but not of others. The importance of peer or reference groups in shaping behaviour and attitudes cannot be overestimated. It has been observed that whereas professional, white-collar workers tend to be influenced by a much wider network than just their co-workers, manual workers form very strong peer pressure groups which have a determining influence on norms and behaviour. This is strongly borne out in the French research. The French steel worker who dismissed learning was expressing a consensus view of a group whose normal behaviour patterns exclude voluntary participation in education. Similar reactions have been encountered in the UK by people initiating work with unemployed men. [. . .] There is substantial evidence that many people from working-class communities are acutely conscious of the fact that attending classes renders them conspicuous and an oddity among their neighbours. Some face hostility and lack of support from spouses, relatives and friends, many of whom perceive their participation as a kind of class betrayal. Hostility or disapproval can be particularly strong if participation is seen to threaten accepted gender roles:

> It is not uncommon to find friends and co-workers who want the learner to remain in the fold . . . there are spouses who fear their mate's educational endeavours will affect the relationship and family members who are concerned that household responsibilities will be traded-off against school obligations.
>
> (Lewis 1988)

It could be argued, therefore, that certain sections of the community do not readily participate in education or training partly because of constraints arising from their personal circumstances, but primarily because voluntary learning is perceived to be part of the culture pattern of higher socio-economic groups. Middle-class dominance in education is a difficult circle to break: members of higher socio-economic groups tend to live and work in environments where they have more scope for influencing their situation than those in lower income groups; where they have access to education or training opportunities; and where there is a positive orientation to education. They often come from families in which education was valued, have themselves been 'successful' in educational terms and have consequently passed on positive attitudes to education to their own children.

Dispositional barriers

As this suggests, reluctance to engage in education may have more to do with attitudes, perceptions and expectations than with any practical barriers. [...] This problem may have been underestimated, partly because research instruments tend to have a bias towards situational and institutional barriers; partly because respondents may not recognize, or wish to admit to, negative feelings towards education. Nevertheless, a number of studies confirm that attitudes and perceptions play a significant role in non-participation. Notably, these include perceptions of inappropriateness and lack of relevance; no awareness of learning needs; hostility towards school; the belief that one is too old to learn; and lack of confidence in one's ability to learn. These have all been repeatedly identified as major reasons for non-participation, particularly among older adults, people of low educational attainment and those on low incomes. In Britain, it is indisputable that a large proportion of the adult population considers education as totally irrelevant: 'for those who believe that education ends with school and real life begins with work the whole concept of adult learning is novel' (McDonald 1984). [...]

Primary and secondary data reveal that a disturbingly large proportion of the public has a stereotyped view of learning dating from school experience. Many believe that all forms of post-compulsory education are formal, inflexible and examination-oriented, and that participants will be judged on their ability to meet certain standards. This perception undoubtedly has a powerful deterrent effect. [...]

Misconceptions exist on both sides. There is evidence that some teaching staff, particularly in further and higher education institutions, have stereotyped views of mature learners, particularly groups such as the elderly, ethnic minorities and women. There is little doubt that the inaccurate view of education held by many members of the public and the inaccurate view of adult learners held by many teaching staff have contributed to keeping education and the majority of adults rigorously apart.

Another powerful psychological barrier has been identified by Hedoux (1981): perceptions of powerlessness linked with the lack of a future perspective. Hedoux argues that decisions to participate in education and training are intimately connected with a person's ability to control his/her own life and anticipate the future. Among the groups he identified as 'radical' non-participants, this ability is blocked, particularly in the case of elderly people and married women whose autonomy and freedom of movement are severely constrained by their partners.

The evidence as a whole, therefore, suggests that dispositional factors – attitudes, perceptions, expectations – constitute perhaps the most powerful deterrents to participation among the groups investigated. When these are added to the numerous practical obstacles that prevent individuals from taking up educational opportunities – lack of time, money, transport, day-time facilities, and childcare – the immense difficulties faced by providers wishing to recruit non-participant sections of the community can be appreciated.

There are, then, multiple obstacles which prevent large sections of the public from seeking or taking up educational opportunities, and there is now a strong consensus that non-participation results from the combination and interaction of diverse factors, rather than one or two obstacles which would be relatively easy to overcome (Darkenwald and Valentine 1985, Scanlan 1986, Hedoux 1982). [...]

MOTIVATIONS

Why do people participate?

Much of the emphasis in participation research has been on what motivates people to learn. [...]

Research into motivation has often involved 'factor analysis' – subdividing a number of item responses or variables into meaningful categories – and 'cluster analysis' – grouping respondents into mutually exclusive clusters according to similarity. One of the pioneers of motivation research was Houle, who identified three categories of adult learner: goal-oriented (to fulfil conscious objectives); learning-oriented (pursuing knowledge for the love of it); and activity-oriented (participation for reasons unconnected to programme purpose or content). Despite a view that researchers have 'clung perhaps a bit too lovingly to Houle's shirt-tails' (Cookson 1987), later studies have found these categories – particularly the first and second – to be generally accurate. A number of American researchers have categorized stated motives for voluntary learning and come up with largely similar clusters (see Table 1.1). These show that, although factor analysis has its critics, there is a certain consistency in survey findings.

Instrumental and expressive motives

Beder and Valentine (1987) distinguish between the extrinsic (such as job advancement) and intrinsic (self-improvement) benefits of participation; Percy (1988) adds a third dimension – social/affiliative. He points out that

Table 1.1 Stated motives for participation in organized adult education

Desire for knowledge
(Johnstone and Rivera 1965, Sheffield 1962, Morstain and Smart 1974,
Ghazzali 1979, Beder and Valentine 1987*)
To meet personal/self-development goals
(Johnstone and Rivera; Sheffield; Ghazzali; Beder and Valentine)
To meet occupational goals
(Johnstone and Rivera; Morstain and Smart; Beder and Valentine)
To meet social/community goals
(Sheffield; Morstain and Smart; Ghazzali; Beder and Valentine)
To comply with external expectations/formal requirements/urging of others
(Morstain and Smart; Ghazzali; Beder and Valentine)
To find activity, escape, diversion, stimulation
(Sheffield; Morstain and Smart; Ghazzali; Beder and Valentine)
To meet economic need
(Beder and Valentine)
To fulfil needs to do with religion or church
(Morstain and Smart; Beder and Valentine)
To fulfil family responsibilities
(Beder and Valentine)
'Launching'/role development
(Beder and Valentine)

Note: *The Beder and Valentine study was of basic education students.

although motives for participation are often a mixture of the three categories, explicitly educational motives are rarely cited as the reason for attending learning activities in voluntary organizations: people engage in voluntary organizations for other than educational reasons and perceive their activities as 'doing' rather than learning.

In most British and North American surveys, the majority of respondents have given instrumental (extrinsic) motives for participation in organized education. From her analysis of US reserach, Cross (1981) found that the major emphasis in adult learning was on the practical – obtaining skills – rather than on acquiring knowledge. She also found that non-participants put as much stress on the instrumental aims of education as did participants.

Other evidence, however, implies that people who engage in voluntary learning have a greater range of motives than surveys sometimes suggest. Research into participation occasionally contradicts widely held assumptions. Hedoux's 1982 survey in French mining communities disclosed that 90 per cent of working-class adults participating in education in their leisure time were engaged in learning activities that were totally unrelated to their work or job-related concerns. In the UK, the Consett education scheme for redundant steel workers also confounded expectations: although participants generally cited retraining or the financial allowance as their motives for enrolment, many eschewed the purely vocational activites and became engaged in a whole range of general and more academically-demanding learning options (Holmes and Storrie 1985). [. . .] In the Scottish survey (Munn and MacDonald 1988), 41 per cent of respondents also cited a personal interest or hobby as their main reason for participation. This confirms another of Cross's (1981) findings: that people are increasingly engaging in education for interest and personal development.

While stated motives obviously correspond to a large extent to the type of educational activites sought, it is possible that instrumental motives predominate in survey responses because of a limited view among the public of the scope of post-school education. It is also clear that some people express instrumental motives to justify participation to friends, relatives or co-workers. Male respondents in particular tend to cite instrumental motives. This may be due partly to an awareness of the link between employment and educational level, and partly to the need to conform to accepted male behavioural norms. In some sections of the community it is not regarded as normal behaviour for men to participate in education without a clear employment-related aim. When actually participating, however, many rapidly develop other interests and put more stress on personal self-development and recreational motives.

Existing research shows that motivations vary according to age and gender: younger adults and men learn mostly for employment-related reasons, while older adults and women learn more for personal satisfaction, self-development, leisure purposes and family or role transitions. The evidence also suggests that there is some correlation between socio-economic circumstances and learning choice, with disadvantaged groups tending to be found on lower level, non-advanced courses.

THEORIES OF PARTICIPATION

The reasons for participation are complex and multi-dimensional and often not reducible to a single motivation. Most explanations of participation involve the interaction of external (environmental, situational) and internal (dispositional) factors. There are a number of well-known theories. [. . .] The following is a brief and far from exhaustive summary of some of the best known.

Needs hierarchy theory

According to theorists such as Miller (1967), participation and non-participation depend on the extent to which an individual has been able to meet a range of primary and secondary needs and the influence of positive and negative forces. As one's socio-economic status improves, basic primary needs are met, higher level needs are activated, and the ratio of negative to positive forces declines. This leads to a situation conducive to engagement in educational or other activities.

Congruence model

Theorists such as Boshier (1971) have suggested that participation is more likely to result if there is some congruence between the learner's view of him/herself (self-concept) and the nature of the education programme and the educational environment.

Force-field theory

According to this theory, people who participate in adult learning believe they are capable of learning and value the outcomes of learning which they see as relevant to their personal needs. Rubenson (1977) proposed that motivation results from an interaction of 'expectancy' and 'valence'. 'Expectancy' refers to expectations of success in learning and its positive consequences; 'valence' refers to the total sum of positive or negative values an individual assigns to learning activities. Both expectancy and valence are determined by an individual's previous experiences, social environment and personal needs.

Life transitions theory

A number of studies find that the decision to participate frequently coincides with changes in life circumstances. Aslanian and Bricknell (1980) found that over 80 per cent of a large American sample were learning because their lives were changing in some way. British studies have also often found that the proportion of participants in organized education who have experienced life change, such as divorce or bereavement, is high in relation to their numbers in the general population.

Reference group theory

This theory maintains that individuals identify with the social and cultural group to which they belong – 'normative' reference group (NRG) – or with another to which they aspire to belong – 'comparative' reference group (CRG). Habitual participants usually belong to an NRG that is positively oriented to education. Several researchers refer to the same phenomenon using other terms, for example 'learning press' (Darkenwald and Merriam 1982).

Other people participate in education in order to achieve the perceived advantages of a group to which they do not belong. A comparative reference group presents a contrast to an individual's personal situation, creating what Gooderham (1987) refers to as 'a sense of relative deprivation'. Individuals with upwardly mobile socio-economic aspirations use the values, standards and attitudes of a comparative reference group to evaluate or change their own socio-economic situation. CRGs may be provided by the mass media, the local neighbourhood or colleagues, but, according to Gooderham, the most potent example is marriage, with women in particular seeking education to keep up with better qualified partners.

According to reference group theory, elements within an adult's current social situation may be a more decisive determinant of participation than comparable elements located in pre-adult years. Anderson and Darkenwald (1979) also believe that an individual's *current* situation should be given more emphasis in attempts to explain participation behaviour. Their analysis of the American National Educational Statistics Database for 1975 revealed that, in contrast to most research findings, factors such as sex, race and initial schooling accounted for only about 10 per cent of variance between participants and non-participants. In view of this, they suggest that participation needs to be explained according to 'more sophisticated personal or situational variables'.

Social participation

A number of other commentators maintain that participation in education should be explained with greater reference to social participation in general. Cookson (1987) criticizes participation theories for their restriction to a purely educational context; their 'narrow psychological view of reality'; and lack of comprehensive, integrative theories or models. He argues that research should make greater reference to broader social behaviour, as does Courtney (1981), who contends that, like most forms of social participation, educational participation is bound up with factors such as occupational status and income which define an individual's standing in the community. Although variables such as age, sex, marital status and place of residence play their part, educational participation is related to the 'perceptions of power and self-worth mediated through the instrumentality of those variables'.

Composite theories

There are a number of composite participation theories or models which integrate some of the theories mentioned above, and which purport to show how a variety of different factors in an individual's pre-adult and adult life interact to promote readiness to participate. Most of the models have some features in common.

'Chain of response' model

Cross's 'Chain of response' model (Cross 1981) incorporates elements from a number of theoretical frameworks in a seven-stage process which starts with the individual and ends with external influences. The seven stages are perceived as interacting links in a chain. The more positive the learner's experience at each stage, the more likely he or she is to reach the last stage – the decision to participate.

1 Learner's own self-evaluation.
2 Learner's attitude to education.
3 Motivation to learn (goals and the expectation that these will be met).
4 Life transitions.
5 Opportunities and barriers.
6 Information on educational opportunities.
7 The decision to participate.

Recruitment paradigm

Rubenson (1977) proposed a recruitment paradigm in which there are three sets of interacting variables, in the following order of importance:

- personal variables (prior experiences, personal attributes, current needs) and environmental factors (control over one's situation, reference groups, study possibilities);
- 'active preparedness': perception and interpretation of the environment; the experience of individual needs;
- the perceived value of an educational activity (valence) and the probability of being able to participate in and benefit from it (expectancy).

Psychosocial interaction model

Darkenwald and Merriam (1982) proposed a similar sequence of interacting variables which influence participation or non-participation:

- early individual and family characteristics;
- preparatory education and socialization;
- socio-economic status;
- 'learning press' (the extent to which current social or working environment requires or encourages further learning);
- perceived value/utility of adult education;
- readiness to participate;
- specific stimuli;
- barriers to participation.

Combination of favourable circumstances

French researchers have also come to the conclusion that participation is most likely when there is a combination and interaction of specifically favourable circumstances and conditions. De Montlibert (1973) contends that only people with a long initial schooling, advantageous professional status, and an entourage with a positive orientation towards education manage to break the 'logic which leads to disparities in access to education'. Hedoux (1981) adds two other favourable conditions: a 'dynamic of upward social mobility' offering future change, and involvement in a range of social and community activities. But he argues that participation will only ensue if, in addition to these favourable circumstances, individuals:

- perceive a need for education/training in their social, professional or non-professional domains;
- know that courses are provided which will respond to that need;
- are ready and prepared to formulate a future learning project (which implies some degree of anticipation and control over the future);
- possess enough social and spatial autonomy and free time to participate;
- possess sufficient basic skills in the area of education chosen to face a group-learning situation.

Hedoux contends that the number of people likely to enrol diminishes with each of these conditions, and, in consequence, relatively few non-participants are potential participants. This gloomy prognosis is perhaps over-pessimistic. [. . .]

REFERENCES

Advisory Council for Adult and Continuing Education (ACACE) (1982) *Adults: Their Educational Experience and Needs*, Leicester: ACACE.

Alloway, J. and Nelson, P. (1987) *Advice and Guidance to Individuals*, Leicester: Scottish Institute for Adult Continuing Education/Unit for the Development of Adult Continuing Education.

Anderson, R. and Darkenwald, G. G. (1979) *Participation and Persistence in American Adult Education*, Papers in Lifelong Learning, College Entrance Examination Board.

Aslanian, C. and Bricknell, H. (1980) *Americans in Transition: Life Changes as Reasons for Adult Learning*, New York: College Entrance Examination Board.

Beder, H. and Valentine, T. (1987) *Iowa's Basic Education Students: Descriptive Profiles Based on Motivation, Cognitive Ability and Socio-Demographic Variables*, Department of Education, University of Iowa.

Boshier, R. (1971) 'Motivational orientations of adult education participants: a factor analytic exploration of Houle's typology', *Adult Education* (US) 21 (2), 3–266.

Cookson, P. S. (1987) 'The nature of the knowledge base of adult education: the example of participation', *Educational Considerations V*, XIV.

Courtney, S. (1981) 'The factors affecting participation in adult education: an analysis of some literature', *Studies in Adult Education* 13 (2), 104–5.

Cross, K. P. (1981) *Adults as Learners*, San Francisco: Jossey-Bass.

Daines, J. B., Elsey, B. and Gibbs, M. (1982) *Changes in Student Participation in Adult Education*, Nottingham: University of Nottingham.

Darkenwald, G. G. (1988) *Comparison of Deterrents to Adult Education Participation in Britain and the United States*, Nottingham: Standing Conference on University Teaching and Research in the Education of Adults.

—— and Merriam, S. B. (1982) *Adult Education: Foundations of Practice*, London: Harper & Row.

—— and Valentine, T. (1985) 'Factor structure of deterrents to public participation in adult education', *Adult Education Quarterly* 35 (4), summer.

Further Education Unit (FEU) (1987) *Marketing Adult Continuing Education*, London: FEU.

Ghazzali, A. (1979) 'Reasons for adult participation in group education activities', *Research in Education* 21.

Gooderham, P. (1987) 'Reference group theory and adult education', *Adult Education Quarterly* 37 (3), spring, 140–51.

Hedoux, J. (1981) 'Les non-publics de la formation collective', *Education Permanente*, 61, Decembre, 89–105.

—— (1982) 'Des publics et des non-publics de la formation d'adultes: Sallaumines-Noyelles-sous-Lens des 1972', *Revue Française Sociologique*, Avril–Juin, pp. 253–74 (citations translated by researcher).

Holmes, J. and Storrie, T. (1985) *Consett: A Case Study of Education and Unemployment*, London: Further Education Unit.

Johnstone, J. W. C. and Rivera, R. J. (1965) *Volunteers for Learning: A Study of the Educational Pursuits of American Adults*, Aldine Publishing Co.

Jones, D. (1988) *Access to the Arts: Adult Education and Cultural Development*, London: Routledge.

Lewis, L. (1988) 'An issue of support', *International Journal of Lifelong Education* 4 (2), 163–76.

McDonald, J. (1984) *Education for Unemployed Adults*, London: DES.

Mee, G. and Wiltshire, H. (1978) *Structure and Performance in Adult Education*, London: Longman.

Miller, H. L. (1967) *Participation in Education: A Force-Field Analysis*, Center for the Study of Liberal Education for Adults, University of Boston.

Montlibert, C. de (1973) 'Le public de la formation des adultes, *Revue Française Soliologique* XIV, 529–45.

Morstain, B. R. and Smart, J. C. (1974) 'Reasons for participation in adult education courses: a multivariable analysis of group differences', *Adult Education* 24 (2), 83–98.

Munn, P. and MacDonald, C. (1988) *Adult Participation in Education and Training*, Scottish Council for Research in Education.

Organization for Economic Co-operation and Development (OECD) (1977) *Learning Opportunities for Adults: Participation in Adult Education*, Paris: OECD.

—— (1979) *Learning Opportunities for Adults: The Non-Participation Issue*, Paris: OECD.

Osborn, M. Withnall, A. and Charnley, A. H. (1980) *Review of Existing Research in Adult and Continuing Education*: Volume 3, *The Disadvantaged*, Leicester: National Institute of Adult Continuing Education.

O'Shea, J. and Corrigan, p. (1979) 'Surviving adult education', *Adult Education* 52 (4).

Percy, K. (1983) *Post-Initial Education in the North-west of England: A Survey of Provision*, Leicester: ACACE.

―――― *et al.* (1988) *Learning in Voluntary Organisations*, Leicester: UDACE.

Rubenson, K. (1977) *Participation of Adults in Education: A Force-Field Analysis*, Center for the Study of Liberal Education for Adults, University of Boston.

―――― (1986) *Old and New Barriers for Participation*, Occasional Papers of the Dutch Open University, 1.

Scanlan, C. L. (1986) *Deterrents to Participation: An Adult Education Dilemma*, National Center for Research in Vocational Education, Ohio State University.

Schuller, T. (1978) *Education Through Life*, Fabian Society.

Sheffield, S. B. (1962) 'The orientations of adult continuing learners', Unpublished thesis, University of Chicago.

Usher, R. and Bryant, I. (1989) *Adult Education as Theory, Practice and Research: The Captive Triangle*, London: Routledge.

West, L. (1987) 'Challenging the WEA: crisis, learning and purpose', *Workers Education* 1 (2), autumn–winter, pp. 7–11.

Woodley, A. *et al.* (1987) *Choosing to Learn: Adults in Education*, Milton Keynes: Society for Research into Higher Education/Open University Press.

Chapter 2

Self-planned learning and major personal change

Allen Tough

Source: R. M. Smith (ed.) (1976) *Adult Learning: Issues and Innovations*, ERIC Clearing House in Career Education, Northern Illinois University, pp. 58–73.

The first item in Table 2.1 outlines the focus or phenomenon that has fascinated me for the last ten years or so. I have called it a learning project, but what I suggest in parentheses would be an even more accurate title – a major learning effort. The focus is on people trying to learn, trying to change. People of course learn without trying, but that is not what I'm looking at. What I suggest that we look at is highly deliberate effort; we define that as effort where more than half of the person's total motivation had to be learning and retaining certain definite knowledge or skill – so that less than half of the person's motivation can be pleasure or enjoyment.

And I've suggested that there has to be a clear focus. The person has to know what he or she is trying to learn. Someone who walks into a museum for an hour knowing that he will learn something but not knowing what, simply does not qualify by our criteria. We have a minimum time period, seven hours – that is, over a period of several months a person has to spend at least seven hours trying to gain this particular knowledge and skill. Now in fact the average learning project is around 90 or 100 hours, so we do not have to use that seven hour cut-off all that often. My reason for choosing the seven hours was partly as a magic number, and partly it's about one working day; and my feeling has been that if someone devotes the equivalent of a working day to trying to learn something, it is worthwhile looking at it.

Number 2 in Table 2.1 gives the various populations of the study interviewed by our group in Toronto and by graduate students and others all across the USA, Canada, Ghana and New Zealand. Combining the results of all these studies we find that the differences are not great. In fact, the data found in each study are roughly the same as data found in the other studies. And that is what number 3 on Table 2.1 deals with – how common this phenomenon is, and how much time it takes. Those figures pertain to the middle or median person (that is, half of the people in these populations have learned more and spent more time learning and

9108

Table 2.1 Learning projects

1 A learning project (major learning effort):
   - highly deliberate effort
   - to gain and retain certain definite knowledge and skill
   - clear focus
   - at least 7 hours

2 Populations surveyed:
   - Toronto: pre-school mothers; elementary school teachers; lower white-collar women and men; factory workers; municipal politicians; social science professors; unemployed men; IBM salesmen; professional men; 16-year-olds and 10-year-olds
   - Vancouver: members of public employees' union
   - Syracuse: suburban housewives
   - Tennessee: large rural and urban populations
   - Nebraska: adults over 55
   - Fort Lauderdale: adults who recently completed high school
   - Atlanta: pharmacists
   - Kentucky: parish ministers
   - West Africa (Accra, Ghana): secondary school teachers; bank officers; department store executives
   - New Zealand: several North Island populations

3 A middle or median person:
   - conducts 8 different projects in one year
   - spends a total of 700 hours altogether at them

4 Who plans the learning efforts from one session to the next?
   - the learner: 68%
   - a group or its leader/instructor: 12%
   - a pro or friend in a one-to-one situation: 8%
   - a non-human resource (records, TV, etc.): 3%
   - mixed (no dominant planner): 9%

5 Out of 100 learning projects, 19 are planned by a professional educator and 81 by an amateur

6 Most common motivation: some anticipated *use* or application of the knowledge and skill
   Less common: curiosity or puzzlement, or wanting to possess the knowledge for its own sake
   Rare (less than 1% of all learning efforts): credit

half the people have spent less). And you will notice that this person conducts eight different learning projects, eight major learning efforts each year – in eight quite different areas of knowledge and skill.

People spend a total of 700 hours at this activity – highly deliberate efforts to learn. The figure is probably low – at least for a great many populations – for two reasons. First, many of our interviewers have failed to get the full number of hours. Almost every interviewer reports missing some learning projects. Then some of the later studies have actually had much higher figures than that 700. That works out to almost two hours a day – an incredible figure when you think about it.

Number 4 describes who planned the learning effort from one session to the next – not who did the intitial planning – the day-to-day deciding about what to learn and how to go about it. And, of course, the majority is self-planned. The learner himself or herself decides which step to take next in the learning effort – the learner plans the path. It is often a zigzag path which seems helter-skelter, but the learner does decide from one session to the next what and how to learn.

Now what has happened I think, looking at the research for the last fifteen years (or even longer), is that until fairly recently people looked only at the tip of the iceberg. Only a small part of the iceberg shows above the water's surface. In adult learning or adult education that small highly visible tip of the iceberg is groups of people learning – in auditoriums, classrooms, workshops, or conferences. That is what adult educators have noticed and paid attention to over the years. Rightly so. That's an important phenomenon. [. . .]

We came along, in a simple-minded way, and interviewed people about all of their learning efforts. We found they couldn't remember them. So we developed probe-sheets that suggested some things that people learn about. And we also took an hour and a half (at least an hour) in most of the interviews to study just this phenomenon.

We really pushed, poked, probed, and helped the person recall. We found it took people about 20 to 25 minutes to really start getting on our wavelength and start to recall their projects, at least beyond three or four of them. [. . .] Nearly everyone recalls quite a few – and it is a rare person who remembers only one or two or three. In the Toronto group we found only one 'zero,' and in most of the other studies there were either no zeros or very few.

We've looked at this total iceberg then and most of it is in the invisible part, the self-planned part. It is invisible to the learners; it is invisible to other people around them. It is a phenomenon that we are just not in touch with; it is not very common at a dinner party to say, 'And what are you trying to learn lately?' It is not something that you talk about. We talk about courses and conferences, but not the other kinds of learning. At least we do not put it all together in a single phenomenon – an effort to learn.

You will notice in Table 2.1 that 12 per cent of all major learning efforts are conducted in groups, planned by the group or the leader, or instructor. Less than 10 per cent are conducted in a one-to-one situation – the way we all, or most of us, learn to drive a car, play the piano or tennis. The figure that surprises me most is the 3 per cent for non-human resources. It was thought that programmed instruction and television series, language records, and so on would be much more popular than they turned out to be. Then there is the 9 per cent that is mixed. Of course, almost all of those are self-planned plus something else, so the self-planned figure of 68 per cent should be raised to something like three-quarters or 77 per cent.

In number 5 I have tried to capture all the figures in one very simple statistic, that is, if you look at 100 learning projects, about 20 are planned by professionals and about 80 by the learner himself or herself or some other amateur planner.

Turning now to what people learn about or learn to do, we find that there is incredible diversity. If you ask a room full of people to make lists of their recent personal learning projects you will find a mind-boggling variety of topics. An implication of this is a very very old one in adult education – that no one institution could possibly meet the needs of all learning projects for all adults. In fact I do not think any institution can even comprehend all of the items you get on such lists. So adult education must be pluralistic; it could not possibly be monopolistic as youth education primarily is. Anyone who has studied adult education knows that this is one of the basic characteristics of the field; there is tremendous diversity of institutions. We begin to see why, because of the incredible diversity of learning needs.

It will perhaps be useful to try to answer some questions frequently put to us about our research.

Question: 'How do you distinguish between activities and learning projects, or are they one and the same?' What we are really looking at is the intention of the acitivity. So that regardless of what the person is doing, if he or she is trying to learn, trying to change through that activity, then we call it a learning project. People do learn in other ways. There are lots of activities that lead to learning. But if that is not the person's primary intention then we do not include it in our definition of a learning project.

Question: 'Do you define learning as change?' Yes, it can be internal change – within one's head – understanding, information, or whatever. I define a learning project as an effort to change.

Question: 'Is some sort of stress a prerequisite for a learning project to begin?' No, perhaps approximately one-third of all learning projects begin because of this, but a lot begin for other reasons – curiosity, for example. The desire to build a porch around my house may not come out of stress; it may simply be something I want to do. Growing vegetables might be initiated because you don't have money to buy them, or it might just be for fun.

Another important factor is that these learning projects can continue over many years. In West Africa we found a great many projects that went back ten or fifteen years. Students at my institution now are trying to trace some of the projects back to see what the origins are, and they are often going back to childhood – so that you can't understand the present learning project without knowing what the learner's previous interests were. There really is a long-term aspect. Some are seasonal, like tennis. Some come and go, like raising kids, in the sense that a different kind of crisis will arise at different times. The kids seem to go through periods of plateau when everything is rather sunny; then things seem to fall apart. He or she won't sleep or eat, or hits people. Then you turn to Dr Spock or your neighbours or paediatrician about how to deal with it. Then you go through another period of several months when you are not learning anything or putting in the effort.

There are other learning projects (I think this is a typical American pattern) that are very brief. I have to make a decision by Wednesday, so I will read everything I can now and ask people about it, and then I'll make the decision. Or with child-rearing, you may have a crash programme for five days. This seems to be the American style. I say that because we were not picking this up in West Africa even among business executives, who did not seem to have so many of these short-term projects.

Question: 'What about variations in the learning as the result of work or other activities that are taken on primarily for reasons other than learning?' It is not always true that people learn from their work. The trend that I see is that people are choosing jobs that seem to be educative, and corporations or employers that will be educative. They are asking a little less now of pension plans and that sort of thing and a little more about the kind of organization it is. General Electric did a survey on the future of business values and they clearly found this shift toward looking at how educative a job or task is. I enjoyed interviewing one fourth-grade teacher who chose things to teach that he wanted to learn about. He knew that was an effective way to motivate himself. I have heard Sunday School teachers say the same thing. So we do choose some of our tasks partly in order to learn. It is a fascinating phenomenon.

MAJOR PERSONAL CHANGE

In the last few years I have begun to focus my own energy on one specific area of learning projects. Not that I think that the others are unimportant, but my own interest is to study major personal change. Major means that the learning effort is designed to produce major changes, significant changes, in the person. Personal change suggests that it is somehow a personal thing. It is a change in life-style, attitudes, emotional reactions, male–female relationships, or whatever it happens to be. All of these seem more personal than learning about what is happening over in the Middle East or something like that. I'm not putting down the importance of that, but just trying to explain my own focus on the major or immediate types of changes.

There follow two tables that deal with this area. Table 2.2 lists the content or curriculum of this area, i.e. what it is that people can try to change in themselves. Table 2.3 lists the how, the paths, the ways, the steps, the techniques and methods. I would like the reader to look over the two tables – try to be aware of your reactions as you do so: your mental, emotional, and intellectual reactions. What do these tables do to you? What do they do to your thinking and what do they do to your feelings?

Here are some common reactions of persons encountering the items listed, followed by my own comments.

Reaction: 'You get down to some very basic things, and I find myself involved in quite a few of them.' This is a very common reaction – to recognize yourself in some of the items.

Reaction: 'Seems to be something you do from childhood through

Table 2.2 What personal changes can someone strive for?

1	Self-understanding
2	Express genuine feelings and interests
3	Close, authentic relationships with others
4	Broad understanding of history, geography, cultures, universe, future
5	Better performance on the job; reshape the job or its meaning; new job
6	Quit drinking; stop beating children; quit heroin
7	Cope better with the tasks necessary for survival
8	Body free from excessive tenseness and wasted energy; physical fitness
9	New priorities among goals (desired benefits); a fresh balance of activities or expenditures
10	Reshape relationship with mate; new mate or partner (or an alternative living arrangement); new circle of friends
11	Capacity for finding a calm centre of peace and inner strength amidst the turmoil
12	Adequate self-esteem
13	Reduction of psychological and emotional problems and blocks that inhibit full human functioning
14	Improved awareness and consciousness; more open-minded and inquiring; seeking an accurate picture of reality
15	Greater sensitivity to psychic phenomena and to alternate realities
16	Freedom, liberation, looseness, flexibility
17	Competence at psychological processing, at handling own feelings and personal problems
18	Zest for life; joy; happiness
19	Liberation from female–male stereotyping, or from other role-playing
20	Emotional maturity, positive mental health; higher level of psychological functioning
21	Spiritual insights; cosmic consciousness
22	Less selfish and more altruistic; a greater effort to contribute to the lives of others
23	Acceptance and love of self and others; accept the world as it is
24	Come to terms with own death

Table 2.3 Some methods for personal growth

1	Books
2	Conversations with a close friend or an informal helper; relationship with mate or love partner
3	Jogging; diet; bioenergetics; massage; acupuncture; biofeedback; sports; movement and dance therapy
4	Yoga exercises; martial arts (t'ai chi; aikido; judo; karate)
5	Individual counselling; individual psychotherapy; group therapy
6	Behaviour modification
7	Encounter groups; sensory awareness; psychosynthesis; Gestalt therapy groups; Transactional Analysis; psychodrama; art therapy
8	Individual use (whenever appropriate) of personal exercises and psychological processing such as thinking, listing wishes and fears, interpreting dreams, keeping a journal, moving to music, contemplation and reflection, listening to one's unconscious
9	Consciousness-raising groups and literature for women and men
10	Out-of-body experience or other physhic experiences; astronauts' experience of seeing the earth from outer space
11	Guided fantasies; directed daydreams; Transcendental Meditation; Mind Games; hypnotic trance
12	Re-living one's birth or infancy; primal therapy
13	Religious, spiritual, cosmic-unity, symbolic, or consciousness-altering experiences – via religious services, spiritual practices, mysticism, psychedelic drugs, Mind Games, prayer, wilderness solitude, music, meditation, sex, chanting, spinning, baptism in the Holy Spirit, Zen, Buddhism, Christianity, Judaism, Islam, Taoism
14	Tarot; I Ching
15	Alert childbirth; living with children; Parent Effectiveness Training
16	Films; television; audiovisual environment; self-improvement tapes and kits
17	Tackling a challenging task or an educative job; working in a growth-facilitating organization
18	Course; conference; discussion group; management training; organizational development
19	Self-help groups and other peer-groups
20	Music; arts; crafts
21	Deliberate change in life-style; new circle of friends; new neighbourhood; expressive clothes
22	Travel or live abroad; live within a commune or some other subculture or culture

adulthood.' Some of these things go all through your lifetime – not like those short-term projects we mentioned earlier.

Reaction: 'Many seem to be types of experiences that many people have not begun to consider.' No one person is going to be involved in all of these things. Probably most of them never will be involved in them. Some of them may 'bother' you. Perhaps some of you would like to change in a lot of these ways, but find you are not using many methods to do so. That is a fairly common reaction.

Reaction: 'Looking at the list, I feel that the majority of them could or would occur outside formal institutions.' Yes, there is change in formal institutions, but many of them tend not to provide these kinds of experiences.

Reaction: 'It seems to me that a lot of these are motivated out of prevailing discontent with materialistic society.' Right, these aren't very materialistic lists. They are also lists that assume that the person isn't scrambling to get enough money to eat, not severely crippled in some emotional way, that some of his basic needs are taken care of. People who do not have enough money would not even know what these lists are all about.

Reaction: 'It seems to me that many of the methods are for the person who is aware that they are available and not necessarily for the guy who is just sitting at home. I can't see him dealing with a lot of these methods.' Many of these methods have been developed in the last ten or fifteen years; so they are not generally known to the public. My own project is to try to develop a bridge between this array of available techniques and people who should know about them. It is partly their recency, and partly that they seem strange to people. Half the methods on the list probably bothered you when you first heard about them – even one like jogging. So there are a lot of reasons that people do not know about these kinds of things. [. . .]

Reaction: It is interesting that almost everything on the personal changes list is a type of assessment or judgement about progress that is very 'individual'. I have to decide for myself whether or not that change has occurred. I might get some feedback from other people, but it is my decision and no one else can tell me whether or not I've pulled it off.' True, most of these items are very hard to measure. We have found that people who are learning on their own are preoccupied with evaluation of how well they are doing and what level they are at. They develop all kinds of ways of dealing with that. One of them is to have a conversation with someone who is an acknowledged expert. There are other ways. Certainly some items on this list are very hard to evaluate. How do I know when my self-esteem has reached an adequate level? These are all subtle matters. The thing that amazes me is that we now have some technologies that produce some of these changes, and that is a big step. Another big step would be to help people know where they are and how far they have moved.

Reaction: 'Though this is geared toward middle-class individuals, I think that for adult basic learners, one of the things that's missing here is learning from one's children.' That's a fascinating notion – learning from one's children.

Reaction: 'There seems to be willingness to risk. You might find out something that you do not like about yourself.' That is right. These are risky patterns, not safe patterns. That is the choice of the learner.

Reaction: 'I have the feeling that educators are pretty much staying away from teaching and talking about values, and our schools are not making these things known as they should.' That is right. Now somebody suggested that adult educators are not experiencing many of these things themselves. That could be one reason. In fact the way that these often get into the curriculum is that a teacher goes to a workshop or something similar and gets turned on to new technologies – rather than through a curriculum guide or something similar.

Reaction: 'I find it very hard to believe a couple of comments, that people don't grow or don't want to grow. I just don't believe that.' I don't know. I do know that there are a lot of risks involved, and we don't always want to take risks. [. . .]

Perhaps I should add that I do not want to be a salesman for any of these methods. I do not recommend them wholeheartedly to all people. I am simply trying to list methods that some people use for growth – that is, methods that a particular person might use in an attempt to grow.

IMPLICATIONS

We can consider now some implications for action – for educators and educational institutions – looking at some better kinds of help that could be provided. What do we do to facilitate, to help people learn more or better things for themselves? Or, how can we help people with major personal change?

I have five answers to that question that I will state fairly quickly. The first one is rather strange. It is to look not at the programme the institution provides for people but to look at the staff of the institution. The concept here is to look at educators or teachers as learners instead of looking at them just as teachers, or people who are facilitating the learning of other people. I think probably the largest change in our institutions will come from learning how to facilitate the learning of the staffs of those institutions.

I don't mean that educators don't learn. We've found that elementary teachers, for example, spend an average of two hours a day learning to be better teachers. But at the same time institutions tend to do very little to facilitate the learning of their own staff members. To me this is just an incredible situation. If any institutions in society should be facilitating learning and change among their own staff, they should be schools, colleges, and adult education programmes. But in fact they don't. One of our doctoral students who had interviewed the elementary school teachers decided to try to put into practice the recommendations at the end of his dissertation. He put himself on the line and became the principal of our campus lab school. He has just transformed that place in three years. He's done it by focusing his efforts on helping these teachers to become better teachers. [...] He is helping the teachers individually, or in groups of two or three, to set their learning goals and go ahead to become better teachers, however they want to do it. One of the first things he did was to give them Wednesday afternoon off – for learning. He brought parents in to handle the kids. It sounds so obvious and so superior to having one day a year 'teacher development day.'

The second suggestion, or implication, is to add 'major personal change' to the curriculum – at whatever level. And as I suggested earlier, this is in fact being done – mostly in an underground or back-door way. That is, an individual teacher gets turned on to the notion and introduces it to his or her class [...]

Now a third implication is suggested by Ivan Illich and Everett Reimer, who have received publicity for saying that the monopoly of the school system should be broken, that education should be more pluralistic. Illich and Reimer make some specific suggestions. They mention three mechanisms; one of these is the skill exchange. The idea of a skill exchange is very simple. If I want to learn how to play the guitar I dial a telephone number and say that I want to play the guitar. Then they give me the names and telephone numbers of two or three people who have phoned in earlier and said that they would enjoy teaching someone to play the guitar. I then meet with one or two or three of these people and decide which one I want to learn from. I might volunteer later to teach someone else. Usually the meeting takes place in a public building or a coffee shop, so that if people don't hit if off there is no great harm done. The system is very cheap and the idea has spread to at least twenty cities in Canada and the USA.

Another suggestion is a 'peer matching service.' This occurs when you are not looking for a teacher – somebody who is better than you – but for someone who is at your level. If I want to improve my chess playing or my tennis playing, I might want to find a partner who plays at about my level. Or, I might want to find somebody to talk to about inflation. The idea is to match people who can learn together as peers, not as one teaching the other.

Then there is a 'directory of freelancers' – people who will want to be paid to facilitate learning. [...]

A couple of other suggestions: these apply specifically to educational institutions. One of them is to increase the amount of choice and increase the amount of help for students. It has to be a two-sided thing. Our first step usually is increasing the amount of choice in *how* people learn. That is not so scary to instructors – saying to the student, 'Here's what you have to learn but there are two or three paths to get there.' The other kind of choice would be to give people freedom in *what* they learn; that is a little scarier unless limited to procedures like giving out a range of assignment possibilities or a list of topics for essays. One way to increase that a little is to make the last item something like, 'Or any other topic chosen by the student and approved by the teacher.' The way I do it in my graduate course in Toronto is to set boundaries about the subject matter. But that is about the only restriction I have on what people learn or how they learn. I simply say that they have to learn about this phenomenon, major personal change, for 130 hours, and then they pass the course. It's deceptively simple, and it seems to be fairly effective for me in that course with that subject matter. I'm not urging all instructors to do it.

The students are creative in the ways in which they go about learning in that course. They read, of course. They also analyse their own learning and changes. Some will deliberately put themselves into the thing that they least desire to learn – or something very threatening (during which they often keep a diary). They also interview each other. My impression is that the range of methods is actually greater when I give them freedom than if I were to try to make up the methods for them. And, of course, what they learn is also incredibly varied. It's a pass–fail course, so I haven't had much problem with grading. One or two persons probably cheat, but I am not planning to drop the system just because of that.

A final suggestion is to decrease the emphasis on credit. Our research found less than 1 per cent of adult learning projects are conducted for credit. So, it is quite clearly demonstrated that people will learn for reasons other than credit. [. . .] Reducing the emphasis on credit could reduce the monopolistic aspect of adult education.

Chapter 3

Adult education policy in Sweden, 1967–91

Kjell Rubenson

Source: This is an edited version of an article that appeared in the symposium issue of the *Policy Studies Review* on 'Adult Education Policy' edited by H.S. Bhola of Indiana University, 1992.

INTRODUCTION

To choose 1967 as point of departure may seem strange, as Sweden has had a long and important tradition of adult education dating back to the breakthrough of the popular movements at the end of the nineteenth century. However, it was not until the 1960s that adult education became central to Swedish educational and labour market policies.

During the years 1967–91, the social, political and economic context has undergone marked changes, which are reflected in shifting policy focuses and reform strategies. It is possible to distinguish five major periods corresponding to adult education policies in Sweden: 1960–9; 1970–6; 1976–82; 1982–91; 1991.

This chapter analyses the direction of government policy on adult education during the five periods with regard to policy context, reform ideology and strategies, and, where possible, outcomes. However, to provide a comprehensive account of the Swedish strategy one also has to include labour market training policy, which, although not under the governance of the Ministry of Education but the Ministry of Labour, affects an important part of the adult education 'sector'. The analyses will therefore start with a general overview of labour market training which in contrast to adult education has been rather unchanged during the period 1967–91.

LABOUR MARKET TRAINING

The active labour market policy developed in Sweden in the 1950s was based on the model developed by the economists Gösta Rehn and Rudolf Meidner (Meidner 1973, Rehn 1985). This model was characterized above all by its assertion that an active labour market policy is a principal factor of economic stability and full employment. The goal is to achieve full employment while minimizing consumer price inflation and wage drift. The specific measures were to include public employment projects (known as 'relief work projects'), sheltered employment, support for firms in regions of high unemployment, and efforts to stimulate the mobility of workers between different localities, sectors, and occupations.

The labour market training system arose out of the need to act swiftly against imbalances in the labour market. First, the system helped under-employed and unemployed workers to improve their employability in occupations with better opportunities. Second, it increased the supply of skills in industries where a shortage of suitably trained personnel tends to exacerbate inflationary pressures.

Labour market training may be defined as any programme for which a special kind of training allowance is granted by the National Labour Market Board (*Arbetsmarknadsstyrelsen*, *AMS*). These allowances are granted for various kinds of vocational training and for such preparatory training as is required for the vocational programme. The following conditions are laid down for receiving such allowances: the applicant is unemployed or runs the risk of becoming so; is difficult to place in employment; has reached the age of 20 (in some cases 18); and, is seeking work through the public employment service and training can be expected to result in permanent employment which would not have been possible without such training. For example, labour market training is required, within certain limits, to help persons who have had little or no training, or whose previous training is out of date, to strengthen their position in the labour market (even if they are not unemployed). It is also intended to help employers obtain staff with required skills.

Labour market training may be divided into four main categories depending on who administers the courses: (1) special courses arranged by a labour market training authority – the AMU Group, consisting of a central AMU Board and twenty-five autonomous regional bodies (commissioned authorities), which succeeded the National Board of Education, with effect from 1986, as the authority responsible for the special labour market training centres (AMU centres); (2) in-house training for established employees, including what is known as bottleneck training; (3) training within the ordinary educational system; and (4) courses arranged by organizations. The special courses account for the major part of all labour market training and are mainly held at some 100 special AMU centres throughout Sweden. The primary objective of labour market training is to ensure steady jobs for the unemployed. Regular follow-up studies show that of those who have completed vocational labour market training, some 60 to 70 per cent have obtained employment in the open sector within about six months. Approximately 80 per cent of these people have, in turn, obtained work within the occupational branch for which they were trained.

Courses used for labour market training must fulfil special requirements. As a rule, the training should lead to specific occupations rather than to occupational branches, and the importance of limiting the period of training is often greater than in other forms of training. The construction of courses on a modular system so they can be freely combined is particularly suitable for labour market training, as is the division of courses into several stages, each with a varying degree of specialization. Specially arranged labour market training is primarily the concern of the AMU Group, as the training supplier, and the county labour boards, as customers. The content, scope, and price of training are negotiated between these two sides. Overriding labour market policy decisions (including the evaluation of activities) rest with the National Labour Market Board and the county labour boards, while the AMU Group deals with the pedagogical and educational aspects.

ADULT EDUCATION, 1960–9

Policy context

The very selective, hierarchically organized parallel school system was seen as a bastion of the old class system that the Social Democrats set out to erase. Directly after the Second World War, reforming the school system became a major priority for the Labour government and a cornerstone in the strategy of building a more just and equitable society.

Already during the early groundwork for the establishment of comprehensive schools, the issue of the older generation – who in their youth had not had the opportunity to continue beyond six or seven years of education – was raised (SOU 1948: 27). The school reforms of the 1950s and early 1960s led to a rapid expansion of the Swedish educational system. The result of this expansion was an ever-widening gap between the older generation, who had received a minimal education, and the new generation, who not only received nine years of compulsory education, but who increasingly chose to continue on to secondary school. As a consequence, the argument, particularly within the Federation of Labour (LO), that the people who were paying for the increase in primary and secondary education should have their share of the increasing educational resources, grew stronger (TCO 1964, LO 1969). The democratization of the educational system was not the only root of the 1967 reform, which also was heavily influenced by contemporary human capital ideas. Within policy circles, human capital theory was widely embraced. The situation in Sweden, with an educational attainment in the population that resembled

Portugal's and a labour market resembling that of West Germany, was seen as most problematic.

Research had shown that there existed a large intellectual reserve in the adult population that was well equipped to undertake secondary and higher education (Härnqvist 1958). It was against this background that the Swedish Parliament launched its adult education policy in 1967.

Reform strategy

The two major innovations of this reform were the introduction of municipal adult education, which would offer education equivalent to primary and secondary school, and the creation of a permanent organization of TV and radio programmes for educational purposes. As a result of such changes, adult education became differentiated: popular adult education was displaced from its former unique position and now became part of the overall 'system' of adult education. No longer was adult education a marginal activity. As a result of the creation of special departments of adult education within the Ministry of Education and the National Board of Education, as well as a separate post in the national budget, it became a distinguishable and separate part of the educational system.

The 1967 adult education reform had its roots in the same elitist conception of equality as that guiding the restructuring of higher education. The basic idea informing this strategy was that everyone should have equal rights to an education regardless of social background, sex or place of residence (OECD 1967). The concept is elitist in that it implicitly argues that society ought to offer higher/adult education to those who aspire to it and who are able to benefit from such education. The starting point for the 1967 reform was the increased demand for education on the part of those individuals psychologically inclined and socially outfitted for study. Evening class students served as models for the target group of the newly introduced municipal adult education. These students belonged to the so-called 'pool of talent': they had a high level of aspiration, they were motivated to study, and they were often successful in their self-tuition. The 1967 reforms were not aimed at reaching new target groups but were designed to cater to the increased demands from this existing group.

Adult education literature on recruitment isolates three categories of obstacles to participation in adult education (Cross 1981):

1 institutional obstacles (access to education, content of education, admission rules, financing, etc.);
2 situational obstacles (time, child care, etc.);
3 psychological obstacles (attitudes to study, self-esteem, etc.).

The 1967 reforms can be seen as an attempt to tackle what Patricia Cross has termed institutional obstacles to participation, and thereby to help transform the demand for adult education into actual participation. Neither psychological nor structural obstacles to participation were addressed in 1967, for two reasons. First, given that the 1967 reforms were occasioned by an increased demand for adult education, the problem was characterized as one of increasing educational opportunities. Second, adult education was intended as a largely self-taught, leisure-time activity; the increased use of radio and TV made it more likely that students would be able to study at times convenient to them.

The degree of congruence between the measures taken and the intent of the 1967 reforms to overcome situational obstacles was comparatively high. It must be remembered that the aim was not to recruit new target groups but to correct earlier inadequacies of access within the system, and to satisfy the expressed needs of a group with an already established propensity for study. The desired results of the reform were (a) an increase in participation by the so-called intellectual reserve, and (b) an increase in human capital.

The 1967 reform was the result of a process which was underway as early as 1946; at the time of its implementation, the policy context had already started to shift.

ADULT EDUCATION, 1970–6

Policy context

The debate which accompanied the 1969 reform of adult education, in combination with general social developments, made LO (The Swedish Confederation of Trade Unions) and TCO (The Swedish Central Organization of Salaried Employees) take an increasing interest in adult education policy. LO's opinion was presented in a report that attracted much attention, *Fackföreningsrörelsen och Vuxenutbildning* ('The Trade Union Movement and Adult Education') (LO 1969). This report argues that there are two main themes informing its attention to adult education: equality and justice. It further points out that adult education is one of several channels for moving society towards the ideological goals of the Labour Movement. These early ideas were developed further and made concrete in a subsequent report, *Vuxenutbildning. Fakta-Erfarenheter-Förslag* ('Adult Education. Facts–Experiences–Suggestions') (LO 1971). This publication documents that adult education has been used primarily by those already well prepared to study and that, accordingly, no positive privileges can be seen to accrue to the LO collective from adult education.

In order to change the existing patterns of participation, LO demanded high priority be given to measures aimed at neglected groups. This was expressed in terms such as 'A just distribution in the field of adult education does not mean equal shares for everyone, but more for those that have received less' (LO 1971: 206). The LO demand for action in the adult education field was not an isolated event but an expression of the general radicalization of the trade union movement at the end of the 1960s.

Korpi's analysis of the working classes in Welfare-State capitalism shows that the reformist strategy which had been a guideline for Swedish Social Democracy came to be questioned (Korpi 1978). For example, criticism was aimed at the Labour Movement's shift from a popular movement whose ideal was a total reformulation of society to its role as an administrator of the mixed economy. In the mid–1960s there was within the Labour Movement a growing awareness that social developments designed to lead to equality tended instead to preserve inequality. In 1965 the government set up the so-called Low Income Commission, the aim of which was to analyse the distribution of welfare and to make proposals for redistribution strategies.

The wildcat strikes which occurred during the late 1960s strengthened LO's opinion that there was a need for far-reaching changes in working life. This development should be seen as a reappraisal of the Labour Movement's relationship to the question of economic democracy. When the Social Democrats came to power in 1932, the issue of direct state control over the means of production gave way to issues of social democracy, particularly to the emergence of the Welfare State. Politics had come to be based on the assumption that the possession of political power would create sufficient opportunities to make fundamental changes in working life without necessarily abolishing private ownership of the means of production. However, in light of post-war experiences and because of tensions in the labour market and within the Labour Movement, LO began to make far-reaching demands for changes in working life.

In order to bring about cultural changes to parallel the changes in working life, the trade unions called for measures to democratize political and cultural life. In official letters to the government, ABF (The Worker's Educational Association) and LO demanded two things: first, that the government set up a committee to carry out experimental study trying various outreach models to increase participation of the under-educated in adult education; and second, that the present sitting committee on adult study finance be given additional instructions to act for those with less than nine years' education.

The government reacted promptly to the demands from LO and ABF. In Bill 1970:35 a change of action was announced: the Bill stated that in further reforms of adult education one of the most important issues to be addressed would be how to reach those who have little or insufficient education (Government Bill 1970:35: 1).

Following Korpi's argument, a shift in the balance of power between social collectives and classes can be supposed to influence both the distribution of opportunity between different classes in society and the social consciousness of the people. Similarly, changes in power resources can be expected to be reflected in changes in social institutions and their *modus operandi*. Therefore, it seems reasonable to suggest that the increasing social power of the trade-union movement in Sweden explains the state's altered ways of acting in adult education matters. These aspirations that adult education act as an agent of social reform emerged simultaneously with growing cynicism about the ability of formal schooling to effect social reform.

The view that the reform of childhood education was insufficient was reinforced by analyses made by a Royal Commission on the Financing of Adult Study, which indicated that it would take more time than expected for reforms of childhood education to make themselves felt in Swedish society (SOU 1971: 80). Moreover, there were already warning signals indicating that childhood education reforms had not had the equalizing effect that had earlier been hoped for. With this in view, it is possible to see the intense focus on adult education as an attempt to broaden an earlier strategy which had aimed at remodelling class society by remodelling childhood education. What the early 1970s offered was an alternative strategy for social change based on a resocialization of adults rather than the socialization of children. There are parallels between this approach and that of literacy campaigns where initial efforts are directed towards adults in the knowledge that literate parents seldom have illiterate children.

In the period 1970–5, the tenor of the government policy became more pronounced: the overall aim of adult education policy was to bring about parity in standards of living. The government's concept of the resources necessary to an adequate standard of living was in turn informed by the definition offered in the Royal Commission on Low Income: 'Resources of money, property, knowledge, psychological and physical energy, social relations, security *et cetera* at the disposal of the individual with the aid of which the individual can control and consciously govern his living conditions.' Thus adult education was intended to achieve a redistribution of resources through which individuals could control their lives. To do so it was necessary that those with limited resources be recruited and that education, directly or indirectly, promote the creation of these resources.

Reform strategy

Government strategy during the 1970s was to attempt to come to terms with the bias in the recruitment to adult education through a comprehensive package of measures that covered several sectors of society. In addition to measures within the adult education sector itself, this strategy included social benefits for adult students and the introduction of subsidies for outreach activities. The work was based on previous measures which had shown that to increase the participation of groups of limited means, it is necessary to support recruitment as well as to offer education. Support need not be financial alone: it can be any form of compensatory action aimed at helping students overcome their psychological and situational obstacles to study. Ultimately, recruitment was and remains an issue of creating demand for education among groups traditionally disinclined to study.

In contrast to the 1967 reforms, then, it was not the institutional but rather the situational and psychological obstacles to participation that came to the fore of Swedish educational reform policy in the 1970s. Ultimately, the government's task was to remove situational obstacles to participation, particularly factors of timing and of expense that tended to counteract enrolment. The problem was generally characterized in terms of the balance between targeted and general measures, given the knowledge that the consumers of adult education were generally those with ample resources of all kinds.

A similar focus on outreach activities and study assistance for adults informed the selective measures presented in the 1974 Bill on adult education (Government Bill 1975:23). These outreach activities were meant to serve as instruments to bring about the desired change of attitudes in the adult population. If success were achieved, study assistance for adults would then guarantee that the target group realized the very real possibility to continue their education. The complete package of measures, consisting of the laws on the right to study leave, on the position of shop stewards, on state subsidies for outreach activities and on study assistance for adults, was in complete harmony with the stated goals of the Bill.

While the selective measures of the 1975 Bill largely followed the recommendation of the Royal Commission on Outreach and Adult Study Aid, they were somewhat less stringent than the Commission had suggested. Nor did the Bill contain any indication of the pace at which the measures were meant to proceed. This becomes important, because in any analysis of reform studies it is necessary not only to see to what extent measures have benefited their intended target group, but also to see if these measures could have influenced future development. Outcomes of the 1970s' reform cycle cannot be correctly interpreted without keeping this in mind.

A more fundamental issue is the glaring optimism of politicians' emphasis on the ability of education to create the resources through which individuals can command their lives. In this instance it is interesting to note that cabinet ministers often refer in the texts of Government Bills to the collectivist tradition, and to structural changes in society. The democratization of working life is seen as a motivating fact in individuals' demands for adult education. Therefore it would be wrong to maintain that changes in adult education are without consideration of issues of power and social control. What can be questioned in the initiatives towards more equitable distribution of resources was the scope of the expected effects compared with the reforms that were planned and carried out during the radical period, 1970–6.

ADULT EDUCATION, 1976–82

Policy context

Bill 1975:23 was not meant to be the terminal point of the attempts to redistribute resources, but was intended as the start of a package of measures that would be built upon over a number of years. However, once more there was a change in adult education policy. Two major factors underlie this change: the right-of-centre parties' assumption of power, and a serious deterioration in the Swedish economy.

The major statement in Bill 1975:23 on further reform activity aimed at redistributing cultural and economic resources was based on the assumption that continuously expanding finances would be able to bear the necessary increase of costs this entailed. In fact, the situation was far different: the growth rate declined, inflation increased and the government deficit soared, all of which resulted in a situation where it was difficult to achieve a balanced budget. In this situation there was no room for new ventures in adult education or in any other part of the public sector. Instead, there was a reduction in funding to education. Initially, there was a clamp-down on any increases in funding to certain areas. For example, in the 1978/79 budget year, parliament stipulated that the number of teaching hours in secondary school courses within municipal adult education were to be frozen. Two years later, a similar approach was taken with courses at the compulsory school level. In popular education, probably as an effect of increased course fees, the number of study circle participants steadily decreased during 1978/79, and later stabilized at this lower level.

Reform strategy

Unlike in 1970, there are no declared changes of goal to be found in official documents for 1976–82. If it were the case that the new coalition government shared the goals of earlier adult education policy, then changes in the focus of a redistribution of resources could, on the whole, be explained by the deterioration in public finances.

However, there is reason to suppose that behind the apparent degree of correspondence between earlier and later aims there were, in fact, major hidden differences. Analysis of the political parties' accounts of their aims reveals that all parties maintained that adult education should be given priority of place in the attempt to close educational gaps (Broström and Ekeroth 1977). Yet the right-of-centre parties, especially the Conservative party, emphasized economic and service-policy goals of adult education more strongly than the previous government. The measures suggested by the right-of-centre parties were of a more general nature and contained fewer selective measures than previous government resolutions. In turn, this reflects the differing governments' perspectives on educational equality: the right-of-centre bloc saw the issue as one of justice, while the Social Democrats regarded it as an obstacle to their ambitions to change the structure of working life and to remodel society in a Socialist direction.

The original strategy for the policy of a redistribution of resources was based on the assumption that structural change and collective action by social movements are important in any improvement in individuals' living conditions. This was indicated by the close ties between adult education reform and the democratization of working life during 1970–6, and in the emphasis on activities rooted in social movements. These collectivist efforts were toned down by the coalition government, which again threw more emphasis on individuals – rather than on society – and on the impact of education on individuals' ability to change their conditions of living. After the right-of-centre parties' assumption of power, the broader aspects of social change received scant attention, while issues concerning educational content and its control came to the fore. During the period 1976–82 major reforms of the curriculum in municipal adult education were introduced.

ADULT EDUCATION, 1982–91

Policy Context

The Social Democrats' resumption of power in 1982 did not lead to a return to the expansionist and radical period of 1970–6. On the whole, the policy for which the preceding government had set out the basic principles was continued. This meant that the growing discrepancy between reform ideology and actions of 1976–82 was just as marked in the period 1982–91, if not more so. A large public deficit forced the government to undertake severe austerity measures and prevented expensive reforms in adult education. However, more important, there was a questioning of and a gradual shift away from the 'Swedish model' (see Petersson 1991). Instead of being seen as a solution, the public sector has increasingly come to be regarded as the problem. Other changes included a shift away from the centralized form of social organization and in many fields decentralization replaced centralization. The power of the labour movement, particularly LO, which has been the strongest proponent for social equality weakened. During the 1980s Swedes changed their values. The general trend was in the direction of more emphasis being put on personal freedom and less on equality. The support for the trade unions weakened and in general there was a shift away from collective solidarity.

Between 1981 and 1990 the share of the adult Swedish population that had confidence in the labour unions and gave priority to the values of equality dropped from 23 per cent to 12 per cent (LO 1991a). Returning to Korpi the broader societal changes during the 1980s and the consequences hereof on the distribution of power was very different from the 1970s.

During 1982–91, the relationship between adult education and the economy as well as working life again took precedence. Developments towards an information economy caused a return to human capital thinking, now under the heading of human resources development, in the whole OECD world. In Swedish policy documents the link between higher and adult education, technological change and economic growth is a common theme.

A major difference between this thinking and the human capital strategy of the 1960s was that no longer was expansion of education for youth the sole interest. Instead, equal if not more emphasis was put on education of adults, particularly those in the labour force.

Reform strategy

In order to respond to the economy's demands for greater human resources without increasing public expenditure, the government allowed public educational institutions to sell education (Government Bill 1984/ 85:86). This reform constituted a major break with earlier policy in that (1) education could now be commissioned by external bodies, primarily by employers in the public and private sectors, and (2) these employers could then decide on who would participate in education. This has resulted in a situation where individuals' opportunity to receive adult education at public institutions partly depends on circumstances and decisions in the workplace.

Two major problems in Swedish adult education became evident during this period. One had to do with the consequences of the diversification of publicly financed adult education that occurred in 1967 and which also involved the creation of adult education as a separate sector. The other policy problem arose as a result of the fast growth of employer-sponsored education and the subsequent increase of educational inequalities in society.

The issue of overlap between the various publicly financed forms of adult education arose soon after the 1967 reform. As the economy deteriorated and the demands for adult education rose, efficient use of existing resources became a crucial policy issue. Linked to the general problem of who should do what was the question of how to strengthen the popular movements' influence on popular adult education. As a result of increased state involvement and the use of popular adult education as an instrument in the redistribution policy, the link to popular movements had become less visible.

Turning to the second policy issue, employer-sponsored education was responsible for most of the growth that occurred in adult education participation. Within the trade union movement the control over education and training of the work-force has come to be one of the most central issues (LO 1991b, TCO 1988). For a government, trying with limited resources to decrease the educational gap, a fast-growing sector outside its direct control was problematic. During 1982–91 tensions within the system became more pronounced and the need for new reforms more evident.

THE 1991 ADULT EDUCATION REFORM

Government Bills 1990/91:68 and 1990/91:82, passed in June 1991, drastically changed the structure of adult education in Sweden. The process that began in 1967, when adult education became a unified· policy area, was abandoned. From 1967 to 1991, popular adult education and municipal adult education had been governed as the two main components of an activity called adult education, and the bureaucracy was organized accordingly with special departments of adult education.

As a result of the 1991 reform, municipalities would no longer receive separate funding for municipal adult education but would be allocated a general block grant for youth and adult education. The other major change was that governance for popular adult education no longer rested within state bureaucracy (the National Board of Education) and a separate board totally controlled by the popular movements was established. With these changes adult education stopped being a unified policy area.

The reform could be interpreted as a move towards renewed marginality for adult education. However, the case is rather the opposite. With somewhere between 40 and 50 per cent, depending on the estimate, of the adult population participating in some form of adult education, and with constantly increasing demands on the 'system', the learning society is no longer a poetic phrase but a reality. The separation of front-end and adult education is no longer possible and the concept of recurrent education as presented by the OECD and the Swedish Commission on Higher Education (U 68) in the early 1970s has come to the fore again.

It is important to note that the reform of municipal adult education was introduced as a part of a general restructuring of secondary education as a whole, and is very much in accordance with the principle of recurrent education. The Bill also stresses the need for experiments with closer co-operation not only between municipal adult education and regular secondary education but also between these and labour market training and institutions of higher education. Since the radical period of adult education in the 1970s, adult education and secondary and higher education have been governed by different concepts of equality (see above). This is recognized in the 1991 reform (Government Bill 1990/91:85) in so far as a change is made to the school law, stating that each municipality has direct responsibility to offer its educationally disadvantaged citizens basic adult education (years 1–9) and that the latter have a right to this form of education. The law further states that the municipality must use all available resources, including outreach, to recruit the target group, all in accordance with the more radical interpretation of equality that has governed adult education.

The creation of a free-standing board for popular adult education, which has to set the goals and directions for this activity and to assume responsibility for governance, while the Parliament restricts itself to setting the goals for state subsidies, is done in order to revitalize the popular movements and to strenghten their influence on popular adult education. In the Bill, the following reasons for providing state subsidies for free and voluntary popular adult education that is self-governing are presented (Government Bill 1990/91:82: 6):

Popular adult education:

- stimulates democracy, equality, and international solidarity and understanding;
- starts from the individual's own voluntary search for knowledge;
- is characterized by democratic values and co-operation;
- aims at strengthening individuals' ability to influence their own life, and to be able, together with others, to change society in accordance with their values and ideas;
- helps develop a popular culture;
- stimulates the development of an idea-oriented adult education within the popular movements;
- helps provide all, but particularly the educationally disadvantaged, with good basic knowledge, and helps stimulate further search for knowledge.

The two Bills address the internal tension created by the 1967 reform and the increased involvement by the state in popular adult education since the Second World War. However, they do not directly deal with the other major policy problem of how to relate to the explosion in and demand for employer-sponsored education. A separate parliamentary commission was struck to address the question of competencies in the Swedish labour force.

THE ALLOCATION OF RESOURCES TO ADULT EDUCATION

For reforms to be effective, good intentions and bold policy statements are not enough. Unless reforms are accompanied by major resource

Table 3.1 State subsidies for different kinds of education
(based on 1970/71 = 100)

Year	Compulsory school 70/71 = 2977 mkr	Secondary school 70/71 = 1210 mkr	Higher education 70/71 = 1228 mkr	Adult education 70/71 = 304 mkr
1970/71	100	100	100	100
1975/76	114	98	81	176
1980/81	168	109	105	275
1985/86	121	82	102	208
1989/90	121	97	130	228

Source: The State Register.

allocations, they seldom amount to much more than rhetoric. Table 3.1 presents general trends in the allocation of funds to the various forms of education for the period 1970–90.

The central role of adult education in Swedish educational policy during the 1970s is reflected in the amount of state subsidies that went to this sector. Thus during the period 1970–80, particularly 1970–5, adult education did well in comparison with the other sectors of education. For example, while actual resources for adult education increased by 76 per cent, resources for higher education decreased by 19 per cent. The introduction of austerity measures in the beginning of the 1980s hit adult education hard, although no harder than compulsory and secondary education. The downward trend was broken in the middle of the 1980s and since then a slight increase has occurred. However, the increase for adult education has been proportionally substantially lower than for higher education.

During the right-of-centre term of office, municipal adult education received marked increases in resources and a larger share of the total amount spent on adult education. This trend has continued since the Social Democrats resumed power. In 1976/77, popular adult education received almost three times as much money as the credit-oriented municipal adult education. By 1989/90, the latter received a slightly higher subsidy. This development is interesting, given the importance that was earlier placed on popular adult education as an instrument with which to reach disadvantaged groups.

Besides the general subsidies to education, including adult education, presented in Table 3.1, a special adult education payroll tax was introduced in 1976. The purpose of this tax is to provide funding for the earmarked measures used to recruit the target group: adult study assistance and special funds for outreach activities. As the payroll tax has not been affected by the general austerity measures, its relative contribution to the total financing of adult education has increased. In 1977/78, the earmarked subsidies amounted to 22 per cent of the general subsidies; by 1989/90, this share had risen to 42 per cent. Thus in relative terms, increasing resources have been allocated for reaching the disadvantaged. However, this is mainly a result of decreasing allocation of general resources and not of a conscious policy decision. In fact, some of the payroll tax has been used to cover activities traditionally funded by general resources.

EFFECTS ON RECRUITMENT

In order to realize the goals of a redistribution of cultural and economic resources it is necessary that those with limited means are recruited and that education improve these resources. Since those of limited means had earlier been under-represented in adult education, any real change would demand an over-representation of people with limited means. Judging this goal from the present vantage point, we are left with the following:

1 The 1975 reforms did not become a point of departure but were rather the terminal point in ambitions to realize a redistribution of resources.
2 Research literature clearly shows that readiness to participate is unevenly distributed in the population and that this has to do with living conditions, socialization during the life cycle, and the rules of society for the distribution of education.
3 The under-educated group is getting older all the time and is therefore more difficult to recruit.

With these background factors in mind, it would be unreasonable to expect that adult education would be able to counteract the educational disparities that have been created during the life cycle.

Table 3.2 Participation in main forms of adult education by educational attainment: 1975, 1979, 1988/9 (percentage)

	1975					1979					1988/89				
	1	2	3	4	5	1	2	3	4	5	1	2	3	4	5
<9 years	10	2	1	1	1	11	4	2	1	1	9	6	2	1	–
9 years	14	4	2	1	2	14	8	3	3	3	11	12	4	3	1
Secondary – 1 yr	18	6	2	2	2	22	10	2	2	2	16	15	4	3	1
Secondary 1–2 yr	15	7	2	1	2	18	13	5	2	2	14	18	6	2	2
Secondary >2 yr	15	11	2	1	2	14	19	6	2	2	15	20	4	3	1
Postsec. <3 yr	18	10	2	2	3	21	16	4	2	4	16	26	4	3	1
Postsec. 3 yr–	17	12	2	1	2	20	18	5	1	3	16	29	5	2	1
Total	14	5	2	1	2	16	10	4	1	2	14	17	4	2	1

Source: After Andersson 1991.
Notes: 1 = Study circles (popular adult education); 2 = Employer; 3 = Trade union;
4 = Labour market training; 5 = Municipal adult education.

Table 3.2 presents participation in the main forms of adult education for 1975, 1979 and 1988/89 by educational attainment for the population 20–74 years of age. In view of the figures in Table 3.2 it is safe to infer that no major results have accrued as a result of the policy of a redistribution of social, economic and cultural resources. However, it should be noted that some of the earmarked measures like special adult study assistance for longer studies worked well in the sense that they were awarded to members of the target groups. The problem was the number of available awards (Lundqvist 1989).

One positive development in spite of the perpetual bias in recruitment is that the overall proportion of adult students in the educational population increased substantially between 1975–89 (see Table 3.3) and that this did not result in any dramatic increases in inequality.

Table 3.3 Participation in adult education by age and sex 1975, 1979, 1988/9 (percentage)

Age	1975 Women	Men	1979 Women	Men	1988/9 Women	Men
16–19	82	76	66	68	70	66
20–24	47	39	46	32	51	44
16–24	63	56	55	49	60	53
25–44	39	34	47	41	49	48
45–64	25	20	31	29	39	34
65–74	13	7	19	9	22	16
Total	35	30	39	35	44	41

Source: After Andersson 1991.

To a large extent, the increase is due to the explosive development of in-service training. This is problematic as the socio-economic differences are by far the largest in this form of adult education.

Looking at older adults where the most dramatic increase occurred among men, the change can be attributed to successful recruitment of older adults to study circles. This occurred during a time when younger and middle-aged adults' participation in this form of adult education decreased, particularly among women. In fact looking at the whole population, the number of participants in study circles decreased from 16 per cent in 1979 to 14 per cent in 1989, the same as in 1975.

Regardless of expectations, it should also be noted that the greater opportunity for adults to study has been of significance for women in their struggle for equality. As a consequence, there has been considerable over-representation of women in municipal adult education and also in study circles. During the periods in question there have also been favourable developments for women in trade-union and employer-sponsored education.

As far as is possible, it is interesting to compare these results with those of other countries; unfortunately, there are few statistics on adult education in most countries. Despite this, data exist from Norway (Statistik Ukeskrift 15/Statistical Weekly. 1985: 1) and Canada (Secretary of State 1984) that are interesting to consider. Participation has been defined in similar ways in Sweden and these countries, enabling a rough comparison to be made.

Table 3.4 reveals that people in Sweden with fewer than nine years of compulsory schooling participate in adult education to about the same extent as those with secondary education in the other two countries. A similar relationship exists between Swedes with secondary education and the university-educated of Norway and Canada. It should be pointed out that Table 3.4 shows only enrolment as such, and does not indicate the length of the courses. In fact, the structure of Canadian adult education is comparable to that of Sweden in terms of the length of the courses offered.

Table 3.4 Proportion of participants in adult education in 1983 in groups with different backgrounds of formal education (percentage within each cell respectively)

Educational background	Norway	Canada	Sweden
Fewer than nine years of schooling	8	5	21
Upper secondary school	19*	19	46
University education	36	45	64

Note: *Refers to upper secondary school 1. As for upper secondary school 2, the corresponding figure was 28 per cent.

Table 3.4 shows (a) that Swedish public policy, with its strong emphasis on equality expressed through earmarked programmes, can increase participation by disadvantaged groups (this conclusion is based on comparisons across countries), and (b) that even far-reaching efforts like those in Sweden have limited ability to counteract inequalities established in the family and increased through schooling and working life (comparisons within Sweden).

CONCLUDING REMARKS

The discussion above ought to have underlined the close link between adult education policy in Sweden and developments in the broader social, economic and political spheres. These links are more visible and noticeable than is the case in the formal educational system. This can be explained by the long history of popular adult education, as branches of the popular movements, being involved in collective struggle to create a more equitable and civil society characterized by a more just distribution of social, cultural, political and economic resources in the population. The radical reform of the 1970s, with its emphasis on study circles, reflects this tradition. The recent decline in public support for study circles mirrors the changing value pattern in Sweden towards a more individualistically oriented society.

It is interesting to note that the Swedish debate over adult education has centred around whether or not the disadvantaged participate, and not on the type of adult education in which they participate. In other words, discussion has addressed only one of the two prerequisites for a redistribution of economic and cultural resources.

In assessing the actual effects either in the creation of resources or in the intention of bridging educational inequalities, it is worthwhile noticing that most adult activities are in the form of short courses. The voluntary associations' study-circle activities, the main component of popular adult education, usually last a maximum of thirty hours. Courses organized by the trade unions and in-service training courses tend to vary in length. In most cases, however, the courses are of short duration especially in-service training courses for the under-educated (SCB 1990). Thus, with a certain amount of exaggeration it can be argued that more than 80 per cent of Swedish participation in adult education has little or no effect on educational disparities in terms of the number of years of education people acquire. As for the remaining, almost half are in post-secondary education where few of the under-educated can be found.

One is forced to ask if it is meaningful to draw parallels between formal or childhood education and adult education when considering the effects of education. One objection to this would be that our understanding is based on studies of the formal system. Researchers have not observed the effects of non-formal adult education such as popular adult education and in-sevice training. Popular adult education is especially significant as several scholars have shown its importance to various popular movements and its place in the development of the Welfare State (for example, Arvidson 1985, Johansson 1985). The emphasis on popular adult education, it is argued, is justified by its ability to reach and activate groups with little or an insufficient education and the fact that its particular teaching method, the study circle, is suited to the new groups. However, this reveals certain assumptions about popular adult education: that it works in a socializing way by giving practical insight into the rules of democracy; that it confers knowledge; that it acts as a springboard to more advanced studies; and that it introduces the individual into the world of popular movements with its collective resources for action.

In the absence of more profound research on the collective effects of adult education one can only call attention to the fact that the results presented in this chapter show that, from the traditional perspective of individual mobility and academic credentialism, the gap between the educated and the under-educated has not decreased. In order to be able to answer the question of how different forms of adult education effect a redistribution of social, economic, cultural and political resources, a better knowledge of the long-range effects of education is needed, especially in the arena of non-formal adult education.

The enormous expansion in employer-sponsored education during the last decade has created a major policy dilemma. As discussed above there are major inequalities in access to this kind of education which is linked to work hierarchy. Thus in 1988 the participation rate varied between 69 per cent for some academic groups to 15 per cent in some unskilled blue-collar groups (SCB 1990). Not only does rate of participation differ greatly by level of occupation but so does the nature of the educational training. Those in higher positions more often follow academically oriented, often externally organized courses, while unskilled workers receive some shorter form of on-the-job training. This development caused concerns among labour unions (see LO 1991a, 1991b; TCO 1988) and in government. In the present fiscal situation there is no room for a major increase of subsidies for adult education in general or popular adult education in particular. Instead the development will to a large degree depend on what happens in working life and the extent to which unions will be successful in getting more control over employer-sponsored education. One expectation is that central and local agreements will increasingly contain clauses on education and training of the work-force. The Federation of Labour (LO) has been hesitant to ask for general periods of paid educational leave. Rather than a general leave LO would like to see special arrangements focusing on those with the shortest education. This is in accordance with the experience from the 1967–91 reform cycle that has shown that unless the reforms are earmarked for the intended target group the already better educated will make use of the resources. The salaried employees' union (TCO), whose members are better educated, is more positive to a general clause on paid educational leave.

In the discussion the criteria for being targeted as under-educated has surfaced. The 1970s reform had nine years as a criterion. As a result of the expansion of secondary education it is now more reasonable to use eleven or twelve years as the norm. One solution that is being discussed as an answer to this problem as well as to the need for a more skilled work-force is to introduce a new programme under labour market training set up in such a way that it would provide the educationally disadvantaged with a broader general education and at the same time provide training in company-specific matters. The Committee on Competencies is presently examining the feasibility of such a scheme.

The interesting thing with the recent development is that it further underscores that in a learning society the borderlines between various forms of education, as well as between the world of work and the world of education, are becoming fuzzy. What will happen in this situation with regard to who gets access to what kind of education-learning opportunities and under what conditions will, according to the theoretical approach embraced in this chapter, to a large extent depend on the balance of power between the two major collectives, capital and labour.

With Sweden's long and, compared to other countries, rather unique interest in adult education and with the 'Swedish model' in transition, it will be of great interest to follow the developments in adult education in Sweden as we are approaching a new millennium.

REFERENCES

Andersson, L.-G. (1991) *Vuxenutbildning 1975–1989*, Stockholm: SCB.
Arvidson, L. (1985) *Folkbildning i rörelse*, Malmö: Stockholm Institute of Education.
Broström, A. and Ekeroth, G. (1977) *Vuxenutbildning och fördelningspolitik*, Uppsala: Uppsala Universitet.
Cross, P. (1981) *Adults as learners*, San Francisco: Jossey-Bass.
Härnqvist, K (1958) *Beräkning in Reserverna för högre utbildnung*, Statens Offentliga Utredningar (SOU), 11.
Johansson, I. (1985) *För folket genom folket*, Stockholm: Liber.
Korpi, W. (1978) *Arbetarklassen i välfärdskapitalismen*, Stockholm: Prisma.
LO (Federation of Labour) (1969) *Fackföreningsrörelsen och vuxenutbildning*, Stockholm: Prisma.
—— (1971) *Vuxenutbildning*, Stockholm: Prisma.
—— (1991a) *Rättvisan i vågskålen*, Stockholm: LO.
—— (1991b) *Det utvecklande arbetet*, Stockholm: LO.
Lundqvist, O. (1989) *Studiestöd för vuxna*, Göteborg: Studies in Educational Sciences.
Meidner, R. (1973) *Samordning och solidarisk lönepolitik under tre decennier*, Stockholm: Prisma.
OECD (1967) *Educational Policy and Planning: Sweden*, Paris: OECD.
Petersson, O. (1991) 'Democracy and power in Sweden' *Scan. Political Studies* 14 (2), 173–91.
Rehn, G. (1985) 'Swedish active labour market policy: retrospect and prospect', *Industrial Relations* 24, 62–89.
SCB (1990) *Deltagande i personalutbildning 1985–1989*, Stockholm: SCB.
Secretary of State (1984) *One in Every Five: A Survey of Adult Education in Canada*, Ottawa: Supply and Services Canada.
SOU (1948) '1946 aårs skolkommissions betänkande med förslag rill riktlinjer för det svenska skolväsendets utveckling'.
—— (1971) 'Vuxna–Urbildnung–Kludiefinansiering'.
Statistik Ukeskrift 15, 1985: 1.
TCO (Central Organization of Salaried Employees) (1964) *Utbildningspolitiskt program för tjänstemannarörelsen*, Stockholm: TCO.
—— (1988) *Färdigutbildad*, Stockholm: TCO.

Chapter 4

Access, not access courses
Maintaining a broad vision

Malcolm Tight

Source: This is a substantially revised version of an earlier paper, 'Access – not access courses', which first appeared in 1988 in the *Journal of Access Studies*, vol. 3, no. 2, pp. 6–13.

INTRODUCTION

Access, which until comparatively recently was an interest shared by only a select few, is now without doubt one of the major policy issues in post-school education (see, for example, Ball 1990, Fulton 1989, Parry and Wake 1990, Smithers and Robinson 1989, and Tight 1990). Thus, in its most recent public expenditure white paper, the government identified the following as one of its five principle aims for education as a whole:

> To increase and widen participation in further and higher education and to make institutions more responsive to the needs of the economy.
>
> (The Secretary of State for Education and Science,
> Chief Secretary to the Treasury 1991a: 5)

Despite the inevitable economic caveat, such a statement with such prioritization would have been startling only a few years ago. Now it seems a commonplace, and all involved – students, staff, employers, funding agencies, politicians – seem reasonably happy to accept the government's plans for increasing the number of full-time equivalent students (FTEs) in higher education by 50 per cent by the end of the century (see the Secretary of State for Education and Science *et al*. 1991b).

This whole interest in access has both positive and negative aspects. On the one hand, there are those who are concerned with opening up study opportunities to more and to different people. Frequently, this concern is linked with a desire to restructure further and higher education in what are seen as being more relevant, flexible or adult ways (Usher 1986). On the other hand, there are those who are anxious about the fluctuation and decline in the size of the conventional further and higher education entry cohort: the 16- to 19-year-olds. These anxieties have provided an impetus for seeking out, at least in the short term, alternative sources to make up student numbers; an impetus strong enough to curb worries about 'falling standards' or 'more being worse'.

However, it is not my purpose in writing this chapter to rehearse once again the various advantages and disadvantages associated with widening access to further and higher education. What I want to argue here is the importance of maintaining a broad perspective on the access issue. For there has been a growing tendency in many quarters to equate 'access' with 'access courses', which are a narrower concern. This tendency has been made manifest in government policy:

Three routes into higher education are generally recognized:
– traditional sixth-form qualifications;
– vocational qualifications;
– access courses.
            (The Secretary of State for Education and Science *et al.* 1987: 9)

More recently, the government has identified access courses, along with award-bearing courses and special-needs provision, as being worthy of receiving support from the proposed Further Education Funding Councils (Secretary of State for Education and Science *et al.* 1991c, vol. 1: 8). Such clear statements are naturally welcomed by those committed to the 'access courses movement', even though their aim is social change rather than economic growth (Brennan 1989). I believe, however, that the simple equation of access with access courses is harmful and should be resisted.

It is perhaps significant that similar debasements in meaning have occurred in recent years in the use of related educational concepts. For example, 'continuing education', initially thought of as encompassing all systematic learning which took place post-school (Advisory Council for Adult and Continuing Education 1982: 2), was taken by the government to apply to profit-making, post-experience short courses for those in employment (DES 1980). Similarly, 'open learning', a term intended to suggest the removal of barriers and the opening-up of the structure of formal education (Lewis 1986), is now frequently thought of as applying primarily to packages of learning materials designed for updating technical and managerial skills (Paine 1988, Rumble 1989). To take a third case, 'experiential learning' often tends to be viewed in terms of the accreditation of work-based learning, rather than in the broad sense of life experience as a source and means of learning (Evans 1988, Weil and McGill 1989).

It would be a great loss if 'access' were to go the same way, subverted in most people's minds to mean just 'access courses'. I accept, of course, that access courses can provide a rewarding and useful experience for many people who might otherwise have been 'failed' again by the educational system. But access courses have their faults, which have become more and more apparent as the access courses movement has mushroomed and developed its own burgeoning bureaucracy. And they are far from being the only alternative methods of enabling mature access to further and higher education.

A CRITIQUE OF ACCESS COURSES

Five linked educational criticisms may be levelled at access courses.

- they are often unnecessary;
- they are often over-elaborate;
- they help to create and sustain ghettos;
- they overemphasize higher education;
- they sustain conventional perceptions of further and higher education.

Access courses are often unnecessary

The typical access course involves one year of full-time study or two years of part-time study and requires no formal qualifications for entry. Yet many, perhaps most, mature students who are seeking entry to further or higher education already have some qualifications (indeed some have the minimum higher education entry requirements), and almost all have a good deal of experience and understanding. Many of these students do not need to undertake an access course in order to demonstrate – whether to themselves or to their receiving institutions – their ability to cope with further or higher education. Other, quicker and more relevant, means for enabling access should be available to them, as indeed they are in some cases and at some institutions.

Most further and higher education institutions are now involved as authorized validating agencies (AVAs) in the Access Courses Recognition Group (ACRG) scheme run by the Council for National Academic Awards (CNAA) for the accreditation of access courses. All validated access courses are – at least in theory – almost universally accepted as satisfying higher education institutions' general entrance requirements. This has led to a growing pressure to assume that all mature applicants should now go through the access course route. The aspiring mature student is likely to be advised by an admissions tutor to take an appropriate access course, almost regardless of their background and circumstances. This represents a distortion of the egalitarian principles which underlie the concept of access.

Access courses are often over-elaborate

An increasing standardization of practice – in terms of the aims, contents, length, organization and certification of access courses – has been imposed by the ACRG on the AVAs and, through them, on the actual providers of access courses (CNAA 1989/90). In the words of one commentator, this standardization 'could if not watched very carefully become a straitjacket' (Wagner 1990: 96). And with standardization has come an increasing complexity. I am thinking here in particular of multi-level, modular access course schemes, usually organized by 'open college federations', which are becoming more and more common. Four or five levels of study are typically recognized, and individual students may be issued with 'passports' which are stamped as they accumulate credits at the different levels.

These schemes are, of course, intended to be flexible, and open college federations do vary in their approach and methods (see Kearney and Diamond 1987). Many of those who join them may only take one or two modules, or may not be seeking to undertake further formal study. But I find the idea of someone working steadily through different modules and levels over a period of years with the aim of securing entry to, say, a degree course profoundly disturbing. Might they not be better advised to simply take a few A-levels? After all, as Avis points out: 'the notion of levels . . . through their hierarchical structure, reflect traditional educational categories and connive in the production of a relation to knowledge that is hardly progressive' (Avis 1991: 48). What I fear we are witnessing here is the creation of an alternative further education system, hierarchy and bureaucracy. This is just as likely to create additional barriers to access, and reinforce existing ones, as it is to enable access to and through further and higher education (Waterhouse 1987).

Access courses help to create and sustain ghettos

Many access courses focus their recruitment on specific social or cultural groups, such as women, ethnic minorities and the unemployed (Edwards 1990, Lyon 1988). Indeed, it was a primary aim of the access course developments encouraged by the DES in 1978 to enable the greater involvement of such under-represented groups in further and higher education (Brennan 1989).

Two-thirds of access courses only have formal links with a single higher education institution (CNAA 1990, Educational Counselling and Credit Transfer Information Service 1989). Most focus on a limited range of academic disciplines in the social sciences and humanities. Most successful access course students will be recruited into these departments in currently existing polytechnics and colleges, rather than universities. At the end of their studies, most of those who entered further or higher education through this route, and who then enter or re-enter the employment market, are likely – like mature students in general – to end up as teachers, social workers or local government officers (Brown and Webb 1990, Graham 1989, Tarsh 1989).

The success of the local links between further education courses and
degree courses . . . should not blind us to their limitations. The educational opportunities open to the successful student are severely restricted compared to those open to an A-level student . . . The chances of
getting a good degree and, beyond that, a good job are generally lower
for students entering public sector institutions (i.e. polytechnics, colleges
and universities).

(Brennan 1989: 61)

The emphasis in education is now being placed more and more on performance indicators and monitoring. In the area under discussion, there is a
particular concern to ensure the standards of access courses and their
students when compared to more conventional routes (Bourner and
Hamed 1987). Consequently, access course students are identified as such
throughout their careers in further and higher education, and will probably
be evaluated as such by most prospective employers. They are effectively
in an educational ghetto, with a restricted set of opportunities open to
them, both during and after their studies.

Their 'ghettoization' reflects, of course, the prevailing attitudes and
prejudices of students, teachers, educational institutions and employers;
though it certainly does not excuse them. What it means is that, in the
same way as the Open University system was exploited in the 1970s and
1980s to enable the teaching profession to become effectively graduate-
only, so the access course movement is now providing the qualified personnel required to staff increasingly undesirable and low status professional
jobs in the local government sector.

Access courses overemphasize higher education

Access courses do not exist simply to prepare and accredit mature students
for entry into higher education. Some, perhaps many, of their clients may
wish to leave their learning at that, or to enter vocational forms of education and training, or to explore the learning opportunities available to
them outside formal educational institutions. This seems to have been the
pattern on some of the longer-established and more generic access courses
(Hutchinson and Hutchinson 1986), and may increasingly become the case
within open college federations. But there is a strong tendency for access
course providers to emphasize their function with respect to higher education, a tendency which has been encouraged by the work of the ACRG
and the AVAs. The prospect of obtaining a degree is used as a major, and
usually *the* major, selling point in the marketing of access courses.

Higher education, by definition, is not meant for everyone. Indeed, it
is arguably only a suitable or worthwhile experience for the minority of
the population, though this will likely be a substantial minority. There is

still a great deal of scope for enabling under-represented groups to enter higher education, as the United Kingdom has a relatively elite system of higher education. But there is surely much more scope for developing worthwhile participation in forms of education and training other than higher education, and to have a much more significant social and economic impact by so doing. While it is understandable that, for reasons of status and income, further education institutions and staff should want to develop their links with higher education institutions through access courses and other means, this should remain only a small part of their function.

Access courses sustain conventional perceptions of further and higher education

Within higher education, the dominant model of teaching remains the three-year, full-time, residential, specialist honours degree (Tight 1989). This model rests firmly on expert/novice forms of presentation – the lecture, seminar and laboratory session – and on established frameworks of disciplinary knowledge and understanding. While the great majority of those involved in the access courses movement would probably wish to change this dominant model, there is little evidence that they are doing so. After all, higher education institutions offer a product for which there is a strong and growing demand: why should they alter the basis of their provision? In so far as access courses impact on higher education providers, it is the latter who have the whiphand: they decide who enters, and they have a great influence on the nature of access courses themselves through their involvement in AVAs.

Access course providers are, because of the emphasis they place on higher education, in a position analogous to that of the car components producer with respect to the major car manufacturer. They have little control over the relationship, and can only hope for steady, incremental change to take place within higher education. Whatever their aims, access course providers find themselves in the position of accepting, whether explicitly or implicitly, higher education for what it is. Their role, at least for the foreseeable future, is to provide an alternative means of entry for a limited number of people to what is a relatively unchanged process of higher education, which may result in tensions for access course students:

> By adopting a highly flexible, understanding, and supportive posture to students, access tutors may do a disservice to women in two respects: firstly, a flexible pedagogy may also be a non-demanding pedagogy . . . Secondly, an understanding, kindly and hand-holding pedagogy fosters dependency. It suggests that students cannot cope and makes the transition to the tough world of higher education much more difficult.
>
> (Green and Percy 1991: 155–6)

Unless they are appropriately prepared, the subsequent experience of access course students in higher education can involve disappointment as well as discovery (Weil 1986, Wisker *et al.* 1990).

SUSTAINING A BROAD VISION OF ACCESS

Access courses are not an end in themselves; they are a means to an end and that end is to facilitate the widest possible entry routes to higher education. These courses began as *an* alternative to A-levels for mature students. We must guard against them becoming the *only* alternative . . . all of us involved in this work should be as imaginative as possible in devising access routes into higher education, and not get hooked into one route only. We must keep our eye on the ball, which is wider access, not access courses *per se*.

(Wagner 1990: 96)

The previous section was deliberately over-critical of the current state of access courses. Some (though by no means all) of the criticisms made could, after all, also be levelled with some justice at some other forms of access provision. The point, however, is to stress that access courses should not be permitted to become the only alternative route into higher education apart from the established routes of A-levels, Scottish Highers and vocational qualifications. Access to and through further and higher education is possibly by many other routes, and we should aim to sustain and develop this broader and more variegated vision of access.

What then does, or should, this broader vision consist of? A whole series of alternative forms of access may be recognized and encouraged (Michaels 1986, NIACE 1989). These include access through examination or assessment, through liberal adult education provision, through the assessment of prior learning, through probationary enrolment, and through open entry schemes. All British institutions of further and higher education currently use one or more of these methods, sometimes in combination.

Access through examination or assessment

When the University of London received a new charter in 1858, access to its national (and international) system of examinations was opened up to all-comers through the matriculation examination. If this was passed, the student could proceed to degree level examinations; no course attendance or other formal preparation was required (Bell and Tight 1992, Harte 1986). This tradition still has its echoes today, even though the original matriculation examination has now become, after many changes, the General Certificate of Secondary Education (GCSE) examinations, which secondary school pupils normally take at the end of their fifth year (Kingdon

1991). Universities still retail the notion that students should 'matriculate' in order to satisfy their general entrance requirements.

In many institutions and departments, regulations allow for the matriculation of mature students who lack the standard entry requirements, or their equivalent, but who are judged capable of benefiting from higher education. Thus, in the five Joint Matriculation Board (JMB) universities – Birmingham, Leeds, Liverpool, Manchester and Sheffield – a varied approach has been taken to mature student matriculation (Smithers and Griffin 1986). After an initial interview, selected applicants may, for example, be asked to submit an essay, take a test or complete a preparatory course. Such methods can offer a quick and flexible means for enabling the access of suitable mature, but under-qualified, students.

Access through liberal adult education provision

Liberal education classes are offered to adults by many organizations: university departments of extra-mural studies, adult education or continuing education, polytechnics and colleges of further education, local education authorities, adult residential colleges, the Workers' Educational Association and similar bodies. Hundreds of thousands of adults follow such classes every year. Although only a minority of them will use them as a means of obtaining access to higher education, this route has been important to a great many individuals ever since the 1870s, when the university extension movement was set in motion (Marriott 1984).

At different times the stress within liberal adult education has been placed on the extended development of its students, through, for example, the tutorial classes system or the certification of courses (Duke and Marriott 1973). The latter approach has returned to prominence in recent years, partly as a result of increasing government pressures towards accreditation. In some cases, students who have successfully followed a certificate course through liberal adult education can now be granted not just entry, but entry with advanced standing, (i.e. crediting their existing learning as part of the degree course).

Access through the assessment of prior learning

This method has also grown in importance during the last decade or so, partly due to the work of the Learning from Experience Trust, but it does have long historical routes (Evans 1983, 1988). A series of related concepts are in current use, including the assessment of prior learning, of prior experiential learning, of prior achievement, and of work-based learning. Underlying them all is a recognition that adults may learn a great deal outside formal educational institutions: in their workplaces, in community organizations, in the library, in their homes.

If this learning, much of which will have been self-directed, can be articulated, recognized and recorded, it may then be assessed and accredited by a further or higher education institution, or by some other body. Various practical issues arise, of course, including whether prior learning is recognized just for entry or also for advanced standing, and whether the credit given for it should be general or specific to particular courses or subject areas. Many schemes are now in operation, particularly in polytechnics and colleges, which allow for the assessment and accredit-ation of both prior learning and ongoing work-based learning.

Access through probationary enrolment

Where an institution (or the student) is unsure of the worth of a student's existing qualifications, or ability to cope with the educational or other demands of a particular course, it can opt to register that student provision-ally. There is a sense, of course, in which enrolment is always provisional; what I am talking about here are schemes which explicitly seek to give the benefit of the doubt to borderline cases. The student's performance during a probationary or filter period can then be used to better assess abilities and needs, and appropriate guidance can be given. Such schemes are, however, likely to be time consuming, and require both careful evalu-ation and a clear mutual understanding of the position by both institution and student.

Access through open entry

This may be viewed as a variant of probationary enrolment, in that it starts from the principle of not wishing to turn away any potential students, but then places the onus both on students and the institution to take action if it subsequently appears that students are unsuited for the course on which they have enrolled. The best known current exponent of access through open entry is probably the Open University, which has been enrolling adults without any formal entry qualifications (though they are a small minority) on its degree course for over twenty years. However, this practice has not been without its problems, particularly in science-based subjects, and increasing emphasis has been placed on counselling students to undergo preparatory study where appropriate.

The 'open' label, with its attendant access philosophy, has been adopted by other educational institutions in more recent years, including the now defunct Open Tech initiative and the Open College, both of which have operated mainly at sub-degree level (Tight 1988). But the same principle also underlies much of the further and adult education provision designed for mature students.

In making this point, we are brought back to a recognition of the continuing importance of what are thought of as the conventional routes for enabling the access of mature students (amongst others) into and through further and higher education. These routes comprise traditional sixth-form courses (for A-levels, AS-levels, and their Scottish equivalents) and vocational qualifications (BTEC courses and their equivalents), plus the long lists of other British and overseas qualifications which are recognized as being of equal standing (Kingdon 1991).

These routes may seem to be more suited to adolescents than to adults, but a good deal more flexibility has been built into them in recent years, and they continue to offer a valid and closely targeted means of preparation for higher education. This is particularly true of part-time forms of provision, typically offered in colleges of further education. These have historically been 'the alternative route' into higher-level study for those from disadvantaged social or educational backgrounds (Blackburn et al. 1980, Bourner et al. 1991, Cotgrove 1958, Halsey et al. 1980, Hordley and Lee 1970, Raffe 1979).

CONCLUSIONS

It may well be the case, of course, that in this subject, as in many others, the terminology used gives rise in itself to many arguments. Some practitioners, for example, undoubtedly interpret the term 'access course' widely. Others argue that the term 'access' is restrictive, viewing it as supply- rather than demand-related, and suggest 'accessibility' as an alternative (Wright 1991). Still others would prefer to talk of 'participation' or 'educational rights'.

I believe, however, that access courses are narrowly interpreted by the majority of policy makers and practitioners involved in further and higher education. If we are to encourage the broadest possible use of our educational resources by adults throughout their lives – with all the individual, social and economic benefits which this may bring – then we need to get away from the notion of 'access courses', or even 'courses' at all, as the only or the predominant form of enabling mature access into the formal educational system. We should instead be seeking to maintain and develop a wide range of alternative access routes or methods – each with their advantages and disadvantages – to be offered to mature students in accordance with their individual needs, experience and circumstances.

REFERENCES

Advisory Council for Adult and Continuing Education (ACACE) (1982) *Continuing Education: From Policies to Practice*, Leicester: ACACE.
Avis, J. (1991) 'Not so radical after all? Access, credit levels and the learner', *Journal of Access Studies* 6 (1), 40–51.

Ball, C. (1990) *More Means Different: Widening Access to Higher Education*, London: Royal Society of Arts.

Bell, R. and Tight, M. (1992) *The History of Distance Education in the British Isles*, Milton Keynes: Open University Press.

Blackburn, R., Stewart, A. and Proudy, K. (1980) 'Part-time education and the alternative route', *Sociology* 14, 603–14.

Bourner, T. and Hamed, M. (1987) 'Degree awards in the public sector of higher education: comparative results for A-level entrants and non-A-level entrants', *Journal of Access Studies* 2 (1), 25–41.

——, Reynolds, A., Hamed, M. and Barnett, R. (1991) *Part-time Students and their Experience of Higher Education*, Milton Keynes: Open University Press.

Brennan, J. (1989) 'Access courses', in O. Fulton (ed.), *Access and Institutional Change*, Milton Keynes: Open University Press, pp. 51–63.

Brown, A. and Webb, J. (1990) 'The higher education route to the labour market for mature students', *British Journal of Education and Work* 4 (1), 5–21.

Cotgrove, S. (1958) *Technical Education and Social Change*, London: George Allen & Unwin.

Council for National Academic Awards (1989/90) *Access Courses to Higher Education: A Framework of National Arrangements for Recognition*, London: CNAA.

—— (1990) *A Survey of Access Courses to Higher Education: Analysis and Prospects*, London: CNAA.

Department of Education and Science (DES) (1980) *Continuing Education: Post-experience Vocational Provision for Those in Employment*, London: DES.

Duke, C. and Marriott, S. (1973) *Paper Awards in Liberal Adult Education*, London: Michael Joseph.

Educational Counselling and Credit Transfer Information Service (1989) *Access to Higher Education Courses Directory*, Milton Keynes: ECCTIS.

Edwards, R. (1990) 'Access and assets: the experience of mature mother-students in higher education', *Journal of Access Studies* 5 (2), 188–202.

Evans, N. (1983) *Curriculum Opportunity: A Map of Experiential Learning in Entry Requirements to Higher and Further Education Award Bearing Courses*, London: Further Education Unit.

—— (1988) *The Assessment of Prior Experiential Learning*, London: Council for National Academic Awards.

Fulton, O. (ed.) (1989) *Access and Institutional Change*, Milton Keynes: Open University Press.

Graham, B. (1989) *Older Graduates and Employment*, London: Careers Services Trust.

Green, M. and Percy, P. (1991) 'Gender and access', in C. Chitty (ed.), *Post–16 Education: Studies in Access and Achievement*, London: Kogan Page, pp. 145–56.

Halsey, A., Heath, A. and Ridge, J. (1980) *Origins and Destinations: Family, Class and Education in Modern Britain*, Oxford: Clarendon Press.

Harte, N. (1986) *The University of London 1836–1986*, London: Athlone Press.

Hordley, I. and Lee, D. (1970) 'The "alternative route": social change and opportunity in technical education', *Sociology* 4, 23–50.

Hutchinson, E. and Hutchinson, E. (1986) *Women Returning to Learning*, Cambridge: National Extension College.

Kearney, A. and Diamond, J. (1987) 'Access courses: a model for discussion', *Journal of Access Studies* 2 (2), 33–43.

Kingdon, M. (1991) *The Reform of Advanced Level*, London: Hodder & Stoughton.

Lewis, R. (1986) 'What is open learning?', *Open Learning* 1 (2), 5–10.

Lyon, E. (1988) 'Unequal opportunities: black minorities and access to higher education', *Journal of Further and Higher Education* 12 (34), 20–37.

Marriott, S. (1984) *Extramural Empires: Service and Self-interest in English University Adult Education, 1873–1983*, Nottingham: University of Nottingham Department of Adult Education.

Michaels, R. (1986) 'Entry routes for mature students: variety and quality assessed', *Journal of Access Studies* 1 (1), 57–71.

National Institute of Adult Continuing Education (NIACE) (1989) *Adults in Higher Education: A Policy Discussion Paper*, Leicester: NIACE.

Paine, N. (ed.) (1988) *Open Learning in Transition: An Agenda for Action*, Cambridge: National Extension College.

Parry, G. and Wake, C. (1990) *Access and Alternative Futures for Higher Education*, London: Hodder & Stoughton.

Raffe, D. (1979) 'The "alternative route" reconsidered: part-time further education and social mobility in England and Wales', *Sociology* 13, 47–73.

Rumble, G. (1989) ' "Open learning", "distance learning", and the misuse of language', *Open Learning* 4 (2), 28–36.

Secretary of State for Education and Science, Secretary of State for Wales, Secretary of State for Northern Ireland, Secretary of State for Scotland (1987) *Higher Education: Meeting the Challenge*, London: HMSO, Cm 114.

——, Chief Secretary to the Treasury (1991a) *The Government's Expenditure Plans 1991–1992 to 1993–1994: The Department of Education and Science*, London: HMSO, Cm 1511.

——, Secretary of State for Scotland, Secretary of State for Northern Ireland, Secretary of State for Wales (1991b) *Higher Education: A New Framework*, London: HMSO, Cm. 1541.

——, Secretary of State for Employment, Secretary of State for Wales (1991c) *Education and Training for the 21st Century* (2 vols), London: HMSO, Cm 1536.

Smithers, A. and Griffin, A. (1986) *The Progress of Mature Students*, Manchester: Joint Matriculation Board.

—— and Robinson, P. (1989) *Increasing Participation in Higher Education*, London: BP Educational Service.

Tarsh, J. (1989) 'New graduate destinations by age on graduation', *Employment Gazette*, no. 97, 581–98.

Tight, M. (1988) 'Open learning and continuing education', in P. Jarvis (ed.), *Britain: Policy and Practice in Continuing Education*, San Francisco: Jossey-Bass, pp. 75–83.

—— (1989) 'The ideology of higher education', in O. Fulton (ed.), *Access and Institutional Change*, Milton Keynes: Open University Press, pp. 85–98.

—— (1990) *Higher Education: A Part-time Perspective*, Milton Keynes: Open University Press.

Usher, R. (1986) 'Reflection and prior work experience: some problematic issues in relation to adult students in university studies', *Studies in Higher Education* 11 (3), 245–56.

Wagner, L. (1990) 'Adults in higher education: the next five years', *Adults Learning* 2 (4), 94–6.

Waterhouse, R. (1987) 'The access possibility: barrier or bridgehead?', *Journal of Access Studies* 2 (2), 15–21.

Weil, S. (1986) 'Non-traditional learners within traditional higher education: discovery and disappointment', *Studies in Higher Education* 11 (3), 219–35.

—— and McGill, I. (1989) *Making Sense of Experiential Learning: Diversity in Theory and Practice*, Milton Keynes: Open University Press.

Wisker, G., Brennan, L. and Zeitlyn, A. (1990) 'The interface: access students, access courses and higher education', *Journal of Access Studies* 5 (2), 162–76.

Wright, P. (1991) 'Access or accessibility?', *Journal of Access Studies* 6 (1), 6–15.

Chapter 5

Adult literacy and basic education in Europe and North America

From recognition to provision

Leslie Limage

Source: This is an edited version of an article which appeared in *Comparative Education*, vol. 26, no. 1, 1990.

Adult illiteracy as an extensive social and educational issue in industrialized countries is of fairly recent origin. This chapter examines the growth of recognition of this complex issue in Western European countries and North America since the early 1970s. It looks at various criteria for gauging a national commitment to ensure a literate society: awareness-raising, public commitment of resources, partnerships to increase adult literacy/basic education provision and political will. While reference is made to both northern European and southern European countries, an in-depth analysis will be confined to the British, French and United States contexts. [. . .] Parallels are drawn between future prospects in these industrialized countries and certain developing nations' efforts to provide universal literacy.

An initial distinction has to be made between the countries of southern Europe, Spain, Portugal, Italy and Greece, which have long recognized that a significant proportion of their adult populations are semi-literate or illiterate, and the countries of northern Europe, some of which still do not perceive illiteracy as an important social problem. According to a study prepared for the European Economic Communicy (EEC) by Pierre Freynet of the University of Angers (France), the problem was first formally recognized in the United Kingdom (1973), then by Ireland. In 1977, The Netherlands began to address illiteracy publicly. In 1979, Flemish-speaking Belgium followed suit. In 1981 the Federal Republic of Germany began to give public attention to illiteracy, followed in 1983 by French-speaking Belgium and in 1984 by France. Luxembourg and Denmark appear reluctant to take a public stance. These dates, of course, refer a variety of categories of recognition: the publication of official reports or research findings commissioned by governments, a national awareness-raising campaign, public subventions for voluntary or charitable associations' literacy efforts.

One might begin by wondering why semi-literacy or illiteracy among large sectors of the adult population (15 years and over) could have gone unrecognized for so long. There are a wide variety of reasons. [. . .] Some reasons for the invisibility of the problem are related to the invisibility of the populations most usually concerned by illiteracy. Another factor which has tended to hide the issue is the ambivalence of national commitment to ensure a literate society as either a basic human right, a social obligation or a necessary prerequisite for economic and social development. [. . .]

LITERACY AND POVERTY

[. . .] An abundant literature documents the cycle of illiterate and impoverished parents who cannot afford and are unable to assist their children (Hunter and Harman 1979, Alden 1982, Aide à Toute Détresse (ATD)-Quart Monde 1984, Kozol 1986, Vélis 1988). The poverty in significant portions of the industrialized world is not dissimilar to that which can be found in developing countries. Regional disparities are scarcely affected by the measures taken in both centralized and decentralized countries.

The linkage between poverty and illiteracy is indisputable; but it is not enough to assume that all the impoverished are semi-literate or illiterate or that illiteracy is necessarily a factor of socio-economic status in industrialized countries. What we can say with some conviction, and without resort to irresponsible statistics, is that all forms of illiteracy are highest among school leavers who have not obtained a school-leaving certificate, among ethnic or linguistic minorities, among the long-term unemployed, in regions with high levels of unemployment and among those populations which are most severely disadvantaged. Just because illiteracy is discovered among recruits for the military, or the incarcerated in penal institutions or in young people remanded for juvenile delinquency, does not mean that these populations are always illiterate. Basically, these contexts change the invisibility of the illiterate to a visibility which might not otherwise occur.

Also, economic transformations bring new forms of illiteracy to light. For example, when copper mining in the state of Arizona in the United States proved uneconomical and miners who had worked for generations in this industry were thrown onto the labour market, the need for retraining this population revealed a population with basic skill needs. It is certain that these kinds of transformations are going to continue throughout the industrialized world, and what was irrelevant or functional in one context may not apply in another time and place.

The invisible poor, the invisible illiterate

In certain industrialized countries, such as France or Switzerland, the awareness of illiteracy linked with poverty has been drawn from the work of a charitable body, ATD-Quart Monde. This group is implanted with the most disinherited populations, not only in these countries but in a number of other Western European nations and North America. Their publications describe the isolation, hopelessness and sense of shame which is the daily lot of the hard-core poor. Illiteracy is only one factor in a whole range of disadvantage. Thus the image of the single-parent family, drug or alcohol abuse, wife-battering, juvenile delinquency and so forth are all intertwined in the portrait of the impoverished illiterate. Many of these problems do indeed affect the lives of the most disadvantaged. Indeed, these populations are rarely reached by existing forms of remediation and adult basic provision in any country. But the accumulation of disadvantage is not so representative of people who come forth for assistance with the acquisition of basic skill. In other words, when awarenessraising campaigns and the opening-up of increased adult basic skill provision occurs, as during the British campaign of 1975, we find that adults who do come forward for assistance are not the most marginal members of society. They are articulate, know exactly what they need to learn and why they want to acquire literacy and numeracy skills; they are actually functioning in their families, community and workplace. Indeed, the most frequently met adult with learning needs who comes forward for assistance has proved extremely skilful in hiding his or her difficulties (BBC 1975, Limage 1975).

Thus, as Jonathan Kozol has eloquently argued in *Illiterate America* (1985) or the journalist Jean-Pierre Vélis in *La France Illettrée* (1988) has described, the adult illiterate is usually invisible in society either because of his or her highly marginal status for socio-economic reasons or because the individual has successfully hidden semi-literacy or illiteracy.

Unfortunately, these are the citizens in industrialized societies who are least vocal on their own behalf, and their image and needs as conveyed by the mass media and a number of well-intentioned awareness-raising efforts distorts their plight on occasion. The press and the television 'package' reality to invite sensationalism, and have difficulty in presenting complex situations. It is the mass media in each country which clamour for figures on the size of the problem when no reliable estimates actually exist (Hunter and Harman 1979, Limage 1986a, Kazemek 1988, Freynet 1988).

Prior to the British literacy campaign of 1975, the lobbyists for 'A Right to Read', were pressed for a figure. The figure selected, 2 million adults needing assistance, was relatively meaningless but was seized upon by the press. In 1984 when the media in France were also clamouring for statistics, the newly created interministerial group to deal with illiteracy (Groupe Permanent de Lutte contre l'Illettrisme) also offered the figure of 2 million. This figure has been amended in recent years, but none the less it is interesting that the French chose the same figure as the British when pressed to supply some statistics in a context in which nothing was clear. Figures in the United States range from 23 million to 64 million, according to estimates and differing definitions. Unfortunately adult literacy prac- titioners who are committed to improving the quality and quantity of publicly funded provision for learners in need do not denounce the abuse of statistics (Kazemek 1988). [. . .]

The television and the press are also prone to presenting illiteracy in a highly personalized fashion, the testimonial approach, reminiscent of Alcoholics Anonymous or some other similar socially stigmatized prob- lem. It is easier to show vignettes of individual cases of failure and shame than to analyse the global problem in its social, political and economic dimensions. By showing primarily individual testimonials, the image of the illiterate as responsible for his or her own failure is inadvertently reinforced. [. . .]

The image of the adult illiterate is further distorted, perhaps inadver- tently, by the initiatives taken by private enterprise. For example, the 'Give the Gift of Literacy' programme sponsored by the booksellers of Canada and the United States invites book buyers to contribute their small change to support literary efforts. 'Contributing is easy . . . just look for the distinctive Gift of Literacy coin box. Your change can change a life'. The underlying assumption is that the illiterate is an object of charity, a welfare recipient. Private generosity can help those who cannot or will not help themselves. Once again, the victim is at fault. The political agenda is clear. Basic skill acquisition for all members of that society is not a *public* priority. Whatever is done should be left to philanthropy and private charities. An illusion that something is being done is easily conveyed by the media and this type of awareness-raising effort.

It is indeed of grave concern that so-called national literacy initiatives or campaigns generate millions of dollars for advertising and awareness- raising but negligible public funding for long-term programmes and specialized personnel. By looking more closely at what is occurring in specific industrialized countries such as France, the United States and the United Kingdom we may better understand the complexity of the situation.

WHAT IS BEING DONE: LEVEL OF COMMITMENT

France

France is the most recent country to give official recognition to the existence of semi-literacy or illiteracy within its native French-speaking population. For years, it was assumed that the 'problem' as such was one confined to the immigrant worker population. After the events of *'mai '68'* in France, numerous politically or charitably motivated groups sprang up to give assistance to immigrant workers from North America, Spain, Portugal, Italy and Turkey. [. . .] Illiteracy among native French-speakers was rediscovered in two ways. First of all, the charitable body Aide à Toute Détresse-Quart Monde mentioned earlier constantly drew attention to the linkages between poverty and illiteracy. A government report confirmed their experience (Rapport Oheix 1981). Second, growing youth unemployment and government response in the form of training schemes starkly showed up the fact that large numbers of school leavers lacked basic literacy and numeracy skills. Pre-vocational training schemes had to be reconverted into basic skill programmes whenever possible. Finally, in January 1984, an official report on the problem was published (Espérandieu *et al.* 1984). The report had been commissioned by the government, and an inter-ministerial committee was created, with its secretariat currently in the Ministry for Professional Training (Ministère de la formation permanente). This intentional perception of the literacy question as a social welfare issue distinguishes the French approach from that of other industrialized countries, which usually created agencies or sub-ministries within their ministries or departments of education.

Another factor distinguishing the French approach from that of other French-speaking countries as well as other industrialized countries has raised considerable controversy. The notion that a significant number of native French-speakers do not possess self-sustaining literacy and numeracy skills seems inconceivable both to the general public and to decision-makers in government. The inter-ministerial committee thus decided to adopt a newly coined word to refer to their illiterates: *'illettrisme'*. The itinerary of this term is extremely interesting and sheds light on another form of misinformation which plagues literacy work in industrialized countries.

In a first instance, ATD-Quart Monde coined the word for two related reasons. The term *analphabète* or 'illiterate' had been used so far only to refer to the plight of immigrant workers from developing countries and thus had a pejorative connotation. The assumption is that there is a more 'noble' form of illiteracy in industrialized countries and a more 'modest' one in the developing world. ATD-Quart Monde was of course well-intentioned in seeking to protect the poor illiterate from further humiliation or shame. But the issue did not stop there. Academics took up the discussion and so did the media. There are now numerous justifications for maintaining that semi-literacy or illiteracy is different in countries such as France which have had public education available for more than a century. These justifications tend to assume that a child has learned to read and presumably to write, and then lost these skills. This argument protects the schools from criticism and resolutely places the blame back on the victim. [. . .] The linkages between inadequate teaching methods and teacher training and illiteracy are ignored (Limage 1975, 1986a, 1986b; Espérandieu *et al.* 1984; Freynet 1988).

The inter-ministerial group and the general public remain untouched by the fact that no other French-speaking country felt it necessary to create a new word to describe illiteracy among its native population. Further-more, the assumption that reading and writing skills are *quantities* which an individual acquires in a set period of time and then can lose betrays serious ignorance of the learning process. [. . .]

A recent study conducted for the Minister of Education in France, the *Rapport Migeon* reveals a highly critical view of reading and writing skills achieved by young people entering lower-secondary schools. It indicates alarm at the large numbers of young people who repeat a year of schooling and shows the negative long-term impact of grade-repetition on a child's chances to reach or complete the *baccalauréat*. This study [. . .] represents one more in a series of efforts to look more closely at what has been going on in schools in terms of literacy acquisition. These studies, however, do not yet make the necessary linkages between youth and adult illiteracy and the school experience.

What appears clear in the French context, however, is that the problem is not likely to receive a high-level national commitment through a publicly funded action. The inter-ministerial group does not have an autonomous budget. Little additional provision has been forthcoming. On the other hand, awareness-raising efforts through the media have given rise to further basic-skill training in youth or long-term adult unemployment schemes. As in the American context, the efforts are intended to adapt the illiterate to some place in the labour market – and this during a long-standing economic recession.

The United States

The existence of adult literacy in the United States has been recognized to a certain extent for many years. The publication of Carmen St John Hunter and David Harman's study *Adult Illiteracy in the United States* in 1979 drew serious attention to the scale of the problem. The authors came up with varying figures concerning up to a third of the population, according to definitions used. Once again, the figures have primarily a shock value.

The earliest formal measures for adult illiterates in the USA came about in 1962 with the Manpower Development and Training Act, which estab-lished a programme with a functional literacy component, adult basic education, for workers unable to take advantage of retraining schemes. In 1964 the Economic Opportunity Act provided direct funding for adult literacy to target groups: such were the unemployed; the under-educated; socially, culturally and economically deprived adults; and migrant and seasonal workers. Federal intervention subsequently took the form of the Higher Education Act of 1965, allowing for the training of teachers for economically disadvantaged areas. In 1966, adult literacy was included in what later became the Adult Education Act. All the endeavours, including the 1971 National Right to Read Programme, aimed to enable adults to become more employable and responsible citizens.

Adult literacy provision currently exists in four different forms. The government officially sponsors provision through Adult Basic Education and the military. It also gives direction through the Adult Literacy Initiative of 1983. Two prominent voluntary bodies, Laubach Literacy and Literacy Volunteers of America provide the bulk of the remaining provision. Many small-scale community programmes exist, but all these measures taken together are in no position to address the magnitude of the problem. Adult basic education is the largest provider of adult literacy tuition. It has had federal funding but at a level that prevents its further expansion. It serves some 2 million adults but has a drop-out rate from its programmes of 4 in 10 and waiting lists in the hundreds of thousands (Hunter and Harman 1979, Kozol 1986, Limage 1986a). Adults who tend to seek this type of provision are, as was found in the United Kingdom, virtually 'functional' in their daily lives but have specific learning-goals for which literacy and numeracy are key tools. The most deprived are never reached by this type of provision. The institutional arrangements are like those of the schools in which these adults failed and the majority of instructors are moonlighting schoolteachers. In sum, however, although there is enormous visible demand for adult basic skill provision both for native speakers of English and for English as a second language, the extent of provision is seriously limited by lack of adequate public funding. [. . .]

Responsibility for basic skils training is fragmented at all levels of government. At the federal level, the departments of Education, Labor and Health and Human Services administer major programs and other departments also have responsibilities in the field. Yet, at most, $1–2 billion is available at the federal level and much less is surely spent. This means that adult literacy has been a very low priority for almost everyone in Washington.

(Chisman 1989; iii)

[. . .] It appears clear that universal adult literacy is no more on the agenda of the most advanced industrialized countries than in so many developing nations, which suffer from so many other grave material needs; but it would only take a manageable effort for the case to be otherwise.

The United Kingdom

In 1973, when literacy lobbyists were presenting their charter 'Right to Read' some 5,000 adults in the United Kingdom were receiving some type of assistance with basic skills. It was also known at that time that some 15,000 young people were leaving school each year without any school-leaving certificate.

The United Kingdom, like many other industrialized countries, has a long history of voluntary and charitable bodies mediating between the wealthy and the poor. This tradition has its roots in nineteenth-century humanitarian efforts to alleviate some of the suffering caused by rapid industrialization and lack of social and labour legislation. [...] The British Association of Settlements was created at that time precisely for this purpose. Canon Barnett of St Jude's had the notion that civil conflict might be avoided if young men from the universities of Cambridge and Oxford established 'settlements' in the heart of working-class areas in order to provide some instruction to these populations. It was thought that these young students would be looked on with less mistrust than actual representatives of the capitalist middle class.

As conditions evolved, these settlements took on a variety of educational endeavours. In the early 1970s the British Association of Settlements was providing basic literacy and numeracy tuition and leading the way for a national commitment in their charter 'A Right to Read: action for a literate Britain' (1974) (Limage 1975). As a gauge of progress since that period, it is useful to look at the charter's demands. First, the charter demanded that the government of the United Kingdom make a commitment to eradicate adult illiteracy by a reasonable date, in particular, 1985. Second, it insisted that any attempt to deal with adult literacy should take into consideration the funding of the Bullock Committee and its report on reading, *A Language for Life*. An analysis of the teaching of reading and writing in schools should be linked to the issue of adult illiteracy. Third, it was suggested that a special fund be created as well as a national body to assist local authorities and voluntary bodies in extending literacy provision. An awareness-raising campaign should also be undertaken to acquaint adult illiterates and the general public with learning possibilities. All provision that would be created should be free of the usual budgetary conditions attached to adult education provision: classes opening and closing on the basis of maintaining numbers, fees waived for participants, usual formalities for enrolment eliminated, and so forth. Tutors and organizers should be recruited, trained and paid according to the usual payscale for teachers in publicly maintained schools in order to ensure their quality and continuity of service. Although volunteers and voluntary bodies had provided virtually all the instruction, excessive dependence on them should no longer be the rule. Finally, the charter requested that other sectors and public services assist educators in identifying needs and providing tuition.

The first response to this charter came from the British Broadcasting Corporation (BBC), which committed itself to a three-year series of programmes and publications to be produced jointly with the British Association of Settlements and other bodies. The programmes produced by the BBC aimed at both potential learners and potential volunteer tutors in an awareness-raising campaign. The programmes were intended to communicate that illiteracy is not a shameful state and that assistance is available. A telephone referral service was included, and the programmes themselves were broadcast at peak viewing times. At the same time, the BBC produced training materials for tutors and organizers jointly with the British Association of Settlements. Subsequently, the Minister of Education, announced a grant of one million pounds sterling and the creation of an Adult Literacy Resource Agency to allocate funds which could be used as a pump-priming source to local authorities and voluntary bodies. [...]

The adult literacy campaign itself, as an awareness-raising effort, was initially very successful in terms of the response from potential learners and tutors. Approximately 20,000 adults responded to the first phase of the campaign. Local authorities were scarcely prepared within the framework of traditional adult education institutes to cater for this new unknown client, the adult illiterate. [...] Thus local education authorities were called upon to undertake a major training effort simultaneous with the opening of the campaign.

In spite of the relatively unfavourable economic climate, the campaign in its initial three-year period drew 155,000 adults to participate in some form of literacy provision: one-to-one tutoring, small group classes in adult education institutes and home tutoring. Hence, approximately one-thirteenth of the estimated target population was reached by the various types of provision.

A mixed reaction was given to the BBC's awareness-raising television programme *On the Move*. Its use of working-class male characters in comic situations and its over-use of publicity/commercial techniques to draw learners were not always well received by potential clients (Limage 1975). The stereotype of the adult illiterate as a male of working-class origin did not always correspond to adult illiterates' images of themselves. Adult learners who first came forward for tuition were essentially functioning well in their professional and family lives. They were not necessarily of working-class background. In any case, their illiteracy was neither a humorous nor a humiliating condition, to the extent that it was compensated for by skilful means of subterfuge or assistance by friends and family. Indeed, the BBC did respond to this criticism and altered its programming as a result of the views of adult illiterates. The central government agency, currently called the Adult Literacy and Basic Skills Unit (ALBSU), has had its mandate and budget renewed on a short-term basis since that time. It has managed, however, to ensure that a high level of provision is available in most local education authorities, and is constantly encouraging innovative teaching methods appropriate for adults and experimenting with strategies to reach the most deprived in rural areas or inner cities.

According to ALBSU, [...] provision in England and Wales is currently stretched to its limit. Provision is uneven, with the best local education authority serving approximately 4 per cent of the estimated need at any given time and the weakest authority offering help to less than 0.5 per cent (ALBSU 1989: 5). Adult basic skill provision has continued to be hit hard by cuts in educational expenditure and fragmentation of provision, as is the case in the United States. In spite of its precarious state as in all industrialized countries, adult literacy and basic education survives and adapts to changing conditions and needs.

A major characteristic of the British experience [...] is its adaptibility and resolutely non-political approach to identifying need and attempting to serve it. In an initial phase, when the literacy movement was seeking its way, provision was focused on literacy and numeracy for native English speakers. Only fairly recently has the Adult Basic Skills Unit stepped into the field of English as a second language, honestly judging its own capacity and the possible confusion between clients. [...] In addition to the fact that adult basic skill provision is already under-provided for in terms of its current target learners, the problem of integrating new categories of adult learners who require specialized tutors is overwhelming. [...]

The key factor in the British adult literacy and basic skill experience since 1973 appears to be its pragmatism in dealing with shifting public awareness and expressed need as well as precariousness of funding. Indeed, this pragmatism and commitment have had to confront increased demand for financial accountability at the local level, as seen in the controversy and debate surrounding the 1988 Education Reform Act. In spite of high visibility, there is no high-level national commitment to eliminate illiteracy altogether in the United Kingdom.

WHAT HAVE WE LEARNED?

Most industrialized countries of the Mediterranean Basin have long recognized that they have not eliminated illiteracy in their populations. The situation in France, however, is not dissimilar to that of certain northern industrialized countries such as Germany, Switzerland, Luxemburg or Belgium in which recognition of the problem is limited. Voluntary bodies are the major actors in these countries. The situation in the United Kingdom could be compared with that of some Scandinavian countries and The Netherlands which are steadily recognizing the problem and acting upon that recognition. For a time, it has appeared that the United States,

Canada, New Zealand and Australia are all tending towards drawing in new partnerships with the private sector rather than increasing public spending. (This generalization is advanced with caution, however, when one looks at the long-standing provision in certain provinces of Canada: Quebec and Ontario in particular.)

Concern for definition, statistics and stereotypes

Across industrialized countries adult literacy practitioners are perplexed. It would appear that protecting the interests of young people and adults with serious learning needs is in conflict with those of policy planners or governments and the mass media. Such practitioners as Francis Kazemek in the United States warn against 'unholy alliances' with the media and business which will draw attention to the issue of illiteracy but at the same time distort it for their own purposes. [. . .] None of the partnerships with busines and the media convey the notion of literacy and education as a basic human right.

Literacy is either a set of skills to obtain a job or an elusive source of personal shame. In that sense, it appears urgent that public opinion in industrialized countries be made aware of the assumptions behind the messages it is receiving concerning the purpose of learning and those who do not succeed. An illusion of much activity to promote literacy may be taking the place of concrete improvements in conditions and teaching in schools and adult basic skill provision. [. . .] It is essential that attention should not be distracted from the only real guarantor of education as a basic human right: high-level national commitment and funding. Attempts to justify education in economic or other terms can and will be countered with projections of the kinds of jobs which will be available in the twenty-first century, for which high levels of literacy throughout the populations of industrialized countries will simply not be necessary. The argument that self-sustaining literacy and numeracy are basic human rights which all industrialized countries can afford is, however, irrefutable.

Reflections on the role of international organization and international co-operation

While recognition of adult literacy as a public issue dates back to the early 1970s in the best of circumstances in industrialized countries, attention by international organizations such as Unesco, OECD, the EEC and the Council of Europe is virtually just commencing. There are historical as well as political reasons why inter-governmental agencies such as Unesco and the EEC have scarcely addressed the issue for these countries. Unesco's experience and concern for expansion of educational opportunity has tended to focus on the developing world, assuming (as did member countries), that there was no problem in the industrialized nations. Also, the EEC's mandate as an economic community has only recently been broadened as a result of a changing political environment. [. . .]

I would like to put forward some thoughts on both the advantages and dangers inherent in developing a concern for literacy in industrialized countries. In an earlier publication (Limage 1980), I recorded the fact that literacy issues concerning developing countries and those of industrialized nations have been kept resolutely separate in most research, in high-level discussion and within international organizations themselves. I have long argued that there are common concerns which apply equally to both countries of the north and those of the south, albeit to different degrees. The role of schooling for social selection is only one issue, which, to my mind, is cross-nationally relevant. Also, the trend has consistently been that the developing world should learn from the industrialized countries' experience in expanding educational provision. It is virtually unheard-of that the literacy and basic education experience of the developing world be examined for lessons relevant to the industrialized countries. Hence, international organizations, such as Unesco, have the weight of history and practice to contend with prior to serving as an 'honest broker' providing a forum for two-way exchange.

Another difficulty inherent in the international organization approach is also linked to its role as provider of technical assistance through projects and programmes. Instead of perceiving literacy acquisition as a lifelong continuous process with different needs appearing according to context and age, the project or programme defines literacy as a quantity to be obtained in a given period of time (usually predetermined by the length of the project or programme itself). Hence, everything that occurs after that period has a special name, 'post-literacy'. Other projects deal with this next stage instead of addressing the issue as one of process. A whole range of terminology has been developed by international organizations to suit the programming constraints of its intervention rather than reality. This distortion has disturbing effects, since agencies such as Unesco are also looked to for normative statements concerning education as a human right. There are numerous intellectual and practical problems when bringing together the normative side of Unesco's mandate with its technical assistance conjunctural action.

One such striking outcome is wholly unintentional but terribly misleading. Unesco, for example, has developed the notion of 'relapse into illiteracy' or 'analphabétisme de retour' indicating what can happen to children or adults who have received a given quantity of instruction and then, basically for lack of use of literacy skills, returned to a state of illiteracy. This potential danger was to be circumvented by the post-literacy notion, that it is essential to provide reading and writing experience after the initial dose of literacy. A whole range of research and publications developing the post-literacy experience testifies to the seriousness with which Unesco, and in particular the Unesco Institute for Education in Hamburg, have worked to develop the content of this notion.

These terms, however, have been used out of context by various countries, both developing and industrialized, to blame young and adult illiterates for their inadequacies. The notion of relapse into illiteracy allows decision-makers and those unfamiliar with reading and writing education as a whole process to assume that schools have done their jobs, and that other factors, essentially related to the individual's motivation, have caused a young school-leaver to be 'functionally' or completely unable to read and write.

These types of confusion are already occurring as international organizations move into concern for illiteracy in the industrialized world. It is striking that the problem bothered no one when it was a matter of the developing countries alone.

So my first concern is one of caution since, first of all, literacy issues in the developing and industrialized worlds have been kept resolutely separate. The second concern is that categories and terminology which have proved useful in dividing up a piece of work to fit an international organization's project or programme should not be used uncritically as though they were normative statements about how we learn (or do not learn) to read and write.

With these words of caution, however, international advocacy of literacy is both appropriate and necessary. In order to ensure the most appropriate action at the local level, however, partnerships and networks with all types of providers and advocacy groups are in order. The bringing into contact in as many ways as possible of both groups can ensure that stereotypes and misinformation gradually disappear from literacy work. Indeed, there is a pool of knowledge sufficient to ensure a literate world. All that is needed is solidarity, commitment and a willingness to address a complex situation without recourse to simplistic notions of what causes and perpetuates illiteracy.

NOTE

The views expressed in this chapter are the responsibility of the author and in no way commit the organization with which she is employed.

REFERENCES

Adult Literacy and Basic Skills Unit (ALBSU) (1989) *After the Act. Developing Basic Skills Work in the 1990s*, London: ALBSU.
Alden, H. (1982) 'Illiteracy and poverty in Canada: toward a critical perspective', Unpublished MA Thesis, University of Toronto.

ATD–Quart Monde (1984) *Analphabétisme et Pauvreté dans les Pays Industrialisés*, Paris: Unesco.

British Broadcasting Corporation (BBC) (1975) *BBC Adult Literacy Handbook*, London: BBC.

Bullock Report (1975) *A Language for Life*, Report of the Committee of Inquiry Appointed by the Secretary of State for Education and Science under the Chairmanship of Sir Alan Bullock, FBA, London: HMSO.

Chisman, Forrest P. (1989) *Jump Start. The Federal Role in Adult Literacy*, Final report of the Project on Adult Literacy, Southport, USA: The Southport Institute for Policy Analysis.

Espérandieu, V., Lion, A. & Bénichou, J. P. (1984) *Des Illettrés en France*, rapport au Premier Ministre, Paris: La Documentation Française.

Freynet, P. (1988) 'L'alphabétisation des adultes francophones, ou 'Lutte contre l'illettrisme', in *Alpha 88*, under the direction of Jean-Paul Hautecoeur, Direction générale de la recherche et du développement, Québec: Bibliothèque nationale du Québec.

Hunter, C. and Harman, D. (1979) *Adult Illiteracy in the United States: A Report to the Ford Foundation*, New York: McGraw-Hill.

Kazemek, F. (1988) 'Necessary changes: professional involvement in adult literacy programs', *Harvard Educational Review* 58 (4), 464–87.

Kozol, J. (1985) *Illiterate America*, Garden City, NY: Anchor Press/Doubleday.

—— (1986) *Death at an Early Age*, New York: Plume.

Limage, L. (1975) 'Alphabétisation et culture: étude comparative. Cas d'étude: l'Angleterre,la France, la République Démocratique du Viet Nam et le Brésil', Doctoral Thesis, Paris, Université de Paris, René Descartes.

—— (1980) 'Illiteracy in industrialized countries. A sociological commentary', *Prospects*, X (2), Unesco.

—— (1986a) 'Adult literacy policy in industrialized countries', *Comparative Education Review*, no. 30, 50–72.

—— (1986b) 'The right to education for literacy: the case of the United Kingdom, the Socialist Republic of Vietnam and Brazil', in N. Tarrow (ed.), *Human Rights and Education*, Oxford: Pergamon.

Rapport Oheix (1981) *Rapport Oheix contre la Précarité et la Pauvreté*, Paris.

Vélis, J. P. (1988) *La France Illettrée*, Paris: Editions du Seuil.

Part 2

The economy, education and training

Chapter 6

Missing, presumed skilled
Training policy in the UK

Ewart Keep

A modern developed economy can only prosper if it has a labour force with the skills and education to compete with the best. Ours patently hasn't.

> Gavyn Davies, Chief UK economist at Goldman Sachs,
> *The Guardian*, 19 June 1989.

INTRODUCTION

The piece that follows attempts to outline what we know about Britain's provision of vocational education and training (VET) relative to what is provided in other developed countries, to chart the development of government polices towards VET in the 1980s, and to examine how far British employers have come in accepting the need for both improved VET and better general personnel management practices. In the space available it will not be possible to deal with these topics in great detail, but the references cited in the text should provide readers who wish to pursue issues in greater detail with a starting point for their enquiries.

It is worth underlining at the outset that the UK's relative economic decline has been linked to its weak provision of VET for over a century. At various times official reports and investigations pointing to the deficiencies in our education and training provision have sparked off cycles of public debate. The fact that the design and development of an effective VET system has for so long eluded the UK indicates that the problem's causes are deep-rooted and structural.

INTERNATIONAL COMPARISONS

The starting point for worries about Britain's VET provision has normally been unfavourable comparisons between our efforts and those of our major overseas competitors. At present, the levels of VET available to the UK population appear to be significantly lower than in most other OECD (Organization for Economic Co-operation and Development) countries.

Table 6.1 Staying-on rates

Full-time education and training	16-yr-olds (%)	17-yr-olds (%)	18-yr-olds (%)	16–18-yr-olds (%)
UK (1988)	50	35	20	35
W. Germany (1987)	69	43	33	47
France (1986)	78	68	52	66
USA (1986)	94	87	55	79
Japan (1988)	92	89	50	77

Source: Statistical Bulletin, 1990.

Education

A number of distinctive features characterize the UK's provision of VET. First, it is clear that our problems start within the system of basic education. International comparisons of staying-on rates in full and part-time education post–16 vary considerably, usually as a result of differing school-leaving ages and varying ways in which part-time students are counted. However, most international comparisons indicate that UK post-compulsory educational provision is weak, a situation that has brought adverse comment from the OECD (OECD 1991).

Part of the cause for this situation is the fact that the UK is almost unique among developed countries in having employers that are willing to offer labour market opportunities to 16-year-olds that carry little or no element of further education and training. Around 100,000 (about 20 per cent) of British school-leavers enter jobs each year that offer no training. By contrast, in 1987, 93 per cent of West German school-leavers entered an apprenticeship, further schooling, or university (Office of the Bundesminister fur Bildung und Wissenschaft 1988). For those in Britain that do remain in education beyond 16, the choices have been between relatively low-status vocational qualifications and traditional academic A-levels. About 30 per cent of those who opt for the A-level route either fail or drop out.

Participation in higher education (HE) in Britain is lower than in most other developed nations, and despite plans to increase HE provision in the UK, overseas countries have set far more ambitious targets. South Korea is aiming for 80 per cent of its young people to reach university entrance standards by the year 2000, and France has set a target of 75 per cent (CBI 1989). The current proportion of British young people reaching higher education entrance standards is approximately 30 per cent. Furthermore, our output of graduate scientists and technologists is significantly smaller than in many overseas countries; between 1981 and 1988 the number listing computing as their first choice of subject when applying to university actually fell by 8 per cent. Even larger falls were recorded in engineering and mathematics.

Training

In terms of training, there are considerable variations in the amount on offer to British employees. These variations span different sectors of the economy, the ages of workers, and their position within the organizational hierarchy. Public sector employees are more likely to receive training than those in the private sector, particularly in manufacturing. Workers aged under 24 are far more likely to be trained than those aged 50 or over (HMSO 1991a). Gender heavily influences the amount and types of training on offer (Cockburn 1987, Payne 1991) as does position in the organizational hierarchy. In fact, only 3.4 per cent of unskilled, and 7 per cent of semi-skilled workers receive any training (Weston 1991).

These variations notwithstanding, one of the most worrying facts that emerges from international comparisons of training is that the UK's training performance is weak in nearly all areas. According to *Training in Britain* (Training Agency 1989) in 1986/7, 52 per cent of the work-force received no training. At the most general level, a far smaller proportion of the UK national work-force holds vocational qualifications than is the case with most of our competitors. In Germany, for example, about 67 per cent of all workers possess vocational qualifications, whereas the figure for the UK is about 36 per cent (Prais 1981). More than a third of UK females of working age (33.8 per cent), and more than a quarter of the males (26.5 per cent) currently have no qualifications (Weston 1991). Even for a relatively favoured group, like managers, UK education and training provision has traditionally been limited. In 1986 about 20 per cent of UK managers held degrees or professional qualifications. In West Germany the figure was 63 per cent, and in the USA 85 per cent (see Handy 1987). Although managers are more likely to receive training than most shop-floor workers, and more money will be spent on this training than on that of manual or semi-skilled employees, still, in 1985, more than half of all UK companies made no formal provision for management training (Mangham and Silver 1986, see also Constable and McCormick 1987).

The organization of training is also weak. In 1987 ony 30 per cent of companies possessed a training plan, only 19 per cent of those establishments that trained made any assessment of the benefits of training, and only 3 per cent attempted to measure benefits against cost (Training Agency 1989).

Perhaps the most graphic illustrations of our poor performance in VET have come from a series of National Institute of Economic and Social Research (NIESR) comparison studies of plants in Britain and West Germany within the metalworking, furniture, clothing, and hotel industries. These have consistently indicated substantial differences in levels of training and productivity between the two countries. In all the studies, the proportion of the UK work-force receiving training was far smaller than in Germany, the levels of qualification and skill being aimed at were generally lower, and productivity in the British companies normally lagged about 50 per cent behind that of their German counterparts (see Daly *et al.* 1985, Steedman and Wagner 1987, 1989, Prais *et al.* 1989). For a compendium of NIESR's work on international comparisons, see Prais (1990). These general international comparisons, as well as company-commissioned studies of overseas competitors (see, for example, Brown and Read 1984), have formed the backdrop to UK management and government policy debates about the need to improve the UK's VET provision (Keep 1991).

In the last few years there have been some signs of improvement in both the levels of educational attainment (particularly in terms of lower-level qualifications) and the amount of training being provided to employees (Training Agency 1989). However, the pace of this change is relatively slow. In 1984 about 9 per cent of workers benefited from job-related training. By 1990 the proportion had risen to approximately 15 per cent (HMSO 1991a). It also needs to be remembered that these increases are starting from a relatively low base.

WHY VET MATTERS

The reasons why an improvement in the education and training of the work-force is important, both to individual companies and to the nation as a whole, are simply stated. The increasing pace of technical change and the growth of competition mean that all organizations are faced with the need to manage their environment in order to secure a number of strategic aims. These include the ability to deliver goods and/or services of higher quality; the ability to innovate, both incrementally and through major steps; the ability to 'get close to the customer'; the ability continuously to enhance organizational and productive efficiency; and the ability to maintain a competitive edge, both short term and long term (Hayes and Fonda 1985).

None of these capabilities is likely to be easily achieved with a poorly educated, untrained work-force. Moreover, in a world where the same technology is freely available to all who can buy it, international competitive advantage is increasingly likely to turn upon the skills, knowledge and commitment of an enterprise's employees (Cassels 1985: 439). A broad political consensus that better levels of VET in the UK are necessary for economic success emerged during the 1980s.

The effects of weak VET provision

In general terms, the following have been suggested as some of the economic effects that stem from the weak provision of VET in the UK. First, because managers are poorly technically educated, they often find it hard to see the advantages of new technologies and production techniques, and are uncertain and conservative in their use of new equipment. Second, machinery in UK factories is poorly maintained, with correspondingly high amounts of 'down time' as a result. Not surprisingly, wastage of materials and reject rates are also high, and the production of quality goods is difficult. Most worryingly of all, the generally low levels of skill in the work-force can trap UK companies into competitive strategies that come to rely on low-cost/high-volume/low-value-added production, simply because the firms lack the skills to produce higher quality goods and move up-market (Prais 1990). Reliance upon such strategies in turn serves to reduce future skills requirements. The lack of a broad technical education among the majority of the population also means that new business start-ups tend to be low tech, and be concentrated in retailing and traditional services (Barsoux and Lawrence 1990).

GOVERNMENT POLICIES

A growing awareness of the UK's deficiencies has led to widespread agreement across the political spectrum that improvement of the UK's skills base is a vital prerequisite for economic success. The means by which such an improvement might best be secured are, unfortunately, not subject to the same degree of consensus. In particular, the role of the state, and the degree to which training policies and provision can be left to market forces, is the focus of a heated debate.

The background of past policies

In the early 1960s, concern at low levels of training, particularly for young entrants to industry, led to the creation by Act of Parliament of the sectoral statutory Industrial Training Boards (ITBs). The boards concentrated their efforts on identifying skill shortages and fostering relevant training by employers through grants financed by a compulsory levy on all firms 'in scope' to their industry's board. By the early 1970s, following pressure from employers, it was decided to exempt from the levy those companies with suitable arrangements for meeting their own training needs, and to concentrate the efforts of ITBs on those companies that had made little progress, and upon improving the forecasting of future skill needs.

In 1973 a tripartite national body, the Manpower Services Commission (MSC) was set up to oversee national manpower planning, the operation of government training schemes, and the activities of the ITBs. In the years that followed, the MSC launched numerous measures aimed at dealing with persistent cyclical skills shortages, particularly in the engineering industry.

Changing policies since 1979

Since 1979 the government has been changing both the policies and the institutional structure of VET in the UK. The government's reforms have been shaped by the following beliefs. First, that market forces, rather than statutory rights and duties, are the best means of determining the type and levels of training undertaken by employers. It is up to employers and, to a lesser extent, individuals, to choose for themselves how much, or how little, to invest in training (HMSO 1988). As a consequence, the government has felt that the role of the state should be confined to the provision of education, with interventions in the training market limited to supporting disadvantaged groups (for example, the disabled, the long-term unemployed), the provision of pump-priming money for developmental purposes, and exhortation. Second, the government believes that vocational education and training provision should be employer-led and employer-controlled. The influence of educationalists and trade unions on training should be diminished.

New training initiative

In gradually putting these beliefs into practice, a bewildering succession of programmes, schemes, initiatives and structural changes have resulted. In 1981, after extensive consultation with employers, trade unions, and training specialists, the MSC produced a set of strategic objectives for UK training under the banner of the New Training Initiative (NTI). These objectives were:

1 *The development of skill training*. This covered the reform and modernization of the traditional route to a skilled job in industry – the craft apprenticeship (see Keep 1989 for details of these reforms).
2 *Equipping all young people for work*. This meant the introduction of structured programmes of initial vocational education and training for all those not on apprenticeship. In the past, the vast mass of young entrants to employment in the UK (that is, all those not on apprenticeships) had received little or no training.
3 *Widening opportunites for adults*. This objective related to the need to provide training and retraining opportunities to the vast mass of the adult work-force, for most of whom training provision tended to be minimal.

Also in 1981, partly in response to rising youth unemployment, and partly in order to meet the second NTI objective listed above, the MSC introduced the Youth Training Scheme (YTS) to provide broad-based work-related training for both the young unemployed and employed (for further details of YTS, see Jones 1988 and Chapman and Tooze 1987). A number of parallel schemes culminating in the Employment Training Scheme, were introduced to help the long-term unemployed.

Vocational qualifications

In the mid–1980s, the MSC launched a Review of Vocational Qualifications (RVQ), which was charged with rationalizing the vast array of uncoordinated VET courses and qualifications. RVQ led to the establishment of a National Council for Vocational Qualifications (NCVQ) to oversee a unified system of competency-based National Vocational Qualifications (NVQs). There are five NVQ levels (with 1 being the lowest level of qualifications and 5 being the highest), and employers in each industry or sector have been asked to identify the skill requirements for each of the five levels as they relate to their industry (see Jessup 1991).

The standards of training for each industry are usually set by the Industry Training Organizations (ITOs). These are groupings of employers within a particular industry or sector. Membership is voluntary, and the ITOs have no power to force their member companies to undertake training

Changes in education

In the schools sector, the MSC introduced the Technical and Vocational Education Initiative (TVEI) to provide opportunities for young people across a wide ability range to prepare for nationally recognized technical and vocational qualifications. It was hoped that this might encourage more pupils to remain in education beyond the age of 16. TVEI was also meant to induce schools to become involved in provision which used the latest technology, and which placed teaching much more in the context of local industry and employment (Ainley and Corney 1990).

The delivery of training

There have also been a series of major institutional changes in the planning and delivery of training. In 1981, following a major review of their activities, the government abolished most of the Industrial Training Boards (ITBs), leaving just seven in operation (of which the most important were construction, hotels and catering, road transport, and engineering). In 1989 it then announced the abolition of all but one of the remaining ITBs (construction). In place of the ITBs the government expected employers to organize and resource Non-Statutory Training Organizations (NSTOs), whose role was to disseminate information on training, help organize group training activities, and encourage training activity in their industry. Government-commissioned research indicates that the majority of NSTOs are 'ineffective' when judged against official targets (Rainbird and Grant 1985, Varlaam 1987, Anderson 1987). Recently, the NSTOs have renamed themselves Industrial Training Organizations (ITOs).

In 1988, following a refusal by TUC representatives to endorse the proposed Employment Training scheme for the adult unemployed, the government announced the abolition of the tripartite MSC. In future, trade union involvement in training decision-making outside the firm will be by invitation from employers directed at individual unions, rather than the TUC. In place of the MSC, came a new, employer-led structure. This involved:

1 A National Training Task Force, comprised of a dozen senior indus-trialists, to offer advice and guidance to the government on the develop-ment of new local training arrangements and the promotion of greater investment by employers in the skills of their employees.

2 Responsibility for training returning to the Department of Employ-ment. The civil servants who formerly staffed the MSC became part of the Department of Employment. Their role is to offer support, advice and developmental services to employer-led bodies, as well as overseeing the running of government-supported programmes of training for disadvan-taged groups.

3 The NCVQ. This is to remain responsible for the national system of NVQs that is meant to provide the standardizing 'glue' that holds together UK training provision. NVQs are also a crucial element in future evalu-ation and monitoring mechanisms for training policy, for individual TECs/ LECs and for companies involved in TEC/LEC sponsored programmes. Policies, institutions and programmes will no longer be monitored by reference to their content or processes, but simply by the outcomes, measured in terms of NVQs attained. The NCVQ has also been charged with developing a set of General NVQ (GNVQs) which are meant to provide broad-based, vocationally oriented qualifications for use in schools and further education, to run alongside A-levels (HMSO 1991b).

4 The Training and Enterprise Councils (TECs). These new, locally based councils will run alongside the national standards machinery. In Scotland slightly different bodies, called Local Enterprise Companies (LECs) have been established. TECs and LECs are employer-led bodies, and are essentially self-appointed. Two-thirds of their members must be MDs or chief executives of local private sector employers, and in legal terms they are limited companies. Their purpose is to administer existing government training schemes for the unemployed, to persuade local com-panies to undertake more training, and to stimulate local enterprise and economic growth. They receive funding from the Department of Employ-ment for those training schemes aimed at the unemployed, plus a small basic grant towards operating costs and promotional activities. A group

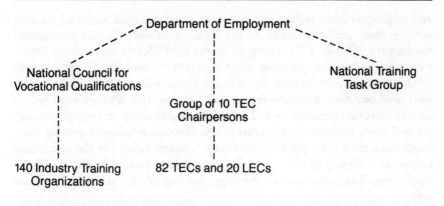

Figure 6.1 The UK training system

of ten TEC chairpersons (G10) represents the TECs in dealings with the Department of Employment.

5 The privatization of government skill centres. Many have subsequently closed.

6 Training credits. By 1996 the Youth Training programme will have been replaced by a national system of Training Credits. These will be vouchers, worth between £1,000 and £2,000, which will entitle every 16- and 17-year-old to education or training, aiming at NVQ Level 2 or higher, or its academic equivalent. The Training Credits will be administered by the TECs (HMSO 1991b).

7 Investors in People. The government has launched an Investors In People (IIP) initiative. This will provide those firms that meet certain criteria identifying them as good trainers with a national IIP 'kitemark'.

8 National training targets. The CBI have established, with government endorsement, a set of national training targets to help bring British VET up to international standards. The new targets include 80 per cent of young people achieving four GCSEs or their NVQ equivalent by 1997. By the year 2000 half of all young people should achieve A-levels or the equivalent NVQ. By 1996 all employees should be receiving training, and half of the work-force should have attained the NVQ equivalent of A-levels by the end of the century (CBI 1991).

In overall terms, the result of the government's reforms has been to shift the focus of decision-making from a national tripartite body (government, trade unions, employers) – the MSC – and industry level bodies (NSTOs and ITBs), towards locally based, employer-dominated TECs. The aim is one of nationally based standards, coupled with local delivery of training.

Within this new institutional framework, the government is rapidly moving to disengage itself from responsibility for the delivery of training, and to progressively reduce the degree of support for all forms of training activity from public finance. As the TECs have been finding out, future funding for YT and ET is going to be reduced (Beavis and Harper 1990). For example, public spending on YT in 1988/9 was £1,020 million. By 1993/4 current government expenditure plans will see this figure cut to £831 million. Any gap between public funding and what is required to deliver existing programmes will have to be made up from savings through more flexible utilization of resources and through employers putting their hands into their own pockets. In future, responsibility for the success or failure of training in the UK will rest almost totally in the hands of employers. The government's message, put baldly, is: 'It's your problem now.'

How the new training system will function

The new projected system is a highly technocratic solution. Its proponents argue that it will enable the UK to make good its deficit in VET relative to most other OECD countries. The overall belief is that the new organizational structure, and particularly the new structure of NVQ and GNVQ qualifications being erected under the supervision of the NCVQ, will produce new attitudes towards training that will drive a virtuous circle of behaviour.

Training Credits offer what is argued to be a substantially more flexible system for dealing with the varying training needs of those young people not remaining in full-time education. NVQs similarly offer the chance for employers to define vocational qualifications in terms that are readily comprehensible and transparent to them, and to design recognized training programmes that have been specified in such a way as to meet the demands posed by employment. At the same time, the five-level NVQ framework allows, for the first time, for comparability between qualifications offered in different occupations and industries. The emphasis within the NVQ framework on accreditation of prior learning (APL) and open access should produce a system through which employers can tie training – whether delivered formally or informally, on or off-the-job – to the award of recognized qualifications. Thus, much training that was previously uncertified and unmarked will lead to the award of nationally recognized qualifications, and hence the overall levels of qualification within the workforce should rise.

The availability of a graduated system of recognized, employer-designed qualifications covering all sectors of employment has also made it possible to envisage tying the award of public funds to the attainment of NVQs by trainees. The move towards 'outcomes-related funding', as it is termed, will, it is hoped, make it far easier for the TECs and LECs to monitor the use of publicly provided training funds, and to force employers to gear their training towards the achievement of national qualifications.

The intention may be to take this a stage further, and to tie the receipt of public funds to the acquisition by companies of the 'Investors in People' kitemark. Firms lacking IIP status would be excluded from receipt of public money for training, which would preclude their being eligible for funding under the Training Credits programme. The hope is that the difficulties likely to be encountered in recruiting young employees by employers not able to offer Training Credits opportunities will force more and more employers to meet the strict criteria set for IIP certification, and they will thus come to integrate training and development into their wider business planning. Once this happens it is argued that training will come increasingly to be seen as a long-term investment vital to the improvement of business performance and achievement of corporate objectives.

Finally, the national Training Targets, allied with the existence of NVQs, offer the ability to tie the strategic direction of training to easily measurable targets. The result – a system where everyone knows what they are aiming towards, and how they are doing in relation to others.

The overall aim of these developments is the creation of a mutually reinforcing, self-sustaining set of pressures that impel British employers to produce what the CBI has termed a 'skills revolution'. Just how realistic is this aim?

PROBLEMS WITH TRAINING POLICY

The 1980s in retrospect

There have been numerous criticisms of training policy in the 1980s (see Benn and Fairley 1986 for a selection of radical appraisals). There are too many to cover in detail here, but some of the most important are outlined briefly below.

One persistent criticism of voluntarist training policies which put employers in the driving seat has been that they have done little to tackle underlying problems of racial (Pollert 1986) and gender discrimination (Cockburn 1987, Payne 1991) in training provision. There certainly seems to be little evidence that government-sponsored training schemes during the 1980s did anything to alter the massive gender segmentation of career routes, or to prevent trainees from ethnic minority communities from receiving less favourable training opportunities than those available to their white counterparts.

The overall failure of the much-vaunted New Training Initiative (NTI) underlines the difficulties faced in trying to achieve any fundamental improvement in UK training performance. The reform of apprenticeship training proceeded more slowly and haltingly than was originally envisaged, and appears to have done little to halt the steep decline in apprenticeship numbers in UK manufacturing industry. The adult training strategy produced little more than government exhortation to employers to do better, with at best limited results. Most worryingly of all, the Youth Training Scheme, once billed by Geoffrey Holland, then director of the MSC, as 'the most significant development in education and training since the Education Act of 1944' (*Times Higher Educational Supplement*, 24 January 1986), failed to provide the promised 'permanent bridge between school and work' that would cover all young people whether employed or unemployed. Despite considerable efforts by the MSC to promote YTS as a universal, high-quality vocational training scheme, the majority of employers continued to see it as a response to youth unemployment (Bevan and Hutt 1985: 10, Rainbird and Grant 1985: 29, Coopers and Lybrand 1985: 12, Roberts *et al.* 1986, Sako and Dore 1986).

Problems also existed at the broader level of policy formation. The government's refusal to provide legislative backing for training met with strong criticism from many commentators. This approach is in marked contrast to other European countries, most of which provide some form of legislative backing to training (Keep 1991), either through individual rights to training and educational leave as in France (Oechslin 1987), compulsory employer membership of training bodies as in Germany (Streeck *et al.* 1987) or the imposition in France of a remissible training tax or levy on all employers.

Despite continuing government policies of disengagement, calls for legislative backing for training are being heard with 'increasing frequency' (Stanworth and Stanworth 1991). A number of major employers have suggested that they see a role for legislation in laying down compulsory minimum standards of training, and the Institute of Directors have recently said publically that they wish to see legislation making it impossible for employers to take on young people without offering them training (IOD 1991).

The abolition of the tripartite MSC and the government's attempts to minimize the role of trade unions in training again took the UK in the opposite direction to most of the rest of Europe. Elsewhere in the EC notions of 'social partnership' mean that tripartite control of training is important (Oechslin 1987, Streeck *et al.* 1987).

The style of VET policy-making in Britain has also been the subject of much adverse comment (Evans and Watts 1985, Kushner 1985, Keep 1987, Ainley and Corney 1990, Chapman 1991). The tendency has been for policy formation to be essentially short-term and *ad hoc* in nature, with little attempt to plan a coherent system from first principles. There have been very considerable problems in integrating research findings into design of new institutions and delivery systems, and attempts to learn from overseas VET systems have been characterized by a 'pick–'n'-mix approach based on crude institutional borrowing (Keep 1991).

Part of the cause of these problems has been the tendency of the political pressures generated by unemployment to override attempts to deal with the shortcomings of the UK training system (Keep 1986, Ainley and Corney 1990, Chapman 1991). Thus, the need for the government to be seen to be doing something about youth and adult unemployment has meant that large amounts of time, effort and public money have been expended on schemes, such as ET, that have little to do with securing long-term improvements in training.

Prospects for the emerging system of VET

Besides the general problems with training policy outlined above, several pillars of the new VET edifice have been the subject of criticism. To begin with, NVQs have not met with universal enthusiasm (Prais 1989). Some commentators have accused employers of defining NVQ skill levels in a narrow and task-specific way, in contrast to their European counterparts who want a broader mix of training and general education (Steedman and Wagner 1989: 48–9, Jarvis and Prais 1989: 62–70). There has also been concern that the levels of skill being specified are very low. The understanding of and commitment to the new system by many employers also appears limited (Hibbert 1990).

The move towards training credits and the abandonment of YT is also arguably problematic. The CBI's enthusiasm (CBI 1989) for the creation of what they term a 'training market' appears to stem from an implicit acceptance that most employers have failed to recognize the importance of initial vocational preparation and training, and that therefore responsibility has to be handed over to the young people themselves. This raises the question of whether the average 16-year-old school-leaver is the best person to make rational and informed choices about training. If training is about personal preference how will it become integrated into companies wider Human Resource Development (HRD) policies? Perhaps more importantly, why should companies that never trained youngsters in the past now be willing to underpin individual training for young employers by supporting the wage costs of day release?

Furthermore, the system of TECs has already proved controversial. The levels of funding available to the Training and Enterprise Councils (TECs) were initially calculated on the basis of declining levels of youth and adult unemployment. The onset of the recession and rapidly rising levels of unemployment rendered these assumptions less than realistic. At the same time, Treasury pressure on public expenditure meant that overall levels of government expenditure on training have been reduced. TEC leaders have warned that, as a result, government guarantees of training places for the unemployed are at risk (*Financial Times*, 3 June 1991), and pressed for additional funding.

When the government decided to develop TECs, it gave little thought to the pattern of relationships between these new training and enterprise bodies and the rest of the VET system. The result has been a certain degree of conflict and confusion. The relationship between TECs and pre-existing local organizations, such as chambers of commerce and local authority enterprise boards, was not thought through, and local rivalries have developed.

Relations with government have also proved to be less than smooth. While the TECs have generally tried to keep their disagreements with ministers and officials at the Department of Employment out of the public limelight, there have been numerous press reports indicating sharp battles, particularly over funding cutbacks and departmental supervision of the TECs activities (Wood 1991a, 1991b). Moreover, the existence of a loose, relatively uncoordinated network of 102 locally based organizations poses a number of problems in terms of its ability to interface with other organizations operating on the national level, such as Industry Training Organizations (ITOs) (Wood 1991a), professional bodies, and large companies (*Financial Times*, 31 July 1991). Plainly, there are tensions between the government's decision to devolve as much responsibility as possible to the local level, and the considerable transaction costs and diseconomies created by the subsequent need for national organizations to enter into a multiplicity of individual negotiations with TECs/LECs.

Initial analysis of the composition of the TEC boards indicates that manufacturing industry is often over-represented in relation to the proportion of employment it provides in the locality (Peck and Emmerich 1991). Involvement by the wider community in the TEC, whether in terms of members of ethnic minorities, local government representatives, public sector employers, or trade unionists, appears to be patchy. The Equal Opportunities Commission has also been critical of the make-up of TEC boards. Their composition, mainly as a consequence of the government's insistence on two-thirds of board members being chairpersons and chief executives of private sector companies, has tended to be dominated by middle-aged white males (*Personnel Management*, January 1991: 11).

Perhaps most importantly of all, it is not clear how the TECs, lacking any statutory powers and with more than 90 per cent of their government funding committed to schemes aimed at the unemployed, can make any significant impact on companies' attitudes towards the value of training. This issue is of crucial importance because the government's introduction of TECs was underpinned by a series of ideological a priori assumptions, the most important of which was that private sector managers have access to a set of techniques, knowledge and skills that are not available to other sections of the population, and that possession of these attributes makes them uniquely qualified to 'solve' a series of deep-seated structural problems in the country's education and training system.

It is not, however, immediately apparent what empirical evidence there is to support these unquestioned beliefs. The evidence available tends rather to cast doubt about the idea that British private sector managers constitute a meritocratic elite capable of fundamental transformation of VET provision. British managers are, according to survey data, poorly educated and trained by European standards. Indeed, British managers and their attitudes towards the value of training are part of the problem which they are now being expected to solve single-handedly.

COMPANIES, TRAINING AND HUMAN RESOURCE MANAGEMENT

If, as has been suggested above, the role of companies is a crucial one in the new scheme of things, what can be said about changes in UK companies' attitudes towards training and development in the last decade? There is little doubt that some firms, particularly those associated with the adoption of human resource management techniques (HRM), have made significant strides in developing a comprehensive approach to training (for a discussion of the concept of HRM, see Storey 1989). In the case of many of these organizations, factors such as increasing international competition, technological change, and customer demands for higher quality goods and services have forced management to recognize that they need to invest in a high-quality work-force and to secure the active commitment of all engaged in the productive process.

HRM in action

If we examine the actions of one (atypical) UK-based company – Nissan UK – we can see the emphasis placed on training as a source of competitive advantage. Nissan UK have defined a number of key business principles, which include the ability to build profitably the highest-quality car sold in Europe; to achieve the target of number one in customer satisfaction in Europe; to meet required volumes of production; and, when introducing new products, to deliver on time, at the required quality, within cost. Nissan recognize that 'these objectives can only be achieved through the people in our organization' (Wickens 1990: 2). Hence, the company has established a number of 'people principles'. These include hiring the highest calibre people, maximizing staff responsibility by devolving decision-making, encouraging teamwork, expanding the role of the individual through multi-skilling, giving workers the 'ownership' of change, ensuring good communications, and treating every worker as a 'first-class citizen'.

Underlying these principles is a commitment to continuous training throughout the organization.

Nissan UK's training budget in 1990 was £1.5 million (approximately 4 per cent of payroll costs), and the company spends more on training each worker than does its Japanese parent. Training is seen as a continuous process, embracing not simply technical skills, but also the concept of ensuring that all workers acquire and utilize 'management skills'. There is a Continuous Development Programme, covering every employee. This comprises a 'company core curriculum' of basic topics, such as total quality and problem-solving techniques; a series of Occupational Skills topics which are common to all those working at a particular occupational level within the company, irrespective of the department in which they work; and a Professional Programme which covers those 'topics people doing a job in a particular department need to know to be able to do their job effectively' (Wickens 1990: 6). Responsibility for training rests with line managers, and the development of subordinates is seen as an integral part of the managerial task.

Other companies, such as the Rover Group, have sought to build an active commitment to 'lifelong learning' into their training and development strategy (Williams 1990, Muller 1991). The Ford Motor Company's much-publicized EDAP scheme (see Hougham et al. 1991) offers another example of attempts to broaden training efforts away from task- or job-specific provision, and to emphasize the motivational benefits of training for all levels of the work-force at all stages of their working lives. The problem, as the national training figures cited above indicates, is that not enough companies have gone down this road. Why should this be the case?

The range of explanations for UK companies' failure to invest in training is extensive, and only a few of the more important arguments can be outlined here. One suggests that the problem with training is that it disrupts existing power relationships and hierarchies within the workplace. A better-trained work-force can be a threat to a poorly educated and poorly trained manager. At the same time, emphasis on the value of skill within organizations assumes the functioning of meritocratic recruitment and promotion systems. Research indicates that this is not always the case, either in terms of selection and recruitment (Collinson 1988), or promotion (Lee and Piper 1988, Grieco 1987, Silverman and Jones 1973).

Another very important reason for UK manufacturing's often apparent disinterest in major improvements in levels of UK skill formation may be the degree to which many of the larger UK companies have transformed themselves in the last twenty years from domestic producers to British-based multinationals. Throughout the 1980s, following the ending of exchange control legislation, UK manufacturing investment in overseas operations, whether through organic growth or acquisition or a mixture thereof, has been spectacular. In 1987, for example, UK firms spent $31.7 billion on acquisitions in the USA (Rodgers and Tran 1988). The result has been a tendency for many major UK companies to find themselves with domestic operations that are increasingly marginal to the overall future of the company, and the majority of their work-forces employed overseas.

A simultaneous development has been the diversification of many major British companies. The results, in terms of internal control structures that place heavy reliance on portfolio management techniques, has been to weaken long-term commitment to any particular business within the company, and to make long-term investment and planning in human resources far harder to achieve (Purcell 1989). This brings us to the long-running debate about short-termism in Britain, and the degree to which pressure from the City for the maximization of short-term profit has made it difficult for UK companies to invest in activities (for example, training, and research and development) which have a lengthy pay back (Cosh *et al.* 1990, Holberton 1990, Marsh 1990). Perhaps the point to be emphasized is that whatever the reality of external pressures on companies to take a short-term view, many corporate headquarters have developed internal financial control mechanisms that 'peer at the business through numbers' (Goold and Campbell 1986) and effectively internalize short-termism (Purcell 1989). These systems encourage managers to maximize short-term profit at the cost of the long-term investment. For example, in so far as performance-related pay systems for managers are related only to the immediate 'bottom line' they may encourage managers to cut back on investment in training (Murlis 1990).

Perhaps most importantly of all, as has been suggested above, the UK's training problems do not simply stem from difficulties with the supply of training and skills. They also reflect the fact that, because of their product market strategies, demand for skills from many employers is weak. The lack of a sufficiently strong demand for skills in the economy limits not only the efficiency of the training supply system, but also the incentives available to individuals to get trained. As Finegold and Soskice (1988) have argued, much of the British economy is arguably trapped in a 'low-skills equilibrium', from which escape will not be easy.

There are two clear dangers that arise from this situation. The first is that current product market strategies of many UK firms mean that, even if the government is able to stimulate an increase in the volume of training, it will occur at the lower end of the skills spectrum. The result will be that British training will produce large numbers of people equipped to: 'perform today's low valued-added tasks . . . while the rest of the European Community focuses on training and education to pursue innovation and value-added business strategies' (Fonda 1989: 7).

Indeed, some (Jarvis and Prais 1989: 70) have argued that many of the

NVQs being specified by British employers target such low skill levels that they run the risk of producing 'a certified semi-literate under-class', and Sir Bryan Nicholson, chair of the National Council for Vocational Qualifications (NCVQ) has admitted that, 'there are jobs in the British economy that can be achieved with only modules of NVQ Level 1' (Nicholson 1991). In this respect, the contrast offered by Lane (1988) between the ways in which British and German employers have been changing production technologies, work organizations, and skill requirements, is illuminating.

The second danger of a tendency to opt for a low skills route is that, faced with increasing international competition from countries with more highly educated and skilled work-forces, British companies will have little choice but to concentrate on competitive strategies based on low-cost production (Fonda 1989: 6). The consequence is that UK producers will face growing competition from low-wage, but increasingly productive, developing countries. How far such a strategy is sustainable is open to question, given that many expert commentators (Streeck 1989, Fonda 1989, New and Myers 1986) have suggested that the high skill, high wage, high value-added route is 'amost certainly the only viable long term strategy for a highly developed economy' (New and Myers 1986: 26).

The longer that the UK delays action to improve its overall skills base, and to increase the length and levels of the basic education provided for the majority of the working population, the more out of step with other developed and developing economies it becomes.

REFERENCES

Anderson, A. (1987) *Non-Statutory Training Organisations: Their Activities and Effectiveness*, Sheffield: Manpower Services Commission (mimeo).

Ainley, P. and Corney, M. (1990) *Training for the Future – The Rise and Fall of the Manpower Services Commission*, London: Cassell.

Barsoux, J-L, and Lawrence, P. (1990) 'Not enough spanners in the works', *Times Higher Educational Supplement*, 29 June.

Beavis, S. and Harper, K. (1990) '£2.5bn training hive-off in chaos', *The Guardian*, 22 March.

Benn, C. and Fairley, J. (1986) *Challenging the MSC on Jobs, Education and Training*, London: Pluto Press.

Bevan, S. and Hutt, R. (1985) *Company Perspectives on the Youth Training Scheme*, Report No. 104, Brighton: Sussex University, Institute of Manpower Studies.

Brown, G. F. and Read, A. R. (1984) 'Personnel and training policies – some lessons for western companies', *Long Range Planning* 17 (2), 48–57.

Cassels, J. (1985) 'Learning, work and the future', *Royal Society of Arts Journal*, 133 (5347), 438–49.

Chapman, P. G. (1991) 'The crisis in UK adult training policy: 1981–1990', *Studies in the Education of Adults*, 23 (1), 53–60.

—— and Tooze, M. J. (1987) *The Youth Training Scheme in the United Kingdom*, Aldershot: Gower.

Cockburn, C. (1987) *Two-Track Training, Sex Inequalities, and the YTS*, London: Macmillan.

Collinson, D. (1988) *Barriers to Fair Selection: A Multi-sector Study of Recruitment Practices*, London: HMSO.

Confederation of British Industry (CBI) (1989) *Towards a Skills Revolution – A Youth Charter*, London: CBI.

—— (1991) *World Class Targets: A Joint Initiative to Achieve Britain's Skills Revolution*, London: CBI.

Constable, J. and McCormick, R. (1987) *The Making of British Managers*, London: British Institute of Managers.

Coopers and Lybrand Associates (1985) *A Challenge to Complacency: Changing Attitudes Towards Training*, London: MSC.

Cosh, A., Hughes, A., Singh, A., Carty, J., and Plender J. (1990) *Takeovers and Short-Termism in the UK*, Industrial Policy Paper no. 3, London: Institute of Public Policy Research.

Daly, A., Hitchens, D. M. W. N. and Wagner, K. (1985) 'Productivity, machinery and skills in a sample of British and German manufacturing plants', *National Institute Economic Review*, February, pp. 48–61.

Evans, K. and Watts, A. G. (1985) 'Introduction', in A. G. Watts (ed.), *Education and Training 14–19: Policy and Practice*, Cambridge: Careers Research and Advisory Service, pp. 3–10.

Finegold, D. and Soskice, D. (1988) 'The failure of training in Britain: analysis and prescription', *Oxford Review of Economic Policy* 4 (3), 21–53.

Fonda, N. (1989) 'In search of a training strategy', *Personnel Management*, April, pp. 6–7.

Goold, M. and Campbell, A. (1986) *Strategies and Styles: The Role of the Centre in Managing Diversified Corporations*, Oxford: Basil Blackwell.

Grieco, M. (1987) *Keeping it in the Family: Social Networks and Employment Chance*, London: Tavistock.

Handy, C. (1987) *The Making of Managers: A Report on Management Education, Training and Development in the United States, West Germany, France, Japan and the UK*, London: National Economic Development Office.

Hayes, C. and Fonda, N. (1985) *Top Management Programme Problem No. 6 – Employment and Training*, London: Cabinet Office (mimeo).

Hibbert, V. (1990) 'System, what system?', *Industrial Society Magazine*, September, pp. 14–15.

HMSO (1988) *Employment for the 1990s* (Cm 540), London: HMSO.

—— (1991a) *Training Statistics*, London: HMSO.

—— (1991b) *Education and Training for the 21st Century and Education and Training for the 21st Century: The Challenge to Colleges* (Cm 1536), London: HMSO.

Holberton, S. (1990) 'The long and short of it', *The Financial Times*, 21 May.

Hougham, J., Thomas, J. and Sisson, K. (1991) 'Ford's EDAP scheme: a round table discussion', *Human Resource Management Journal* 1 (3), 77–91.

Institute of Directors (IOD) (1991) *Performance and Potential*, London: IOD.

Jarvis, V. and Prais, S. J. (1989) 'Two nations of shopkeepers: training for retailing in France and Britain', *National Institute Economic Review*, May, pp. 58–73.

Jessup, G. (1991) *Outcomes: NVQs and the Emerging Model of Education and Training*, Brighton: Falmer Press.

Jones, I. (1988) 'An evaluation of YTS', *Oxford Review of Economic Policy* 4 (3), 54–71.

Keep, E. (1986) 'Designing the stable door: a study of how the Youth Training Scheme was planned', *Warwick Papers in Industrial Relations* (no. 8), Coventry: University of Warwick.

—— (1987) 'Britain's attempt to create a national vocational education and training system: a review of progress', *Warwick Papers in Industrial Relations* (no. 16), Coventry: University of Warwick, IRRU.

—— (1989) 'A training scandal?', in K. Sisson (ed.), *Personnel Management in Britain*, Oxford: Basil Blackwell, pp. 177–202.

—— (1991) 'The grass looked greener – some thoughts on the influence of comparative vocational training research on the UK policy debate', in P. Ryan (ed.), *International Comparisons of Vocational Education and Training for Intermediate Skills*, Brighton: Falmer Press.

Kushner, S. (1985) 'Vocational chic: an historical and curriculum context to the field of transition in England', in R. Fiddy (ed.), *Youth Unemployment and Training, A Collection of National Perspectives*, Brighton: Falmer Press.

Lane, C. (1988) 'Industrial change in Europe: the pursuit of flexible specialisation in Britain and West Germany', *Work, Employment and Society* 2 (2), 141–68.

Lee, R. A. and Piper, J. (1988) 'Dimensions of promotion culture in Midland Bank', *Personnel Review* 17 (6).

Mangham, I. L. and Silver, M. S. (1986) *Management Training: Context and Practice*, University of Bath, School of Management, ESRC/DTI Report.

Marsh, P. (1990) *Short-termism on Trial*, London: Institutional Fund Managers Association.

Muller, F. (1991) 'A new engine of change in employee relations', *Personnel Management*, July.

Murlis, H. (1990) 'A long-term view of reward systems', *Personnel Management*, August, p. 10.

New, C. C. and Myers, A. (1986) *Managing Manufacturing Operations in the UK, 1975–1985*, London: British Institute of Management.

Nicholson, B. (1991) Response given at LSE Centre for Economic Performance/Anglo-German Foundation seminar on the UK and German training systems, 8 October.

Oechslin, J. J. (1987) 'Training and the business world: the French experience', *International Labour Review* 126 (6), 653–67.

Office of the Bundesminister fur Bildung and Wissenschaft (1988) *Development and Improvement of Technical and Vocational Education: Report and Contributions of the UNESCO Congress Berlin (East) 1987*, Bonn: OBBW.

Organization for Economic Cooperation and Development (OECD) (1991) *OECD Economic Surveys: United Kingdom*, OECD.

Payne, J. (1991) *Women, Training and the Skills Shortage: The Case for Public Investment*, London: Policy Studies Institute.

Peck, J. and Emmerich, M. (1991) *Challenging the TECs: The First Year. Interim Report of the CLES TECs and LECs Monitoring Project*, Manchester: Centre for Local Economic Strategies.

Pollert, A. (1986) 'The MSC and ethnic minorities', in C. Benn and J. Fairley (eds), *Challenging the MSC on Jobs, Education and Training*, London: Pluto Press.

Prais, S. J. (1981) 'Some practical aspects of human capital investment, training standards in five occupations in Britain and Germany', *National Institute Economic Review*, November, pp. 46–65.

——— (1989) 'How Europe would see the new British initiative for standardising vocational qualifications', *National Institute Economic Review*, no. 129, August, pp. 52–4.

——— (ed.) (1990) *Productivity, Education and Training*, London: NIESR.

———, Jarvis, V. and Wagner, K. (1989) 'Productivity and vocational skills in services in Britain and Germany: hotels', *National Institute Economic Review*, no. 130, November, pp. 52–74.

Purcell, J. (1989) 'The impact of corporate strategy on human resource management', in J. Storey (ed.) *New Perspectives on Human Resource Management*, London: Routledge, pp. 67–91.

Rainbird, H. and Grant, W. (1985) *Employers' Associations and Training Policy*, Coventry: University of Warwick, Institute of Employment Research.

Roberts, K., Dench, S. and Richardson, D. (1986) 'Firms' uses of the Youth Training Scheme', *Policy Studies*, vol. 6, part 3, January, pp. 37–53.

Rodgers, P. and Tran, M. (1988) 'US feathers ruffled at British invasion', *The Guardian*, 26 April.

Sako, M. and Dore, R. (1986) 'How the Youth Training Scheme helps employers', *Department of Employment Gazette*, June, pp. 195–204.

Silverman, D. and Jones, J. (1973) 'Getting in: the managed accomplishment of 'correct' selection outcomes', in J. Child (ed.), *Man and Organisation*, London: George Allen & Unwin.

Stanworth, J. and Stanworth, C. (1991) *Work 2000: The Future for Industry, Employment and Society*, London: Paul Chapman Publishing.

Steedman, H. and Wagner, K. (1987) 'A second look at productivity, machinery and skill in Britain and Germany', *National Institute Economic Review*, November.

——— ——— (1989) 'Productivity, machinery and skills: clothing manufacture in Britain and Germany', *National Institute Economic Review*, May, pp. 40–57.

Storey, J. (ed.) (1989) *New Perspectives on Human Resource Management*, London: Routledge.

Streeck, W. (1989) 'Skills and the limits of Neo-Liberalism: the enterprise of the future as a place of learning', *Work, Employment and Society*, 3 (1), 89–104.

——— et al. (1987) *The Role of the Social Partners in Vocational Training and Further Training in the Federal Republic of Germany*, Berlin: European Centre for the Promotion of Vocational Training.

Training Agency (1989) *Training in Britain*, Sheffield: Training Agency.

Varlaam, C. (1987) *The Full Fact Finding Study of the NSTO System*, IMS Report no. 147, Brighton: University of Surrey, Institute of Manpower Studies.

Weston, C. (1991) 'Training go-slow puts the brake on skill factor', *The Guardian*, 26 October.

Wickens, P. (1990) *Innovation in Training Creates a Competitive Edge*, Paper Presented to NEDO Policy Seminar on Training, Oxford University, Nissan (UK) Ltd (mimeo).

Williams, M. (1990) 'Learning to win', *Transition*, June.

Wood, L. (1991a) 'Training on trial', *Financial Times*, 10 July.

——— (1991b) 'Tecs look for marriage guidance', *Financial Times*, 10 June.

Chapter 7

Vocational training and new production concepts in Germany
Some lessons for Britain

Christel Lane

Source: This is an edited version of an article which appeared in the *Industrial Relations Journal*, vol. 21, no. 4, 1990.

Recent changes in the international division of labour have forced the advanced countries to approach the problem of competitiveness of manufactured goods on world markets in a new way. Concurrent developments in the field of production technology have provided an additional impetus for a transformation of production organization and marketing strategy, culminating in new production concepts or a new manufacturing policy.[1] The development of such a new manufacturing policy has been crucially influenced both by the societal institutional framework, particularly by the system of vocational education and training (VET), and by the practices of human resource management at the level of the firm. While the latter tend to be decisively shaped by the former, individual managements can sometimes overcome the constraints imposed on them by the structural framework of their society.

This chapter argues that, in the then Federal Republic of Germany (hereafter Germany), both public policy and management practices have created the human resources which make it possible and advisable to adopt the new manufacturing policy. In Britain, in contrast, the institutional framework makes it difficult to follow the same course, and individual managements, who are committed to a new approach to the recruitment, training and deployment of human resources, have to work against the grain of their society and culture.[2] [. . .]

A system of VET is far more than merely an instrument for the production of technical skills. As Figure 7.1 illustrates, the German system creates not only a distinct social structure in business organizations but also a host of behavioural and attitudinal patterns. These shape interaction in labour markets and in the field of employment, in industrial relations and work organization, and even in the area of technological innovation. These various social consequences of the German skill structure constitute strong 'push' and 'pull' factors which, together with recent changes in the market environment and in technology, have led managements to adopt new production concepts. These have enabled enterprises in many industries to maintain or improve their competitive position in world markets. Such economic success has, in turn, confirmed the vital importance of the system of VET and perpetuates the virtuous circle. The following sections of the paper will focus on each element of this circle in turn.

THE GERMAN SYSTEM OF VOCATIONAL EDUCATION AND TRAINING

Apprenticeship training

The system of initial VET is a dual system, consisting of plant-based practical training and college-based theoretical instruction. Training lasts for three years and is offered not only to 16-year-old school-leavers but also to older persons. The cost of training is shared between employers and the state although the former pay about two-thirds of the costs.[3] The training allowance is, however, much lower than in Britain. This means that, in effect, trainees make a significant contribution of their own to the financing of their training costs.

The contents and the standards of training for all occupations are determined in a tripartite manner at the federal level, by the Institute of Vocational-Education and Training. At plant level training is guided by a training contract, and adherence to it is monitored by the works council. Training can only be carried out by qualified foremen (*Meister*). It is examined by local Chambers of Craft and Industry, and examinations cover both theoretical and practical aspects. A pass leads to the award of a certificate which is recognized and respected all over Germany.

Training entails the exposure to a wide range of work situations and problems. Trainers impart not only technical knowledge and skill but also administrative and managerial competence (costing, design and planning of production) and social skills (punctuality, discipline, pride in the product etc.).

The disadvantages of the apprenticeship system, as viewed by the unions and by individual workers, lie in the fact that training often suits the short-term needs of employers and is not sufficiently oriented towards the long-term needs of labour for personal and career development. There occurs a substantial amount of training for dying craft occupations. Individual employers, in turn, may object that they cannot shape training sufficiently in accordance with their local short-term needs. But this may be a necessary price to pay for the extensive benefits of the system for the long-term development of both individuals and the whole economy.

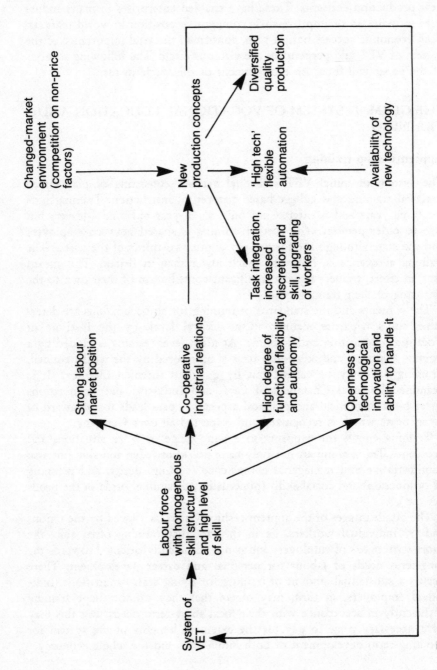

Figure 7.1 Virtuous circle set in motion by the German system of VET

ADVANCED TRAINING OF TECHNICIANS AND FOREMEN

The training of these two groups builds on that of skilled workers and, as a rule, necessitates the part-time attendance of more advanced vocational colleges. Courses of two to three years' duration for technicians and foremen take place at *Berufsfachschulen* and *Fachschulen* respectively. Courses are examined and certified in the same way as those for apprentices. It is at the level of the foreman that German superiority over British qualification and skill levels is particularly glaring. The training received by foremen is both deep and wide, covering not only the technical and managerial aspects of production but also the pedagogical tasks of the foreman in his/her role of trainer of apprentices. The impact of this on the quality of initial VET cannot be overestimated.

Further training

Although further training is not regulated by public policy it is nevertheless well established and widely practised. Training efforts by individual employers receive reinforcement from the regulations of the Works Constitution Act and from Works Agreements. Such training is mainly in-firm and locally standarized, but it has received a lot of financial and moral government support in recent decades. Works councils also take a strong interest in further training. A high proportion of firms (over 50 per cent in the early 1980s) provide such training,[4] and training effort has steeply increased during the 1980s.[5] There is a lively debate about whether further training should receive a higher degree of formalization and institutionalization.

STRUCTURE AND LEVEL OF SKILL IN THE GERMAN LABOUR FORCE

Homogeneity of skill structure in manufacturing enterprises

As Figure 7.2 illustrates, the German system of vocational education facilitates workplace mobility through further study from the bottom to the top of the hierarchy. Conversely, the training of those at the higher levels usually builds on that at the lower ones. This is, of course, not necessarily the case for engineers and managers. But the engineers who have taken the *Fachhochschule* (Polytechnic) route predominate in industry, and a substantial number of German managers are said to have served apprenticeships.[6] Also the payment system rewards such practical experience very highly.[7] Such a highly integrated system of VET makes for a homogeneous skill structure which helps to create the common understandings and sense of solidarity of a craft community. Although the British structure also

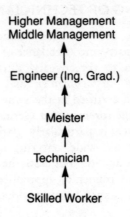

Higher Management
Middle Management

↑

Engineer (Ing. Grad.)

↑

Meister

↑

Technician

↑

Skilled Worker

Figure 7.2 Career progression through VET

permits mobility from the level of craftsman to that of technician or engineer, progression to management level is less common, and apprenticeships are not encouraged and rewarded for aspiring managers. Also the recent greater formalization of technical training has made such upward mobility more difficult to achieve.

LEVEL OF TECHNICAL SKILL IN THE LABOUR FORCE

Table 7.1, showing the proportions of technically skilled German personnel in comparison with those of its main competitors, illustrates the overwhelming superiority of German skill levels not only in relation to Britain but also in relation to other advanced countries.

Table 7.1 How Britain compares: numbers qualifying in engineering and technology, 1985 (per 100,000)

	Britain	*France*	*W. Germany*	*Japan*
Doctorates	1.2	0.5	1.6	0.5
Masters and enhanced degrees	4	11	7	8
Bachelor degrees	25	27	34	50
Technicians	51	63	72	46
Craftsmen	62	167	197	75*

Source: NIESR, quoted by *The Economist*, 13–19 January 1990.
Note: *Excludes building: comparable British figure = 42.

This discrepancy between Germany and Britain in the proportions of the labour force, trained to a high level, applies to all industrial sectors.[8] Conversely, the labour force component without any vocational qualifications is very small in Germany but is high in Britain although the introduction of the Youth Training Scheme in the 1980s has begun to marginally alter this for new entrants to the labour market.[9] German employers intensified their training effort from the mid–1970s onwards to help combat unemployment. This has often led to overskilling and temporary downward mobility of skilled workers but is nevertheless deemed worthwhile by workers affected.[10] This period also witnessed an increase in demand for apprenticeships among better-educated people with 'A' levels. In 1984, 16 per cent of young people with *Abitur* did an apprenticeship, and 1986 figures for the clothing industry give a similar figure.[11] The continually rising skills levels evident in the 1980s and forecast for the 1990s are illustrated by the figures in Table 7.2.

Table 7.2 Changes in the qualification structure in production

Degree of qualification (highest level)	1982 (%)	1990 (%)	2000 (%)
Without initial training	38.1	31.1	24.4
With short or long initial training	54.0	59.9	65.9
Certificate of foreman or technician or equivalent	6.9	7.6	8.3
Degree from polytechnic or university	1.0	1.2	1.5

Source: Progncs AG, Institut f. Arbeitsmarkt- und Berufsforschung. Quoted by Industriemagazin April 1987, p. 174.

The high proportion of skilled labour at all levels of the work-force and the high level and breadth of skill achieved do not only indicate an effective public policy but also point to the almost universal acceptance of human resource management at the level of the firm, regardless of size. Training is not merely seen as an extra cost, as it is mostly regarded in Britain, but as a worthwhile and, indeed, indispensable investment which is as important as investment in technology. Human resource management, particularly in recent decades, has become a part of strategic planning.

It is by now a familiar fact that the relation between financial and industrial capital allows German managers to adopt long-term planning horizons whereas that pertaining in Britain puts considerations of quick pay-back and short-term profit at the forefront of management thinking. Whereas in the past, this explanation has been evoked mainly in relation to capital investment it is now also applied to human resources management. The educational background in engineering of a large proportion of German managers at all levels, the possession of apprenticeships by a sizeable minority, as well as managerial career paths in internal labour markets and the subsequent development of longer-term horizons, all contribute towards a high estimation of the importance of training.

German managements have thus for a long time regarded training as a valuable investment but several more recent events have raised it to an issue of strategic importance. First, the Works Constitution Act, particularly its 1976 amendment, which gives labour numerical parity on the supervisory boards of large (more than 2,000 employees) companies, has raised the discussion of employment issues to board level.[12] This already high profile of human resource management then received added weight by the high-tech competitive strategy adopted in the late 1970s.[13] It was realized that this strategy could only succeed if combined with a further intensification of effort in the field of training.[14] This required both an increase in the proportion of skilled labour in the whole labour force and a raising and broadening of skill levels and contents for both skilled and semi-skilled workers. [...] Lastly, the temporary 'glut' of skilled workers, resulting from the big training offensive during the recession to alleviate youth unemployment, acted as an additional inducement for managements to raise the importance of skill training to strategic level.

It is, therefore, evident that in Germany both public policy and management initiatives at the level of the firm have combined to create a highly skilled work-force whereas in Britain impediments at both levels make it difficult to obtain this result, even when the realization of the necessity for change is strong. The following section will explore the effects the German skill structure has on the attitudes and behaviour of labour and how these, in turn, 'pull and push' managements towards the adoption of the New Production Concepts.

LABOUR MARKET STRENGTH

The wide validity and easy marketability of the 'Skilled Worker' certificate gives German workers strength in external labour markets and convinces them of the indispensability of skilled trades. The big weight of skilled workers among all workers accords them a strong influence in collective bargaining and has raised the costs of both wages and social benefits to the highest among European workers. As is shown by Figure 7.3, wages are nearly double those in Britain. But high levels of productivity ensure that unit labour costs are kept at a level where competitiveness can still be maintained, provided certain production and marketing strategies are being pursued.

The skill structure of the labour force is not only reflected in high wages but also in a much stronger differentiation of the pay structure according to skill than is the case in Britain.[15] The pay structure not only reflects merit but also serves to provide incentives to improve skill levels through further training. Whereas the differential between an unskilled worker and a skilled craftsman in Britain in 1986 was a ratio of 100:113, in Germany the same ratio was 100:121. For foremen it widened even further with a British ratio of 100:136 contrasted with one of 100:169 in Germany.[16] The incentive to acquire further skills is heightened by pro-

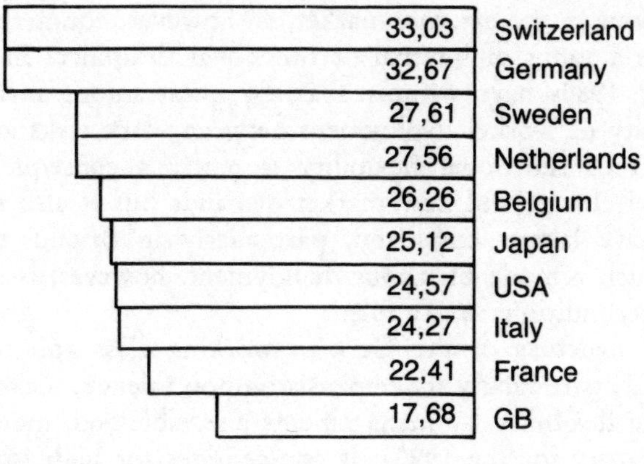

33,03	Switzerland
32,67	Germany
27,61	Sweden
27,56	Netherlands
26,26	Belgium
25,12	Japan
24,57	USA
24,27	Italy
22,41	France
17,68	GB

Figure 7.3 Labour costs: hourly wages plus social payments in DM (1987)
Source: *Der Spiegel*, 17, 1988, p. 128.

motion procedures which emphasize competence rather than seniority at all levels. [. . .]

The system of VET also affects the level of employment security, although other factors contribute to it as well. The sustained training effort of German employers constitutes a considerable investment on their part, and managements are loath to forfeit this investment even during times of economic down-turn. In smaller firms the ideology of the craft community makes economic redundancies difficult to justify and, in some of the large firms, informal policies of no redundancies are operated.[17] But German workers are by no means immune from unemployment. In the crisis industries work-forces have been cut as drastically as anywhere else, and in some industries, such as steel and clothing, the introduction of the new production concepts have, at the least, received a strong impetus from an employment policy which has pared down work-forces to the minimum.

Also the second half of the 1980s, following the Employment Promotion Act, has seen an increase in marginal forms of employment. But, with the exception of one or two industries, these are not common in the manufacturing sector. According to a survey by the German employers' federation, the BDA, only 1.5 per cent of the industrial work-force were on short-term contracts in 1986.[18] But this proportion may increase over time as short-term contracts are very common among new entrants to the labour market.[19] On balance, however, German industrial workers still have a high degree of employment security. In the mid–1980s the average length of employment was second only to that of Japan among OECD countries.[20] In 1984, 46 per cent of the German labour force had been with the same employer for more than ten years, compared to only 30 per cent of the British labour force.[21]

The degree of rigidity created by the relatively strong position of German labour in the external market, is, however, counterbalanced by a considerable amount of internal or functional flexibility. In all advanced societies the 1980s have witnessed a new quest among managements to gain flexibility of worker deployment between work tasks and functions. This pursuit of functional flexibility is partly a consequence of rapid technological change and new market demands but is also motivated by efforts to save labour costs and, particularly in Britain, to raise productivity. Such a mode of labour deployment, however, is only possible if certain preconditions are fulfilled.

The skill structure of the German working class and the nature of German VET, particularly its emphasis on polyvalency, makes the pursuit of functional flexibility by managements a feasible and, indeed, an indispensable strategy for the 1990s. It compensates for high wage costs and for the relatively high degree of external employment rigidity, and it is made possible by the absence of union control over job territories and the negotiation, in the 1970s, of agreements on internal mobility.

Functional flexibility presupposes not only a high degree of polyvalent skill but also co-operative industrial relations. These serve to mitigate the threat of loss of management control, flowing from the indispensability and disruption potential acquired by highly skilled labour in a high-tech production strategy. In Germany the co-operative nature of relations between management and labour is not only maintained by the structure of the system of industrial relations,[22] the relatively harmonious quality of industrial relations also receives considerable support from the system of VET. The homogeneity of the skill structure creates common values and orientations, embodied in a craft ethos. This improves communication between different hierarchical levels, and conflicts of interest between management and labour become mediated by the co-operative culture of a craft community.

TRAINING AND TECHNOLOGICAL INNOVATION

A high level of polyvalent skill positively influences both worker attitudes to technological innovation and the ability to cope with technologically sophisticated machinery and processes. Positive attitudes are, however, also fostered by the expectation of employment security. The latter was demonstrated by a German-British comparison of the 1970s.[23] A more recent comparative study by Daly et al. shows convincingly how the higher all-round levels of skill in German firms have a positive impact on what machinery is bought, its ease of installation and of maintenance, as well as rendering its handling and operation by operatives much less problematic than in Britain.[24] A study by Northcott et al.[25] of the use of microelectronically controlled technology also confirms that German firms use technologically more advanced machinery and processes than their British counterparts. Another comparative study shows that greater technological innovativeness by German firms also extends to products.[26] The study concludes that German firms incorporate microelectronic components in products more widely and more consistently than their British counterparts, and the authors connect this finding with the different skill levels of the two labour forces. In Britain, to sum up, low levels of worker skill encourage the use of low levels of technology which, in turn, perpetuates low training efforts. This form of production organization thus maintains a vicious circle which, if unchecked, bodes ill for the future competitiveness of British industry.

Technological innovation also receives important impulses from the degree of worker autonomy granted which, in turn, is closely related to degree of skill. Worker autonomy in the execution of work tasks in different societies has been measured and compared by establishing the ratio of supervisory staff to production workers or, in other words, the span of control. The latter has been consistently found to be wider in Germany than in Britain. The connection of this greater autonomy with higher levels of skill and greater pride in work, fostered by the system of VET, is obvious.[27]

THE INTRODUCTION OF THE NEW PRODUCTION CONCEPTS

The new production concepts or the new model of industrial organization, as defined by Kern and Schumann and by Piore and Sabel, have as one of their main premises the existence of a highly skilled and polyvalent labour force.[28] The preceding discussion of the wide ramifications of skill training has already made this connection evident. Kern and Schumann's work made it clear that the new production concepts did not herald a return to the old craft idyll and a total abandonment of mass production, as implied by Piore and Sabel, but that they stand for 'diversified quality production'. [. . .] It indicates a blending of craft methods of production with those of mass production.

Numerous empirical studies have shown that the model of diversified quality production enjoys great popularity both among British and German managements, but that the implementation of the model has been pursued both more consistently and more widely in Germany. [. . .] Although there is no doubt that the new production concepts are a reality in German mnaufacturing, it is still being debated how widespread their implementation has become by the end of the 1980s.[29] Recent overviews of developments in Britain show a more hesitant, haphazard and contradictory adoption of some of the elements of the new concept but rarely the implementation of an integrated approach, meriting the term 'model'.[30]

[. . .] At the same time, however, recent case studies show that some individual British managements have succeeded in adopting a forward-looking approach to human resource management and have overcome the many impediments to the development of a more strategic approach to training.[31]

In the German case, it is easy to show that, in terms of industries affected by the new production concepts, coverage is now very wide. The concepts have gained acceptance in both former craft and former mass production sectors and are even beginning to touch the once most Taylorized industries, such as the electro-technical.[32] They have spread beyond the core industries and are now prevalent in former crisis sectors, such as steel and clothing production.[33] The car, machine tool, chemical and electro-technical industries alone were responsible for over 50 per cent of sales of manufactured goods in 1986,[34] and all the industries mentioned are important in export terms. They all contain the basic elements of the new industrial strategy – task integration and job enrichment, unskilling, upgrading and increases in the proportion of skilled workers employed, as well as new or upgraded technology and market strategies. [. . .]

In those areas of production, characterized by both technological and organizational innovation, a new type of production worker – the system regulator, with a level of skill above that of the traditional craftsman – has come into being. The system regulator is engaged in a qualitatively new type of work which requires a high degree of skill and initiative and affords the opportunity to exert independent influence on the content of work. [. . .] Human resources management strategy is oriented towards this assumption.

LESSONS FOR BRITISH INDUSTRY

It is clear that a manufacturing policy of concentration on diversified quality products is the only one for advanced societies in order to remain competitive in world markets. It is equally evident that this strategy can only succeed if certain preconditions are fulfilled. The most basic and influential of these is a sound system of VET. This is now widely realized in Britain, and some politicians and training specialists may argue that the latest British reform of the training system constitutes a large step in this direction. This chapter, in contrast, contends that the new training policy still has such serious shortcomings that it is unlikely to provide the much-needed transformation of the skill structure which will give it parity with the German system. British managers, too, have not moved sufficiently far on the 'human resource management' front to make the new manufacturing policy feasible. Both policy-makers and managers can learn some lessons from German policy and managerial practice in this field.

The setting up in Britain of a National Council for Vocational Qualifications (NCVQ) and the standardization of training levels to be reached are steps in the right direction. But they do not go nearly far enough, nor is the content of training sufficiently wide and demanding. In the light of the German experience, changes are required in the following areas. First, standardization needs to be extended to the testing of skill levels and must be carried out by outside bodies. Otherwise, certificates will not carry any status in the wider society and will not attract the more able and motivated youngsters into VET. Second, training must cover not only practical but also theoretical aspects, as well as contain some general educational content relevant to occupational training. Without such content the training will have little value to the individuals and the wider economy. It will result in limited horizons and will not facilitate the transfer of skills from one firm to another nor to changed situations within a firm. Such narrow training will not enable individuals to build on their initial training and to ascend up the training ladder and hence will remain unattractive to the more able and ambitious potential recruit.

Third, to facilitate career mobility within the enterprise through successively higher levels of training and to gain homogeneity of the whole skill structure there has to be more co-ordination. [. . .]

Fourth, even at the practical level the requirements made of trainees are far too low. This is revealed by Steedman and Wagner[36] in their excellent comparison of training in British and German clothing firms making women's outerwear. It shows that the skills it took YTS trainees two years to learn the German trainees accomplished in the first six months of their training programme.[37] It may be argued that it is unfair to compare German apprentices and British YTS trainees and that it would be more appropriate to compare them with City and Guilds students. In 1986, 6,600 German young people passed stages II and III of the apprenticeship in the clothing industry, compared with only 520 young Britons passing the equivalent levels of the City and Guilds examinations.[38] This makes it obvious that the British clothing industry will not be shaped by workers from the latter category but by lowly skilled YTS trainees. The disastrous impact of this fact on skill, productivity and quality of goods produced, makes it clear that the new manufacturing policy is unrealizable for the bulk of British clothing firms. The high quality of workmanship noted by Steedman and Wagner throughout the German clothing industry, could be discerned in only some dozen British companies.[39] Sadly, this picture is by no means confined to the clothing industry but can be replicated for many others.

While there is certainly an urgent need to provide training for the lower segment of the British educational spectrum the almost exclusive focus on it and the extremely modest objectives adopted are not going to solve Britain's skill shortages and the problems associated with it. Training is still geared to old production concepts, and the new approach pays too little attention to the training needs of existing employees. It should also be noted that even an improved training course will remain ineffective if trainers themselves remain underqualified for their tasks. Hence a greater emphasis on the technical training of foremen must form one plank of any reform of the British training system.

British employers might be more encouraged to engage in high-quality occupational training if the training allowance were to be reduced to the German level of about one third of the adult wage. But any such reduction must go hand in hand with a new conception of training. Such a new approach would regard training as an extension of basic education. It would be designed to provide trainees with a nationally respected certificate of skills which ensures them a lifetime of well-rewarded, relatively secure employment and challenging and autonomous work activity whilst also benefiting the economy as a whole. Such training would be a worthwhile investment for the individual worker, for the employer and for the whole of British society.

CONCLUSIONS

The preceding argument has made it clear that an adoption of the new production concepts depends on a fresh approach to human resources management in which a sound system of skill training constitutes the cornerstone. It has been shown that, in Germany, public policy and the resulting institutional framework have steered managements unambiguously in the direction of high and increasing investment in human resources development. In Britain, in contrast, recognition that labour is the central and most valuable resource in the competitive struggle is not as widespread. Training is still frequently regarded as merely a cost rather than as a source of future opportunity, and its organization remains oriented to immediate need. Even where managements have recognized the pivotal role of training, a translation into managerial practice often proceeds unevenly. Despite some changes in public policy in recent years, the institutional framework of British society continues to impede the widespread adoption of a sound training policy. [. . .]

Without wanting to minimize the difficulty of achieving a break of the historically forged mould, this chapter argues against fatalistic acceptance of structural determinism. Although exhortation is insufficient to achieve a transformation in attitudes and practices it is not superfluous. Recognition of the importance of skill training is not yet sufficiently widespread, and even when it is present among policy-makers the magnitude of the change required is not appreciated. The new training policy still constitutes a reaction to adverse circumstances – a high level of youth unemployment – rather than a strategic response, devised as part of a forward-looking competition policy. But proselytizing about a new approach to training must not only be directed towards governmental and enterprise policy-makers it must also address itself to the unions. Policies of the unions show, as yet, low recognition of the fact that a training offensive will be highly beneficial also for labour.

Recognition of the necessity for radical change is, however, not enough. It will have to be accompanied by a recasting of public policy, aimed at fundamental structural transformation and by a fresh approach towards human resources development by both management and labour. Such changes are, of course, interdependent but not fully determined. Although such radical institutional restructuring seems, on the face of it, incompatible with the present government's professed 'free market' stance, its past record – for example, in the fields of trade unions and labour market policy more generally – has demonstrated that, on occasions, the voluntarist orientation can be cast aside in favour of a highly interventionist approach. In the meantime, the initiative lies with forward-looking individual managements and unions, prepared to work against the cultural grain of their society. It was indicated in other parts of this chapter that such innovative managements exist. It remains to be seen whether they can grow sufficiently numerous to spark off a more widespread training offensive. The long-term benefits to be reaped, by both capital and labour, will certainly make their difficult mission worthwhile.

REFERENCES

1 Kern, H. and Schuman, M., *Das Ende der Arbeitsteilung? Rationalisierung in der Industriellen Produktion*, Munich: Verlag C. H. Beck, 1984.
2 Storey, J. and Sisson, K., 'Limits to transformation: human resource management in the British context', *Industrial Relations Journal* 21 (1), Spring 1990; and Hendry, C., 'New technology, new careers: the impact of company employment policy', *New Technology, Work and Employment* 5 (1), 1990.
3 Roberts, J., 'Apprenticeships in Germany', *Employment Gazette*, March-April 1986: p. 111.
4 CEDEFOP, *Vocational Training Systems in the Member States of the European Community*, Luxemburg, 1984: p. 172.
5 *CEDEFOP News*, December 1989.
6 Handy, C., *The Making of Managers*, A NEDO Report on behalf of the MSC, NEDC and the BIM, London: NEDO, 1987: pp. 44, 46; Lawrence, P., *Managers and Management in West Germany*, London: Croom Helm, 1980.
7 *Manager Magazine*, 11, 1986: p. 343.
8 Prais, S. J., 'Vocational qualifications of the labour force in Britain and Germany, *National Institute Economic Review*, 98, 1981, and numerous other articles in the above journal.
9 Ibid.
10 Streeck, W., 'Successful adjustment to turbulent markets: the automobile industry', in P. J. Katzenstein (ed.), *Industry and Politics in West Germany*, Ithaca: Cornell University Press, 1989: p. 130.
11 Handy, C., *The Making of Managers*, A NEDO Report on behalf of MSC., NEDC and the BIM, London: NEDO 1987: p. 44; Steedman, H. and Wagner, K., 'Productivity, machinery and skills: clothing manufacture in Britain and Germany', *National Institute Economic Review*, May, 1989: p. 47.
12 Streeck, W., 'Co-determination: the fourth decade', in B. Wilpert and A. Sorge (eds), *International Perspectives on Organizational Democracy*, Chichester: John Wiley, 1984.
13 Kern, H. and Schuman, M., *Das Ende der Arbeitsteilung? Rationalisierung in der Industriellen Produktion*, Munich: Verlag C. H. Beck, 1984.
14 Heizmann, J., 'Work structuring in automated manufacturing systems, exemplified by the use of robots for body shell assembly', in T. Martin (ed.), *Design of Work in Automated Manufacturing Systems*, Oxford: Pergamon Press, 1984.
15 *The Economist*, 13–19 January 1990: p. 35.
16 Prais, S. and Wagner, K., 'Productivity and management: the training of foremen in Britain and Germany', *National Institute Economic Review*, February 1988: p. 39, Table 1.
17 Herrigel, G. B., 'Industrial order and the politics of industrial change: mechanical engineering', in P. J. Katzenstein (ed.), *Industry and Politics in West Germany*, Ithaca: Cornell University Press, 1989; and Streeck, W., 'Successful adjustment to turbulent markets: the automobile industry', in P. J. Katzenstein (ed.), *Industry and Politics in West Germany*, Ithaca: Cornell University Press, 1989.
18 Bundesvereinigung der Deutschen Arbeitgeberverbaende (BDA), *Untersuchung der Bundesvereinigung ueber die Anwendung und Auswirkungen des Beschaeftigungsfoerderungsgesetzes von 1985*, BDA Koelln, 1986: p. 14.
19 Lane, C., 'From "welfare capitalism" to "market capitalism": a comparative review of trends towards employment flexibility in the labour markets of three major European societies', *Sociology*, 4, 1989.

20 Streeck, W., *Industrial Relations in West Germany: Agenda for Change*, Discussion Paper No. 5, Research Unit, Labour Market and Employment, WZB, April 1987: p. 19.

21 *Arbeitsmarktchronik*, 24, 1986: p. 1.

22 Lane, C., *Management and Labour in Europe*, Edward Elgar, 1989: Chapter 8.

23 Weltz, F., *Introduction of New Technologies, Employment Policies and Industrial Relations*, London: Anglo-German Foundation, 1978.

24 Daly, A., Hitchens, P. and Wagner, K., 'Productivity, machinery and skills in a sample of British and German manufacturing plants', *National Institute Economic Review*, 111, February 1985.

25 Northcott, J., Rogers, P., Knetsch, W. and de Lestapis, B., *Microelectronics in Industry. An International Comparison: Britain, Germany, France*, London: Policy Studies Institute, 1985: pp. 2, 6.

26 Campbell, A., Sorge, A. and Warner, M., 'Microelectronics applications, product strategies and competence requirements: sectoral strengths and manpower implications in Great Britain and West Germany', Management Studies Research paper 15, University of Cambridge, 1988.

27 Maurice, M., Sorge, A. and Warner, M., 'Societal differences in organizing manufacturing units', *Organisation Studies*, 1: 1980: pp. 67–8; Finlay, P., 'Overmanning: German vs Britain', *Management Today*, August, 1981; Maitland, I., *The Causes of Industrial Disorder. A Comparison of a British and German Factory*, London: Routledge & Kegan Paul, 1983: p. 26; Prais, S. and Wagner, K., 'Productivity and management: the training of foremen in Britain and Germany', *National Institute Economic Review*, February 1988: p. 38.

28 Kern, H. and Schuman, M., *Das Ende der Arbeitsteilung? Rationalisierung in der Industriellen Produktion*, Munich: Verlag C. H. Beck, 1984; Piore, M. J. and Sabel, C., *The Second Industrial Divide*, New York: Basic Books.

29 Voskamp, U., Wittemann, K. P. and Wittke, V., 'Kontinuitaet und Umbruch. Ein Interpretationsansatz aktueller Rationalisierungsentwicklungen in der Elektroindustrie', *SOFI Mitteilungen*, Goettingen, February 1989.

30 Wood, S. (ed.), *The Transformation of Work?*, London: Unwin Hyman, 1989; Elger, T., 'Change and continuity in the labour process: from pseudo-fordism to quasi-Toyotaism?', Paper delivered at the Conference on 'Work, Employment and Society: A decade of Change', University of Durham, September 1989.

31 Hendry, C., 'New technology, new careers: the impact of company employment policy', *New Technology, Work and Employment* 5 (1), 1990; Storey, J. and Sisson, K., 'Limits to transformation: human resource management in the British context', *Industrial Relations Journal* 21 (1), Spring 1990.

32 Campbell, A., Sorge, A. and Warner, M., 'Microelectronics applications, product strategies and competence requirements: sectoral strengths and manpower implications in Great Britain and West Germany', Management Studies Research Paper 15, University of Cambridge, 1988, p. 20; Voskamp U., Wittemann, K. P., and Wittke, V., 'Kontinuitaet und Umbruch. Ein Interpretationsansatz aktueller Rationalisierungsentwicklungen in der Elektroindustrie', *SOFI Mitteilungen*, Goettingen, February 1989.

33 *The Economist*, 10 March 1990: p. 93; Esser, J. and Fach, W., 'Crisis management "made in Germany": the steel industry', in P. J. Katzenstein (ed.), *Industry and Politics in West Germany*, Ithaca: Cornell University Press, 1989; Steedman, H. and Wagner, K., 'Productivity, machinery and skills: clothing manufacture in Britain and Germany', *National Institute Economic Review*, May 1989.

34 Herrigel, G. B., 'Industrial order and the politics of industrial change: mechanical engineering', in P. J. Katzenstein (ed.), *Industry and Politics in West Germany*, Ithaca: Cornell University Press, 1989: p. 187.
35 Schuman, M., Baethge-Kinsky, V., Neumann, U., Springer, R., *Breite Diffusion der Neuen Produktionskonzepte – zoegerlicher Wandel der Arbeitsstrukturen.* (Trendreport Rationalisierung in der Automobilindustrie, im Werkzeugmaschinenbau und in der Chemischen Industrie), Zwischenbericht, Soziologisches Forschungsinstitut Goettingen 1990.
36 Steedman, H. and Wagner, K., 'Productivity, machinery and skills: clothing manufacture in Britain and Germany', *National Institute Economic Review*, May 1989.
37 Ibid: p. 48.
38 Ibid: p. 47.
39 Ibid: p. 42.

Chapter 8

Skills mismatch and policy response

Graham Haughton

Source: This is an edited version of an article which appeared in *Policy and Politics*, vol. 18, no. 4, 1990.

INTRODUCTION

Skills shortages have re-emerged on the British political agenda for the late 1980s and early 1990s. [...] Evidence is accumulating of how skills problems are emerging in a wide variety of occupations, sectors and locations (Haughton 1989a, Labour Market Quarterly Report 1989: 6). What is especially worrying about the skills problem is not just the scale but also the spread. The fifth Annual CBI skills survey, conducted in November 1988, found a total of 45 per cent of firms reporting that shortages would limit their output. [...] White-collar jobs from the low skilled end (P-E Inbucon 1989) to the skilled professional end, in computing, nursing, teaching, planning and many other occupations, have all witnessed problems in recruitment (IER Bulletin 1989).

The reversal of economic fortunes, from decline in the early 1980s to growth later in the decade, highlighted the continuing inadequacies of the British training system. [...] It is, however, too easy to write off the skill crisis as stemming from failures in the immediate past, and in particular from the training system. The true picture is more complex, and is deeply rooted in structural barriers to both employment and training. The intention of this chapter is to examine the policy responses to the emerging skills problems which are really as much to do with skills mismatch as skills shortage. [...]

The essential difference between the two terms is that whilst skills shortage assumes a lack of workers, skills mismatch allows for the fact that in many cases there are potential workers available. For instance, workers may be in jobs inappropriate to their skill and unwilling to revert to their former occupations without sufficient incentive; they may be engaged in domestic work and unwilling to enter into employment unless the conditions and pay are right; or workers may be suffering solely from discrimination in the recruitment process. The intervening factors in creating skills mismatch occupy much of the remainder of the present analysis, involving a concern with both labour market efficiency and labour market equality. [...]

SKILLS SHORTAGE AND SKILLS MISMATCH

Training is often held to be the key issue in explaining British skills problems; in particular, we now recognize ourselves as inferior to most other major industrial nations in terms of both the quality and the quantity of skill creation (National Economic Development Office 1984). Yet this view is too simplistic to be convincing. The whole notion of a massive skills shortage being somehow related to shortcomings in the training system and an emerging 'demographic time-bomb' has increasingly been called into question (Haughton and Peck 1989a, 1989b).

Training, or rather lack of training, is of course vitally important in explaining many skills problems. It is, however, far from the only factor at work, and indeed its explanatory power is improved when it is linked to other factors such as discrimination in training as well as at work. It is the major thrust of this chapter that both the cause and the solutions to current skills problems lie in considerable part outside the training system, and indeed in some part outside the labour market. The 'demographic time-bomb' is of uncertain value as an explanatory variable. Clearly there will be a drop in numbers of school-leavers up to the mid–1990s. The extent of this decline, however, is commonly exaggerated by taking the peak and trough figures to illustrate the likely size of the gap. Taking a longer-term viewpoint, it seems preferable to emphasize not the 1.2 million peak to trough maximum, but a deviation from the mean of around 500,000. Most importantly, it is important to note that this is only a short-term downturn, not a permanent one, with numbers of young people soon beginning to increase once more.

With so many people unemployed still, more workers (older women especially) entering and re-entering the paid labour market, and large numbers of potential workers on government training schemes from which they can be readily released, the question must arise of 'what is all the fuss about?' The answer is not obvious. This is largely because it is difficult to discern one clear policy motivation or direction. Some ingredients in the policy mix might well be: the desire to lend political and economic legitimacy to the unpopular Employment Training scheme which was introduced in 1988; the genuine desire to change employers' perceptions of training as a once-and-for-all investment made solely at an early age; and the desire to ensure that employers are aware of alternative cheap labour sources to replace the falling numbers of young people entering the labour market, ensuring that wages in this and other labour market segments do not shoot upwards. This is important because it is such an important tenet of government policy that young workers in particular 'priced themselves out of the labour market', and readjusting wage expectations downwards has proven a costly and time-consuming task.

'Skills shortages' are clearly not as straightforward as might appear. In spite of the caveats outlined above, skills problems do exist, and will probably worsen. The key to understanding this lies in the nature of labour market segmentation. Jobs previously dominated by reliance on the youth labour market to depress wages will experience enormous adverse impacts from the demographic downturn. In a ratchet effect, other low-paying sectors may also be affected in the short term. Explanations for skills problems in other labour market segments are, however, likely to be very different.

Employment for the 1990s (HMSO 1988) takes the government's analysis forward, proposing three areas for action in eliminating what it refers to as barriers to employment. These three areas are: training, industrial relations, (perceived as a problem of strikes and trade union imposed restrictive practices) and pay. The pay argument is particularly important since it is perceived as a problem of over-pay and workers pricing themselves out of jobs and pricing jobs out of existence.

The clear thrust of these arguments is that the problems of the labour market are essentially those of labour supply, more specifically they are rigidities created by the excessive power of organized labour to distort training, create industrial relations problems and over-price workers. It is a central argument of this chapter that the British government's analysis is a blinkered one: much more attention needs to be focused on other types of barriers to labour supply (e.g. women re-entering the labour market) and also the 'imperfections' in labour demands (e.g. employer stigmatization of the workers, by age, address, sex, race, etc). In the remainder of this section I will develop a wide-ranging five-point explanatory framework for understanding skills shortages and mismatches adaptable to specific local areas. The five key dimensions are: training, recruitment processes, employment practices, public service provision and housing.

Training

Poor training provision undoubtedly contributes to skills problems at both local and national levels. As we have already seen this is not simply a problem of quantity of training, it is also a problem of the quality of training, the relevance of training to the needs of employers and individuals, and also the need to up-grade skills on the job and throughout the careers of individuals. Paradoxically, the effect of the state concentrating its increasing incursion into training provision primarily at new entrants to the labour market and the long-term unemployed has been to discourage some firms from providing continuing training for existing workers – it can be cheaper to hire the new trainees.

One of the key problems facing the training and education sectors is the need to shift fundamentally from the old attitude of 'training for life' to one of 'training for change'. [. . .] This need is already strongly evident; the growth of demand for the flexible, polyvalent worker (Allen 1988; Gertler 1988, Meegan 1988) is part of this same trend. It is not simply, however, a question of flexible production systems, personal flexibility, and obtaining a broader range of skills at entry to the labour market, it is also one of coming to terms with quickly changing skill requirements as technologies change at an increasing pace. The apparent failure of the training system to cope with this change is elusive, and difficult to identify and to take steps against. However, it is possibly the dimension of change which will prove most problematic for policy-makers in the long-term.

Relatedly, there is a very real need to consider the skills content of skilled work as it is currently constructed rather than that of handed down 'heroic stereotypes'. The modern kitchen fitter for example needs to combine the skills of the plumber, joiner and electrician (Haughton and Peck 1988). This said, whilst such new categories are being created, the old ones are far from disappearing (Wood 1985). Indeed, in construction there is some evidence of skills deepening rather than, or as well as, broadening out. The demand for labour then is very poorly articulated, not simply because of problems with poor flows of information, but also because of problems in successfully understanding and identifying which skills are actually required by employers. It is rarely recognized that this issue is far from self-evident to most employers themselves.

Finally, it is important to note that whilst training is potentially a force for improving general labour market equality through positive action in training provision ('frontloading' the system as Haughton and Peck 1988, put it), in practice most state and private sector training and related schemes have served only to reinforce existing discriminatory patterns and practices (Cockburn 1985, 1987, Finn 1987, de Sousa 1989).

Recruitment processes

The multi-layered, multi-faceted notion of labour market segmentation has already been touched upon. Workers' occupational and career mobility is severely constrained by the existence of labour market segmentation based in considerable part on personal characteristics, most notably sex, race, age and disability. This is not simply a problem of employers directly discriminating against certain types of people. The processes are much more complex, much more ingrained and therefore much harder to combat. In what is perhaps the best review of the field, Loveridge helpfully places the combination of discrimination and stigmatization in their broader social and work contexts: 'stigmas are usually given meaning by the demands of social order and by contests between groups and individuals for resources or rewards within such socially imposed constraints' (Loveridge 1987: 3), so that

> stigmatisation arises out of a multiplicity of individual gestures, nuances and planned acts of strategy at various levels of consciousness and deliberation. In aggregation, it is class-related social action that has the effect of maintaining and reproducing social order and a hierarchy of opportunity.
>
> (Loveridge 1987: 13–14)

More concretely, on the supply side of the labour market, social conditioning influences women's job expectations, whilst the division of domestic responsibilities (the sphere of reproduction as opposed to the sphere of production) continues to exert a strong impact on the labour market behaviour of many women. The element of 'self-selection' is in fact pervasive in many parts of the labour market, and is often articulated in the form of acceptance of local cultural norms for career progression – school-leavers tend to emulate their peers, be they family or friends, and end up in similar jobs, often in the same locality (Day 1987, Willis 1977, Lovering 1988). Policies can, and indeed must, be devised to overcome some of the supply-side problems in recruitment – for example, working to help improve the confidence of groups traditionally discriminated against, such as working-class women. However, devising effective policies often requires looking most concentratedly at the problems on the demand side of the labour market, with the employers.

Two studies have been particularly helpful in improving our understanding of employer recruitment practices during the 1980s: Meager and Metcalf (1987) and Davies and Mason (1986). Meager and Metcalf take a detailed look at the recruitment practices of employers towards a specific group: the long-term unemployed.

Regrettably, in its published form as a client-commissioned piece of work, their analysis has little to say about the inextricably linked issues of gender and race. This said, this work does provide some useful findings about the types of factors which employers take into account in their recruitment. Many of the factors cited are predictable and already much discussed, for instance the need for personal flexibility, motivation and reliability (see for instance, Oliver and Turton 1982), training, work experience, and ability to communicate well. There are a number of other specific issues which I want to touch upon briefly. The importance of personal health and fitness in the selection process is not a factor which has generally attracted the attention of either policy-makers or academics. The importance accorded to this factor by employers is echoed on the supply side by the recent findings of three skills surveys in Rochdale. Ealing and Wakefield, where this factor was frequently cited by individuals (P-E Inbucon 1989, Ealing Planning and Economic Development 1989, Campbell *et al.* 1989). The Ealing study of unemployed people was particulalry striking, finding that 42 per cent of those surveyed felt that health problems or disability were restricting their choice of employment. In addition, people with disabilities were found to have particular problems in terms of access to training, often related to transport and communication factors.

Another aspect of recruitment practice which is highlighted in Meager and Metcalf's analysis is the importance of appearance, including factors such as 'earrings on men, nail biting, pink hair' (Meager and Metcalf 1987: 78). This emphasis on conformity to the cultural norms of work behaviour and appearance frequently exerts a discriminatory impact not only on the long-term unemployed, but also more systematically on other groups, for instance headwear and Sikhs, hairstyle and Rastafarians. There are clear policy implications here for the need to educate employers and fellow workers around these kinds of sensitive issues.

Finally, job stability is frequently looked to in recruiting workers. The effect of this is to perpetuate and accentuate the position of groups of workers who are continually discriminated against. Workers who find themselves confined to the secondary sector of the labour market exist in a sector where high turnover of labour is a way of life, often attributable to the employers' side. For instance, secondary sector workers are more commonly hired on short-term contracts, whilst many of the firms are themselves highly volatile, responding rapidly to market fluctuations. An interesting variation on this theme comes from Australia, where a group of female workers laid off from a steel works have successfully fought the company's decision in the courts, arguing that the policy of 'last in, first out' (agreed between the firms and the unions) effectively discriminated against women. Previous discriminatory behaviour had restricted women from working in the steel mills until relatively recently, so that when recession and the redundancies came women were disproportionately affected as a result of their later hiring (Haughton 1989b).

Davies and Mason (1986) take a different approach, concentrating on the attitudes of central London employers to inner-city residents. The 'jobs for locals' issue has become highly topical in recent years, not least because of the apparent failure of inner-city initiatives to deliver jobs to inner-city residents, most notably in Docklands (see Church 1988), but also elsewhere (Haughton *et al.* 1987). [. . .] Davies and Mason (1986) in their study found that many central London employers were actually suffering from their tendency to employ commuters, and some were even considering moving out to the suburbs, where their workers increasingly lived. Others were keen to work with local authorities to improve their take-up of local people and to begin to break down the existing patterns with, for instance, one firm regularly taking all its school-leaving-age employees from one small Essex catchment. The broader problem underlying this, however, was the need to break down the negative stereotypes of local residents which were often strongly present among the employers contacted. [. . .]

Finally, it is important to note at least briefly the filters which can exist prior to formal recruitment, most notably how information about vacancies is transmitted to the labour markets. For many jobs there exists a distinct tendency towards the use of extended internal labour markets, where word of mouth notice of jobs is used (friends and relatives) rather than widespread advertising (see Adnett 1989, Ch. 5). The effect of such exclusive practices is generally to perpetuate any existing discriminatory patterns of employment, though this is by no means a universal, unilinear and unidirectional process working against minority groups (Grieco 1987, Loveridge 1987, Fevre 1989).

Employment practices

A third area in which current practices contribute in a major way to skills shortages is that of employment practices, a broad category which encompasses, amongst other things, pay and conditions; work patterns (shift times in particular); holidays; meaningful, structured career progression, providing career breaks for women; job enrichment; use of job-sharing arrangements; nursery provision; physical access for disabled people; continuing training and taking measures against workplace discrimination and harassment. This list is by no means exhaustive.

Probably the most important dimension of employment practice in contributing to skills shortages and mismatches is pay. The evidence in favour of this is strong, as a digest of research findings published by the Training Agency helps illustrate. The immediate response to shortages of information technology specialists, computing staff and financial professionals was to increase pay, though interestingly this practice was less important to microelectronics firms (Training Commission 1988). Amongst the other solutions adopted by the groups of firms covered in these surveys were: subcontracting work or employing consultants, investing more in training, recruiting staff with less experience, lowering qualification standards, redesigning jobs (job enrichment), improving a company's image and sponsorship of college students.

Public service provision

The public sector can play an important role in overcoming labour market and related blockages which impede the efficient and equitable working of labour markets. Clearly both national and local government can exercise an important role in local labour markets as employers and trainers in their own right. Setting a good example is not to be underestimated. On top of this there are other areas in which local authorities in particular can act positively to improve the labour market situation of many of their residents, though in most cases it must be said that the main constraint tends to be one of finance rather than ideas. Each area will have its own unique set of problems and possibilities for resolving them. Here as in other sections of this chapter, it is neither possible nor desirable to present a comprehensive 'checklist'. The Ealing skills survey (Ealing Planning and Economic Development 1989) looked at the barriers both to employment and training as perceived by the unemployed. The list is extensive, but two elements emerge as particularly critical, both of which could be targeted by local policies – child care provision and transport facilities. At present pre-school child care facilities in most councils are split between social services (only for families in need) and education (usually only for limited hours of the day: 9.30 a.m. to 3.30 p.m. is typical). The number of places are restricted and most importantly there is insufficient flexibility in terms of hours available. Useful though such facilities are, there is an inevitable demand for other facilities, which can be encouraged through private provision, community self-help groups or community co-ops. The extent of the influence which can be exerted on the provision of public transport varies enormously between areas, especially with the advent of private competition for bus routes outside London. There is none the less an important role to be played in establishing the transport needs of employees around the clock. In general, we can expect such problems to be most severe for those living on peripheral housing estates and in rural areas, or where the employers are relatively inaccessible (see Pickup 1988 and Tivers 1988).

In addition to these factors, the Ealing survey highlighted the need for more English language classes, especially through outreach education provision. It was also noted that though fees were not charged for local further education courses for the registered unemployed, this might, if interpreted too rigidly, fail to cover others who were unemployed but not eligible for benefit. Finally, there is much that can be done in planning departments, in particular to ensure that new developments make adequate provision for access by disabled people.

Housing

Over 10,000 workers leave northern England on their weekly journey to the jobs mecca of the South-East (Hogarth and Daniel 1988). Workers crowd onto trains and coaches and into shared cars to transport them from their homes and families in the North to their jobs in the South-

East. Neo-classical labour market theory places great emphasis on the need for geographical mobility in job search, but almost certainly not anticipating this particular type of outcome. The key question is, why do these *Gastarbeiter* weekly migrants not settle down in the South-East? The answer usually is a mixture of not being able to afford to and not wanting to, the latter either because of strong community ties or the fact that many of the jobs created are in any case short-term. Inevitably, cross-cutting these elements is the substantial house price differential between the North and South-East England and the lack of council/affordable rented housing in the South-East for migrant workers (Owen and Green 1989).

In the nineteenth century many industrialists realized the importance of providing rented housing if they were to attract and retain good workers – though it needs to be added that the landlord-tenant relationship was also an important means of exercising social discipline over the work-force. The modern equivalent is to provide subsidized mortgages, though these are usually limited to white collar jobs. Housing for key workers also used to be a strong element of many localities' attempts to attract migrant firms, in the 1950s and 1960s especially. Councils are currently heavily constrained by the government's policies to force them to sell off much of their existing housing stock whilst refusing to allow them to build new stock at the rate at which demand requires it. Part of the government's rationale was that council houses were held to be an obstacle to the geographical mobility of workers (see Owen and Green 1989). The irony is that providing workers with the opportunity to buy their own homes with a relatively low mortgage has impeded North–South movement in the short to medium term. There is little incentive to leave a good home in the North which you have every chance of owning outright, to move to the South-East and inevitably, given the higher prices there, face at best a massive mortgage increase to remain in owner-occupation, more usually to move back into the (increasingly expensive) rented sector.

POLICY RESPONSE

Skills mismatch and skills shortages continue to pose problems for policy-makers. Even in the depths of the 1980s recession they could be found in the most unexpected places and sectors – wool dyers in Bradford, mining engineers in County Durham: the examples are many. Emerging from recession the true costs of many employers regarding training as a readily expendable overhead cost have become apparent, whilst the dismantling of much of the apprenticeship system in favour of state training schemes is proving to be not wholly beneficial to employers.

The state-led restructuring of youth training, with its parallel goal of reducing youth wage rates, has combined with the continuing inability of many employers to provide a training system which caters for other than short-term needs. For training the policy implications are in one sense clear: better training needs to be provided in terms of quantity and quality, and access to training broadened to encompass all social groups. The need to provide training for many traditional skills remains undiminished, as the problems in the British construction industry through the 1980s well illustrate. Recent experience suggests that though the time may be ripe to remould traditional apprenticeships for higher-level skills, they none the less provide a more appropriate starting point than any of the new state training schemes which have been introduced.

As we have already seen, there is also considerable scope outside the training system to ease barriers to both skills supply and skills demand. In terms of the recruitment practices of employers there is considerable scope for policies which will break down existing barriers. Central to this must be strengthened anti-discrimination legislation, exemplary demonstration schemes and the political will to ensure adherence to, for instance, the recommended proportional representation of the disabled in the workforce of larger firms. Legislation and exhortation need to be combined to influence employers in particular, but also to assist in breaking down inherited rigidified occupational stereotyping by individuals themselves.

On employment practices, the clear need is to move towards creating attractive employment conditions, sensitized to the needs of particular target groups, such as single parents or the disabled. Central to this will be greater attention to factors such as work patterns, career breaks and access for the disabled. In addition, there are a number of supportive mechanisms in the sphere of public service provision which need to be more clearly integrated into local labour market policy, most notably involving pre-school child care, public transport and personal safety in public areas (involving, for instance, lighting, path design, policing). Finally, housing and labour market mismatches continue to impede labour mobility, contributing to local and regional skills problems. [. . .]

SUMMARY

What emerges from this critique is the very complexity of the problems of skills shortage and skills mismatch. The analysis quickly moved away from the narrow view of skills problems being largely related to imperfections in the training system and emerging demographic problems, to consider the fuller context of problems in creating, utilizing and retaining skilled workers, covering training, recruitment, employment practices, public service provision and housing.

Policies to combat skills problems need to be formulated coherently and consistently across traditional government department boundaries, since the problems themselves are so multifaceted and inter-linked, often lying outside the labour market as such. For local authorities too, attitudes to skills problems may have to change, requiring action on much broader fronts than hitherto, albeit fundamentally constrained by resources.

The full range of policy implications which emerge from this framework are in reality only hinted at here. Interestingly, some of the more telling aspects of the analysis, such as the need to overcome discriminatory labour market structures and practices, have been gaining widespread recognition recently. The emerging problems in creating and retaining skilled labour are causing employers and government alike to look hard at some of the policy directions mentioned in this chapter – with measures to help attract and retain women and ethnic minority workers now rapidly emerging (e.g. Simms 1988). The challenge for the future, however, is how to make such changes permanent features of British local labour markets. [. . .]

ACKNOWLEDGEMENT

This work owes much to my collaborative work with Jamie Peck and the two ESRC grants which supported aspects of my work on local labour markets between 1984 and 1987. John Shutt, Dave Carter and an anonymous referee all made helpful comments on an earlier draft. The usual disclaimers apply: any problems with this chapter are solely my responsibility.

REFERENCES

Adnett, N. (1989) *Labour Market Policy*, London: Longman.
Allen, J. (1988) 'Fragmented firms, disorganized labour', in J. Allen and D. Massey, *The Economy in Question*, 184–228.
Campbell, M. *et. al.* (1989) *Wakefield Skills Survey*, Policy Research Unit, Leeds Polytechnic.
Church, A. (1988) 'Urban regeneration in London Docklands: a five year policy review', *Environment and Planning C: Government and Policy*, 6, 187–208.
Cockburn, C. (1985) *Machinery of Dominance: Women, Men and Technical Know-how*, London: Pluto Press.
—— (1987) *Two track training: Sex Inequalities and the YTS*, Basingstoke: Macmillan Education.
Davies, T. and Mason, C. (1986) *Shutting Out the Inner City Worker*, Bristol: SAUS.
Day, B. (1987) 'Rites of passage: education policy from the perspective of school leavers', *Policy and Politics*, 15, 147–55.
de Sousa, E. (1989) 'YTS – the racism riddle', *Unemployment Bulletin*, issue 29, Spring, pp. 23–4.
Ealing Planning and Economic Development (1989) *A Study of Unemployment on Housing Estates in the London Borough of Ealing*, London: LB of Ealing.
Fevre, R. (1989) 'Informal practices, flexible firms and private labour markets', *Sociology*, 23 (1), 99–109.

Finn, D. (1987) *Training without Jobs: New Deals and Broken Promises*, Basing-stoke: Macmillan Education.

Gertler, M. S. (1988) 'The limits to flexibility: comments on the post-Fordist vision of production and its geography', *Transactions, Institute of British Geographers*, 13 (4), 419–32.

Grieco, M. (1987) 'Family networks and the closure of employment', in G. Lee, and R. Loveridge, (eds), *The Manufacture of Disadvantage: Stigma and Social Closure*, Milton Keynes: Open University Press, pp. 33–44.

Haughton, G. (1989a) 'Skills shortage and labour shortages into the 1990s'. Paper presented at the conference 'Skills mismatch and labour market policy into the 1990s', Leeds Polytechnic, May.

—— (1989b) 'Community and industrial restructuring: responses to the recession and its aftermath in the Illawarra region of Australia', *Environment and Planning A*, 14 (2), 233–47.

—— and Peck, J. (1988) 'Skills audits: a framework for local economic development', *Local Economy* 3, (1), 11–19.

—— —— (1989a) 'Local labour market analysis, skills shortages and the skills audit approach', *Regional Studies*, 23 (3), 271–6.

—— —— (1989b) 'Understanding local labour markets: the strengths and weaknesses of skills audits, *Local Government Policy Making*, March.

——, —— and Steward, A. (1987) 'Local jobs and local houses for local workers: a critical analysis of spatial employment targeting', *Local Economy*, 2 (3), 201–7.

HMSO (1988) *Employment for the 1990s*, London: HMSO.

Hogarth, T. and Daniel, W. (1988) *Britain's New Industrial Gypsies*, London: Policy Studies Institute.

IER Bulletin (1989) 'Skills shortages', *IER Bulletin*, no. 2.

Labour Market Quarterly Report (1989) 'Skills supply and demand', *Labour Market Quarterly Report*, January, p. 6.

Loveridge, R. (1987) 'Stigma: the manufacture of disadvantage', in G. Lee and R. Loveridge (eds), *The Manufacture of Disadvantage*, Milton Keynes: Open University Press, pp. 2–17.

Lovering, J. (1988) 'The local economy and local economic strategies', *Policy and Politics*, 16 (3), 20, 145–157.

Meager, N. and Metcalf, H. (1987) 'Recruitment of the long term unemployed', *IMS Report 138*, Brighton Institute of Manpower Studies.

Meegan, R. (1988) 'A crisis of mass production?' in J. Allen and D. Massey, *The Economy in Question*, 136–83.

National Economic Development Office (1984) *Competence and Competition: Training and Education in the Federal Republic of Germany, the United States and Japan*, London: NEDO.

Oliver, J. and Turton, J. (1982) 'Is there a shortage of skilled labour?', *British Journal of Industrial Relations*, 20, 195–200.

Owen, D. and Green, A. (1989) 'Spatial aspects of labour mobility in the 1980s', *Geoforum*, 20 (1), 107–26.

P-E Inbucon (1989) 'Rochdale Taskforce: realizing the potential, Final report', February.

Pickup, L. (1988) 'Hard to get around: a study of women's travel mobility', in J. Little, L. Peake, and P. Richardson, *Women in Cities*, 84–97, Basingstoke: Macmillan Education.

Simms, J. (1988) 'Giving women a chance to fill the growing skills gap', *The Guardian*, 21 October, p. 20.

Tivers, J. (1988) 'Women and young children: constraints on activities in the urban environment', in J. Little, L. Peake and P. Richardson, *Women in Cities*, Basingstoke: Macmillan Education, pp. 84–97.

Training Commission (1988) *Skills Monitoring Bulletin*, August.

Willis, P. (1977) *Learning to Labour: How Working Class Kids Get Working Class Jobs*, Farnborough: Saxon House.

Wood, S. (1985) 'Work organization', in R. Deem and G. Salaman, *Work, Culture and Society*, Milton Keynes: Open University Press, pp. 77–101.

Chapter 9

The changing role of the in-company trainer

An analysis of British trainers in the European Community context

Karen Evans, Veda Dovaston and Diana Holland

Source: This is an edited version of an article which appeared in *Comparative Education*, vol. 26, no. 1, 1990.

INTRODUCTION

'Alternance' training has, since 1980, become a permanent feature of the vocational education and training arrangements for young people in the member states of the European Economic Community (EEC). In this type of training, the trainer or supervisor working with the trainee in the workplace has a crucial part to play – not least in maintaining the balance between the practical and theoretical, on- and off-the-job learning. It is surprising, therefore, that, while much research has been undertaken into formalized off-the-job training, relatively little has looked at company-based training, the roles and functions of work-based trainers, and the skills and qualities such trainers need to possess.

A previous EEC – sponsored study (CEDEFOP 1983) noted that the size of the population of in-company trainers of young people in the private sector was difficult to quantify but could amount to hundreds of thousands, depending on how the role was defined. So varied were the roles and functions of trainers that it was not possible within the con-straints of that original study to profile them. Recent developments emphasizing the importance of structured work-based learning and assess-ment, including the Youth Training Scheme in Britain and national systems of vocational qualifications, highlighted the need to fill this information gap. For this reason, the European Centre for the Development of Vocational Training, Berlin, launched six national studies focusing on in-company trainers of young people. Research teams in France, Greece, Ireland, Italy, the United Kingdom and the then West Germany were commissioned to examine the characteristics and functions of in-company trainers, and the provision made for their training and development, within their respective national contexts.

The project brief was to examine trainers engaged in in-company training programmes for young people of at least one year in duration, prefer-ably leading to qualification and/or employment. This led the UK team to focus its study on:

1 the British two-year Youth Training Scheme (YTS);
2 forms of long-duration systematic initial training undertaken outside the YTS, through company-funded apprenticeships, traineeships and equivalent schemes.

Trainers were identified as all those with a training role, part-time or full-time, in relation to young trainees – whether or not they are formally designated as trainers by their company (see MSC 1986a). Workers and managers responsible for the day-to-day support and guidance of young trainers in the on-job element of their training were therefore included.

In common with other countries, the UK placed its emphasis on trainers involved in the relevant types of training schemes in private sector enter-prises of medium size, reflecting the view that information on trainers is most lacking in this economic sector.

The research was based on data collected from four main sources:

1 Literature search and review of information and course materials sup-plied by government bodies, sector training bodies, Accredited Training Centres, trade unions, and industrial and professional training associ-ations provided a backcloth of information on policy and trends.
2 Visits to a sample of 25 selected companies, regionally spread and employing between 100 and 900 employees, provided more detailed qualitative data on roles and functions of in-company trainers and allowed the team to explore these within the company context. [...]
3 Nine interviews were conducted with staff training co-ordinators from regional Accredited Training Centres, organizations which have a spec-ific 'training of trainers' role for Youth Training Schemes. These were selected to reflect the regional distribution of the 25 companies. The style of interview [...] was designed to elicit information on the extent of workplace trainer-training and patterns in the take-up of trainer-training opportunities in the YTS from the perspective of the 'official' providers.
4 Exchange visits to Greece and France enabled the team to experience trainer-training developments in other national contexts, and have informed our interpretations and recommendations. A number of visits to companies and training providers were undertaken in each country, with opportunities to interview key staff.

IN-COMPANY TRAINING FOR YOUNG PEOPLE IN THE UK: THE CONTEXT

The government's White Paper *Education and Training for Young People* (DE/DES 1985), drew attention to the fact that British employers have to recruit from a population which, at age 18 and over, continues to include a higher proportion of people, relative to international competitors, with 'limited vocational or academic attainments'. For the many young people in Britain who continue to leave school or college at the age of 16 or 17 the Youth Training Scheme (YTS) has been introduced with the stated intention of providing new training opportunities for many who would otherwise have received no vocational training, and to offer an alternative route to qualifications.

The YTS, originally launched by the Manpower Services Commission in 1983 as a one-year scheme designed to provide a 'permanent bridge between school and work', was extended in 1986 to provide a guaranteed two years of training for 16-year-olds.

Learning in the workplace through 'on-the-job' experience is a central feature of the scheme. The credibility of the scheme largely depends on the quality of the work-based learning that it is seen to deliver. In practice, the quality of schemes has been judged to be highly variable. [. . .]

TRAINING FOR IN-COMPANY TRAINERS: THE UK NATIONAL CONTEXT

Much of the literature assumes that in-company training is the responsibility of full-time designated trainers.

The policy developments in vocational training since 1980 have substantially increased the numbers of adults involved in the training of young people, and created a dynamic and uncertain environment for companies providing the training. Many of these 'trainers' are part-time or 'occasional' trainers whose roles are not defined by the training activity itself (Law and Caple 1985). Recent studies and reviews have revealed a number of current problems to be addressed: the persistence of 'narrow' perceptions of training focused heavily on the development of specific occupational skills while neglecting broader competences such as team working and communication; lack of structure and progression in some work-based programmes; little awareness of the need for 'training competence' among supervisors who may see training as a minor adjunct to their role rather than integral to it (Davies and Burgoyne 1985); and resistance to policy-led innovations among first-level trainers (Evans *et al.* 1986).

Training and development of in-company vocational trainers can face serious logistical difficulties because of the number of trainers, their dispersal (Varlaam and Pole 1988), difficulties in getting release for training, staff mobility, and 'trainers' attitudes where responsibilities for training young people are seen as temporary. Logistical problems are likely to be compounded in small- to medium-sized enterprises, where the cost of training is proportionately higher than it is in larger companies.

A host of reports (e.g. Coopers and Lybrand 1985, IFF Research 1985) have drawn attention to the continuing reluctance of British industry to invest significantly in training, and have highlighted the urgent need to improve the performance and status of in-company trainers at all levels. In Britain, the training of trainers may be undertaken through in-house arrangements, the use of external consultants, specific-industry training centres; bodies such as British Institute of Management (BIM); the British Association for Commercial and Industrial Education; colleges; and Further and Higher Education Institutions. The MSC, pointing to the inadequacy of the existing 'piecemeal' approach to the training and development of trainers, proposed an agreed national strategy in which independent agencies could contribute to a 'coherent and comprehensive' approach (MSC 1986c).

Recognition of the pressing need for training of YTS trainers led to the establishment of Accredited Training Centres in 1983. These centres were funded by the Manpower Services Commission to service the trainer-training needs of YTS schemes in their geographical areas, through provision of certificated courses (such as the 90-hour City and Guilds Youth Trainer Award), short courses and consultancy. Take-up of these services by companies is voluntary, in recognition of the fact that many will want to use their own arrangements. [. . .]

Industrial, economic and geographical context

Companies were selected from contrasting industrial sectors and geographical regions to allow the effects of context on the roles, functions and development of trainers to be identified. The sample included companies in areas which have a relatively depressed economic profile, as well as in areas of relative economic growth. This geographical picture was also compounded by some industry-specific decline and growth.

In companies located in areas which have a relatively depressed economic profile (and particularly those companies also suffering industry-specific decline) a number of features were in evidence. One effect of decline is to increase staff stability, reduce staff turnover and reduce recruitment and training for young people. In-company training – for trainers, managers, 'adult' staff – often takes into account the likelihood of long-term employment with the same company, and a person's 'training and career profile' will be built up slowly over time. Cuts in the number of young people taken on seem to have reduced the number of full-time training posts and, inevitably, the overall number of people involved in training.

There was some evidence in two of the companies on Merseyside that trainers were again being taken on in small numbers after substantial gaps in youth training programmes lasting several years.

Even in 'economic growth' areas and industries, a similar picture emerged of lack of training, particularly for young people. Economic pressures, the need to be competitive, and the demise of the Industrial Training Boards were all given as reasons to explain past losses of training and training positions within companies in growth areas. A picture emerged of a period in which companies have been taking a very short-term view of investment in training and in young people.

In terms of training posts and training of trainers in economic growth areas, there was evidence of recently increased interest in training. Training Departments were being 'revived' and full-time training posts filled after having been left vacant. There was also evidence of an increase in the profile of training generally and a shift in the role of training more closely in line with specific new management strategies developing in the growth areas of the economy.

CHARACTERISTICS, ROLES AND FUNCTIONS OF UK TRAINERS

The main trainer functions identified in the 25 sample companies were:

- direct training (on- and off-job);
- managing, planning, co-ordinating trainees' programmes;
- liaison with outside training organizations.

Differences emerged between companies in the way in which these responsibilities were allocated to individuals and the relative emphasis which they received. In some companies, those managing and planning the programme would also be direct trainers. In others, there was a sharp distinction between managers of training and direct trainers, with most on-the-job training done by skilled workers.

'Full-' and 'part-time' training staff

Fourteen out of 25 sample companies employed at least one member of staff with an exclusively training role. These have been classified here as 'full-time' trainers.

Companies with 'full-time' training staff:
Of the 25 full-time trainers 14 combined 'off-job' direct training in company with co-ordination of training; 1 had full-time 'on-job' training responsibilities; 10 had mainly co-ordination and managing responsibilities.

Companies without full-time training staff:
In the 11 companies without full-time training staff 2 had no clear training co-ordination, despite reasonable funding levels for external courses. Responsibility for training was spread across several managers, with nominal overall responsibility resting with a director. In 9 companies, responsibility for training lay with a named individual who combined it with other (in many cases, personnel) responsibilities. In three of these the same 'part-time' person both provided in-company direct training for managers and co-ordinated training programmes for young people.

Types of trainers

Managers of training generally had responsibility for the overall management of training at either company or programme level. The position either was exclusively involved with training or, as was more often the case, incorporated training as one aspect of wider managerial responsibilities. This type of in-company trainer showed very wide age variations between the 20s and 60s. Younger full-time trainers usually had personnel/management backgrounds, while other staff tended to have a 'skills' background. The results indicated the emergence of a younger group of training managers whose own background was in training rather than in the industry – i.e. the emergence of the 'professional trainer'.

Supervisory trainers in all cases had an industry-specific background, and had moved up within their professional skills to take on responsibility for staff and, ultimately, for training staff. These trainers were usually departmental or section managers. The position carried with it training-management responsibilities and possibly some on-job direct training on a one-to-one or group basis. Day-to-day programme development and assessment of the effectiveness of training together with liaison with training and personnel managers were typical responsibilities. Young trainers in this group often appeared to be in a transitional career phase, combining skill-specific and managerial responsibilities. Their training role appeared to be a key element of this transitional identity.

Worker trainers were skilled workers whose training responsibilities related exclusively to the tasks and skills in which they had established competence: trainees were allocated to 'worker trainers' to acquire the same skills or to learn how to do a particular task. Worker trainers usually decided on how to transmit their skills, explain or demonstrate them and informally judge the effectiveness of learning. Sometimes they were involved in more formal work-based assessments of competence. The length of time spent with the trainee varied, but might be substantial. Worker trainers normally had a background in the industry and saw their career evolution as within their company or industry. Increasing seniority might bring with it junior management or departmental supervisory responsibilities.

Needs and provision for trainers

The official view of training needs is that direct in-company trainers of young people need to be developed in training and coaching skills as well as in co-ordinating skills and knowledge of areas such as health and safety and equal opportunities. Managers of training need to be competent in programme design and review, needs-identifiction and skills of programme management.

In the sample of companies, training of trainers in the training role (where it was undertaken) was found to be confined almost entirely to training managers and supervisory trainers. Worker trainers received only technical training.

Training managers and other trainers were asked to rank-order attributes required by trainers in terms of priority. The five attributes were: practical experience in the area in which training is being carried out; technical expertise and qualifications; ability to relate to young people; experience as a trainer/teacher, and knowledge of the company and world of work generally.

Overall, clear priority was given by both training managers and other trainers to:

- ability to relate to young people;
- practical experience in area in which s(he) is training

These views are reflected to some extent in the selection and recruitment of trainers and their subsequent training and development. Expertise in training skills and methods was not found to be a priority either in recruitment or in subsequent development of supervisory or worker trainers. While ability to relate to young people was highly rated, there was evidence that, in practice, this is not a prime consideration in identifying trainers. Supervisory trainers were selected primarily for their management potential rather than for their interpersonal skills with young adults, while worker trainers were selected for skills in specific tasks.

These findings held in both manufacturing and service sector companies and are reflected in the assessments made by staff training co-ordinators (officially responsible for training YTS trainers). The reluctance of many workplace trainers to undergo training for the training role was pointed to in interview, and attributed to the belief of these trainers that their competence as skilled and experienced workers equipped them fully to help trainees to learn to carry out tasks. The weakest areas identified were assessment and counselling skills, and resistance to developing these skills had been often encountered.

Training for trainers

Training activities, courses and programmes undertaken within the sample companies were varied, including:

- *formal* training courses, either within company, out-of-company or within a consultancy group, sometimes accredited;
- *company supported* self-directed development, e.g. through open learning resource centres;
- *informal or self-initiated* development or programmes, e.g. events, meetings, own reading, experimentation, own-initiative external courses.

It should, however, be stated that there were significant numbers of people involved in the training of young people who had received no training in their role, particularly 'worker trainers'.

Formal training courses or programmes which helped to prepare trainers for training were sometimes directly and exclusively focused on the training process. In other cases, 'training' may have been a primary or secondary aim of technical or management courses, where the overall aim shaped the 'training' component. Courses seemed to fall into three categories: industry-skill specific; 'person-management' focused; and 'training process'.

Informal development activities, some of which included focused 'training for training', were often referred to as suiting the company context. They were seen as enabling self-direction, and presenting fewer problems of time and timing.

When direct trainers were asked to identify the two courses they would choose to go on if given the opportunity, the priorities given to management training were again apparent. Management courses were mentioned 31 times; advanced technical courses 16 times; training skills and methods 15 times; while 7 other types of courses were mentioned.

Despite this, in approximately one-half of the companies, some training of trainers in training skills and methods had taken place, often in the context of wider management training. In only a small minority however, did there seem to be a systematic programme or 'policy' on the training of trainers.

The managerial emphasis on the development of staff as trainers reflected a trend among sample companies towards new management strategies in which greater importance was attached to the role of first-line supervision in motivation, monitoring and assessment of the work-force.

In-company training and new management strategies

The main developments in management strategies brought out through the research were:

1 *An increasingly important role for first-line supervision*: The stated aim in a number of companies was for most in-company training to be organized at the level of first-line supervision. Supervisory trainers are being seen as responsible for identifying training needs, setting up on-the-job training arrangements, and evaluating the effectiveness of training through monitoring standards of work.

2 *An increase in 'team' or 'group' working with the supervisor as 'group leader'*: There were examples of a number of companies where, within departments or sections, workers were further divided into smaller working groups with an appointed 'group leader' (either an existing supervisor or a possible future supervisor). In these cases, 'training' was further devolved to the 'group leader', who again had responsibility for identifying training needs, carrying out or organizing the training needed, and monitoring standards of work following this training.

3 *The appointment of in-company trainers within new management strategies*: A number of companies involved in these changes in management practice were embarking upon major developments in the numbers of workers with training responsibilities. This move to an increased number of 'in-company trainers' clearly reflected the growing importance placed on the role of first-line supervision and the growing importance of 'team-working' and 'group leaders'.

   Criteria for appointing 'in-company trainers' in these companies was in the main found to be informal, and based on leadership abilities, commitment to the company, and abilities to do the job, rather than on qualifications, years of service or specific training skills. It was clear that selection of trainers was related to managerial potential and commitment. [. . .]

4 *Role of in-company 'trainers' in new management strategies*: The role of an in-company trainer, in terms of the new management strategies, is closely associated with:
   • *Motivation* of the work-force, either as a small team or by department (e.g. by the introduction of inter-departmental training competitions);
   • *Constant assessment* of the work-force to establish the effectiveness of training provided, and to indentify cases for merit-related pay increases; 'corrective' training; discipline where training has proved ineffective.

5 *Training for trainers as part of new management strategies*: There was evidence that those companies committed to these changes in management strategies also tended to place a higher premium on training for in-company trainers. Some companies were undertaking major training operations with the aim both of increasing the numbers of workers regarded as 'trained trainers' and of raising the profile of training and, consequently, standards of work within the company.

It was clear that the programmes and content of such training concentrated to a far greater extent on the 'motivation' and 'assessment' aspects of training as part of new management strategies, than on the 'teaching methods and skills' aspect of training for trainers.

Overall, the UK study concluded that training for the role of trainer needs greater recognition and emphasis. Training courses for trainers of young people need to recognize the importance of developing the ability to relate to young people, as well as the distinction between supervisory/managerial and training skills and responsibilities. Practical and relevant means of providing training for trainers of young people responsible for day-to-day on-the-job training need to be developed and emphasized as a priority.

THE EUROPEAN COMMUNITY DIMENSION: INTERNATIONAL ACTIVITIES AND OBSERVATIONS BASED ON EXCHANGE VISITS

The synthesis report of the 1984 CEDEFOP study on the 'Professional situation and training of trainers in the Member States of the European Communities' concluded that throughout the EEC most in-company trainers worked on a part-time or occasional basis and had obvious needs for training in pedagogical skills, and that flexible continuing training models were required if these needs were to be met in reality.

The Community dimension of our 1988 study enables the current positions of in-company trainers in different national contexts to be reviewed and compared in greater detail. [. . .] Processes which could ultimately enable international comparison and synthesis were built into the research programme at the outset. As part of the method chosen, the UK team participated in a programme of bilateral visits with the French and Greek teams. In the early stages of the study, representatives of both Greek and French teams spent one week in the UK, participating with the UK team in discussion, and in visits to companies and training centres. Return visits were made by the UK team to Greece and France, respectively.

As a result of the initial visit hosted by the UK team, arrangements were made to exchange background information; materials used for trainer-training; definitions of different types of trainers as relevant to national contexts, and interview schedules. Subsequently, written information was exchanged and liaison took place over the finalization of the interview schedules and data-gathering procedures. Although research approaches contrasted, agreement was reached on 'key' questions which should be asked. It was felt that this was a flexible way of ensuring compatibility without constraining the individual research approaches adopted – an essential part of collaboration, given that the differing national contexts resulted in inevitable variations in research style. Return visits by members of the UK team to Greece and France in the ensuing months resulted in greater understanding of in-company training programmes and trainer-training issues in these countries, and continuation of exchanges on the respective 'systems' and findings of the research.

The following section briefly reviews some of the insights gained by the UK team through this programme of international visits (see Tables 9.1 and 9.2).

Insights gained from contacts with the French team and visit to France

In the French context, apprenticeship schemes and 'alternance' training schemes and contracts were identified as the focus of the study. The 'alternance' schemes are for young people 'in a situation of occupational transition' – typically disadvantaged, and experiencing prolonged spells of unemployment after leaving school at 16, the end of compulsory schooling (Boru and Barbier 1988). In France, as in the UK, existing information of the nature and role of the trainer was confined to trainers in educational/ training institutions and to full-time trainers in larger companies. The study aimed to examine the position of employees in the workplace as mentors, monitors and supervisors of young people. These were collec-tively termed 'tutors'.

Areas of common interest between the UK and French teams were identified. These included:

1 The need to establish the overall status of training within the company.
2 The need to identify at what levels training for young people is being provided and who is involved, in order to evaluate the most effective types of training for trainers of young people.
3 The importance of the identification of 'variables' and their effects on training provision, e.g. industry; occupation within the industry; level of innovation; stability/mobility of the work-force and training per-sonnel; local economic background: unemployment levels, etc.; nature of the company – public/privately owned.
4 The attitudes towards training for trainers/workplace supervisor.
5 The importance of establishing the extent to which training and support were being provided informally (and therefore, possibly, less visibly).
6 The relationship of training to managerial/disciplinary structures.

In interviews with French researchers and training professionals, it became apparent that thinking on new qualifications in France differed substantially from that underpinning the system of Vocational Qualifi-cations in Britain in that a prime aim of the Opérations Nouvelles Qualifi-cations appears to be the development of relevant qualifications for young people considered to be disadvantatged in France. Important similarities were, however, apparent. Recognition of competence in new and develop-

Table 9.1 Target group: trainers of young people

	UK	Greece	France
1 Managers of training			
Characteristics identified:			
(a) Status (full- or part time training responsibilities)	✓ Full- and part-time	✓ Most part-time	✓ Most part-time
(b) Background	Industry/personnel and training	Industry/management	Personnel management
(c) Management of external training of young people	✓	✓	✓
(d) Conducting internal training of young people	Some	x	x
(e) Qualifications	Technical/personnel	Technical/management	Professional/management Varied
(f) Age	20s–60s	—	—
(g) Sex	Men and women	✓	✓
2 Supervisory trainers			
Characteristics identified:			
(a) Status	Part-time	Part-time	Part-time
(b) Background	Industry	Industry	Industry
(c) Management of external training of young people	Some	x	Some
(d) Conducting internal training of young people	Some	✓	✓
(e) Qualifications	Technical/vocational	Technical/higher education	—
(f) Age	20s–60s	Average age 42	30–40
(g) Sex	Men and women	Mostly men	✓
3 Worker trainers			
Characteristics identified:			
(a) Status	Part-time	Part-time	Part-time
(b) Background	Industry	Industry	Industry
(c) Management of external training of young people	x	x	x
(d) Conducting internal training of young people	✓	✓	✓
(e) Qualifications	Technical/vocational	—	Technical/vocational (to level young people are aiming at)
(f) Age	20s–60s	—	30–40
(g) Sex	Men and women	—	—

Responses: (✓) yes; (x) no or little; (–) no information supplied.

Table 9.2 Current training of trainer arrangements

	UK	Greece	France
1 Trainer–training status	Generally low	Generally low	Some high, some low
(a) State requirement	x	Some	Some
(b) Company policy	Some	Some	Some
(c) Industry policy	Some	x	Some
(d) Informal	Some	–	Some
2 Trainer–training programme aims			
(a) Industry-skill specific	Most	–	Some
(b) Person management	Some	✓	Some
(c) Training process	Some	✓	Some
3 Trainer–training curriculum			
(a) Educational methods	Some	✓	Some
(b) Relating to young people	x	–	x
(c) Alternance	x	–	x
(d) Contact with outside organizations	x	–	x
(e) Training and the labour market	x	–	x
(f) Equal opportunities	x	–	
(g) Legal foundations of training programme	x	–	x
4 Type of training			
(a) Formal courses	Some	Some	✓
(b) Company supported 'open learning'	Some	–	x ✓
(c) Informal arrangements	'Self-directed'	–	✓
5 Trainer–training provider			
(a) External education/training body	Some	Most	Some
(b) External industry	Some	Some	Some
(c) Company	Most	Some	Some
(d) Voluntary organization	Some	–	Some
6 Target group			
(a) Managers of training	Most	Most	✓
(b) Supervisory trainers	Some	Some	✓
(c) Worker trainers	x	x	x
7 Accreditation			
(a) Nationally recognized qualification	Some	Some	Some
(b) Industry qualification	Some	Some	Some
(c) Company accreditation	Most	Some	Some
(d) No accreditation	Some	Some	Some
8 Role of trade union	Monitoring training representing trainers and trainees, social partner	Context and organization of training representing trainers and trainers	Social partner on tripartite bodies

Responses: (✓) yes; (x) no or little; (–) no information supplied.

ing areas was central, as was the principle that workplace learning, if effectively structured and managed, would be highly motivating to young people, and that workplace supervisors play an important role in this. Visits to selected companies illustrated these ideas in practice, and provided examples of ways in which workplace supervisors developed their role informally through experience. Feedback and support were obtained through periodic 'review meetings'. These were meetings in which trainees, training managers and workplace supervisors worked through aspects of the trainee's individual 'training plan'. More generally, though, it was reported that company managers often appeared to regard the training of young people as a burden rather than an investment, and attitudes towards the training of supervisors as 'tutors' were consistent with this. Tutor-training was often perceived in terms of further expense and 'lost time', rather than in terms of the advantages to be gained in upgrading and expanding employees' skills.

Discussions with trade union representatives in France also highlighted common ground with the UK. Key issues were:

- the increasing number of programmes including work-experience;
- problems with programmes being used as a form of job substitution;
- the increasing involvement of workers in a supervisory/training role towards young people;
- the numbers of young people involved in training programmes, schemes and contracts.

Training for workplace supervisors was also seen by trade union representatives as an important area for recognition. One reservation about the development of a formalized training/accreditation system was that it could act to exclude those people who are now most effectively doing the job, as they would not necessarily have the academic background that such a system might require.

The three types of trainer identified in the UK appeared to have direct parallels in the French system. Overall, the visits and discussions gave an opportunity to analyse different training roles and were particularly helpful in establishing parallels between the UK and France in the role of the worker trainer. The visit also illustrated how trainer-training was provided – the highly centralized and formal French education and training framework exists alongside a range of informal 'actions' such as meetings, briefings, conferences, etc. which provide training for trainers. It was also apparent that developments in open learning for training were more advanced in the UK than in France, and this was seen by French counterparts as a potentially important area of development.

Insights gained from contact with the Greek team and visit to Greece

In-company training of young people was described as a relatively new concept in Greece. It was reported that, until recently, attendance at vocational school followed a full day's work in the company for most young apprentices. With the entry of Greece to the EEC, the 'alternance' concept is being introduced in the form of full-time attendance at vocational school in the first year of training, followed by day-release to vocational school (IVEPE 1988).

National Service delays the entry of many young men to work until the early twenties. Young women are generally not employed in manufacturing, and not even in office work in large numbers. Consequently, several companies visited seldom had trainees under 25 years of age. In-company trainers interviewed were principally involved in training adults in the work-force, although some provided 'top-up' training for new entrants from apprenticeship schools, intended to bring the new entrants up to company standards and to introduce them to the company's ways of working.

Criteria for appointing trainers seemed to be comparable with those in the UK – the system was to select on the basis that solid industrial experience was the first priority. Previous training experience was seen as being of lower priority. *Trainability* in communication skills and the ability to simplify for those who have had little formal training were seen as important by those we met. the 'typical' in-company trainer was identified as an experienced employee, usually highly qualified in the technical field, but probably not well prepared in the skills of training and not necessarily well motivated towards the role.

Of particular interest to the UK team were the arrangements for training and recognizing trainers.

Four types of training for in-company trainers could be identified in Greece: longitudinal (6–12 months) training at the Pedagogical School of SELETE; accelerated training through a 15-day seminar run by the national manpower agency; training offered by private companies specializing in personnel developments; training offered abroad. In practice few companies can afford to release personnel for the SELETE course, while the demand for the 15-day programme was described as overwhelming – reflecting the fact that participation is compulsory for companies wishing to qualify for EEC and national government support for their in-company programmes.

The main criticism we heard of this latter programme (from company personnel) was that it was too brief and more training was needed in training methods. This is of interest when one compares the lower level of 'training in training' and awareness of needs in this area found in the British companies. Discussions with full-time trainers showed that the latter recognized pedagogical skills training as essential to their role – it was what the job was about. Release for trainers to undertake materials development and updating in training skills and new ideas was in some cases substantial. (It should be noted that these were trainers from larger enterprises than those defined as medium-sized in the UK study.) At the levels of the in-company supervisor and departmental manager, the need to develop expertise in training skills and methods was considered to be inadequately catered for.

Overall, the system by which training of trainers in pedagogical skills is compulsory for companies seeking public funding support appeared to be linked with a greater awareness of the importance of these skills among those interviewed.

GENERAL OBSERVATIONS

In the context of a parallel feasibility study on the training needs of trainers in industry and commerce, Varlaam and Pole (1988) have observed changes in all aspects of training in UK Companies, from 'the place of training within the organisation, through training roles and who fills them, to training context and modes of delivery'.

These findings are consistent with those of the study reported here. Both studies illustrate how increased awareness of the place of Human Resources Development in organizational effectiveness, together with the expansion of various forms of youth and adult training programmes, have given a particular stimulus to the development of training in the private sector in the UK. Similar trends are noted in Western European counterparts.

Changes in training roles arising from greater diffusion of training responsibility, as noted in Varlaam and Pole's study, are illustrated specifically here by the growth and significance of the 'supervisory trainer' and the 'worker trainer'. Trainer identity is an important dimension worthy of further attention.

Distinctions have been found between personnel for whom training responsibilities are part of a transitional career phase in management, and the emerging group of training 'professionals' whose background and identity are in training rather than in management or in the industry. Davies and Burgoyne's 1985 work on career paths of trainers found similar distinctions, observing in addition that training roles can become dead-ends or side-tracks for those seeking senior management positions, if training is a segregated and peripheral function.

The findings of these and other contemporary studies, taken together, confirm the new status of training as a potential 'agent of change', reflected in moves towards more strategic models of training embedded within organizational development. [. . .]

REFERENCES

Boru, J. J. and Barbier, J. M. (1988) *Tutors and the Tutorship Function in the Enterprise in the Alternance Training of Young People*, Paris: Conservatoire National Des Arts et Métiers.

Companies' Association for the Industrial and Professional Training of Staff (IVEPE) (1988) *The Case of Greece*, Athens: IVEPE.

Coopers & Lybrand Associates (1985) *A Challenge to Complacency: Changing Attitudes to Training*.

Davies J. and Burgoyne, J. (1984) *Career Paths of Direct Trainers*, Sheffield: MSC.

Department of Employment/Department of Education and Science (DE/DES) (1985) *Education and Training for Young People*, London: HMSO.

—— (1986) *Working Together – Education and Training*, Sheffield: HMSO.

European Centre for the Development of Vocational Training (CEDEFOP) (1983) *The Vocational Trainer of Young People in the United Kingdom*, Berlin: CEDEFOP.

Evans, K., Brown, A. and Oates, T. (1986) *Developing Work-Based Learning*, MSC Research and Development Series No. 39, Sheffield: MSC.

IFF Research Ltd (1985) *Adult Training in Britain*, Sheffield: MSC.

Law, C. and Caple, T. (1985) Developing the part-time trainer, *Training and Development* 4 (2), 24–7.

Manpower Services Commission (MSC) (1986a) 'Classification of "Trainers in industry and commerce"', in *Developing Trainers*, Sheffield: MSC.

—— (1986b) *Guide to Content and Quality on YTS/Approved Training Organisations*, Sheffield: MSC.

—— (1986c) *Developing Trainers*, Sheffield: MSC.

Varlaam, C. and Pole, C. (1988) *The Training Needs of Trainers in Industry and Commerce*, Sheffield: MSC.

Chapter 10

From new vocationalism to the culture of enterprise

Bob Coles and Robert F. MacDonald

Source: The British Sociological Association, 1990.

This chapter reviews the activities of the Manpower Services Commission (MSC) and the Training Agency (TA) in the fields of education and youth training. In particular it evaluates the role of the MSC/TA in the promotion and institutionalization of 'vocationalism' and 'enterprise culture'. Much literature has focused attention on the growth of 'new vocationalism' as a response to high levels of youth unemployment (Bates *et al.* 1984, Brown and Ashton 1987, Coles 1988, Pollard *et al.* 1988, Raffe 1988). Less attention has been given to the activities of the MSC/TA in promoting 'enterprise' (Rees 1986). The chapter will argue that the rationale, organization and mode of delivery for 'enterprise initiatives' illustrates a new and changing role for the TA in managing social and economic change.

In describing the development of cultures such as 'enterprise' or 'new vocationalism' five interrelated elements must be involved (Coles 1988). First, we have a detailed understanding of the institutional innovations themselves. We will argue that apparently separate programmes in different institutional areas reflect a more general pattern. Not all the individual programmes which constitute 'vocationalism' and 'enterprise' can be covered in detail in this chapter. Rather, we have taken specific examples from youth training and education to illustrate how particular schemes reflect the more general trends of 'vocationalism' and 'enterprise'.

Second, we must pay close attention to the changing structural relationships which the initiatives have brought about: relationships of advice, consultation and policy-making, the monitoring of aims and objectives, and methods of attaining financial control. Here we trace the ways in which the MSC/TA have developed management strategies which have increasingly shifted power and control towards private industry.

Third, we must directly examine 'cultures' – the rationale underpinning schemes and initiatives, the values they espouse and try to promote, together with the procedures through which schemes and initiatives are developed, delivered and legitimized. This 'culture' gives shape and direction to what, in administrative terms, may be discrete, sometimes almost *ad hoc*, policy initiatives.

Fourth, we must examine the economic context in which changes occur. It is clear, for instance, that the development of 'new vocationalism' was stimulated by steep rises in youth unemployment in the 1970s. In the current promotion of 'enterprise', however, it should be recognized at the outset that *nationally* there is now a very different economic context. Repeated government White Papers on employment now see the major problem facing the country as being 'skill shortage' rather than unemployment (White Paters 1988a and 1988b). We will argue that 'new vocationalism' and the promotion of 'enterprise culture' must be understood as responses to these different economic contexts.

Fifth, close attention must be given to the ways in which nation-wide initiatives articulate with local conditions. National 'blueprints' rarely simply reproduce themselves at a local level. Rather, they become mediated through local cultures and economic contexts (MacDonald 1988a). In the final section of this chapter we will focus attention on Cleveland which, whilst having high rates of unemployment, has also become a key test site for 'enterprise' initiatives. First, we turn to the promotion of 'vocationalism' in youth training and education.

YOUTH UNEMPLOYMENT AND THE GROWTH OF YOUTH TRAINING

The growth of Youth Training provision has been well documented elsewhere (Atkinson and Rees 1982, Brown and Ashton 1987, Raffe 1988, Ainley 1988). The Youth Training Scheme (YTS) has been referred to as 'the jewel in the MSC crown' (Finn 1986). It is, however, the culmination of a series of youth unemployment measures reaching back almost to the foundations of the MSC in 1974. In these early days the MSC saw its role as helping the young unemployed to compete more successfully with adults for work in an increasingly competitive labour market. What made them uncompetitive was the lack of experience of work and this, of course, at the time, required employment. 'Special measures' through work experience programmes (WEP) attempted to break the cycle. Despite these measures, however, youth unemployment in the mid–1970s continued to grow; and so, too, did the number and variety of schemes.

The Holland Report set the scene for the development of youth training throughout the 1970s and 1980s and provided the basic framework for the main precursor of YTS, the Youth Opportunities Programme (YOP) (Department of Employment 1977). There are several elements to note in the diagnosis of 'the problem' made by Holland and the consequent approach to policy formation. First, the issue of youth unemployment was seen as both a 'demand side' and a 'supply side' problem. There was a worry about the demand for youth labour in part because of competition from adults. The answer to this was to give young people skills and work experience. Second, there was a problem concerning the 'lumpiness' of supply; it was not spread evenly throughout the year. 'Training' could, therefore, be used as a form of seasonal 'warehousing' of young people until such time, during the year, that demand picked up. Third, there was an acceptance of 'supply side deficiency' – the young unemployed were unqualified, and considered to be unprepared for the world of work, poorly motivated and displaying the wrong attitudes. The young unemployed were, thus, regarded as being the problem and as such *they* needed to be 'remedied'.

Fourth, Holland recognized the need for a large-scale nation-wide network through which training could be delivered. Even a large bureaucracy like the MSC could not do this alone. The Report argued for a 'single, coherent programme, comprehensive in its coverage and responsive to the differing needs of unemployed young people in different parts of the country' (3.1b). To deliver such a programme the MSC considered it expedient, at least in the short term, to give training agents, in both the public and private sectors, power and initiative in the hope that this would provoke responsibility and involvement. They were to be left in charge of the management of funding.

The content of YOP was not outlined in the Holland Report. What emerged was a variable mixture of three core ingredients: work experience, skills training and social and life skills teaching. These were to remain the staple diet of youth training for the next ten years.

On most criteria YOP was failing by the early 1980s. It all but destroyed the youth labour market for 16-year-olds in a few short years whilst presiding over rapidly increasing rates of youth unemployment. The number of 16-year-olds with jobs fell from 61 per cent in 1974 to 18 per cent in 1984 (Roberts *et al.* 1988). By 1982 the number of 16-year-olds on schemes accounted for more than a fifth of the age group (Raffe and Courtenay 1988). But of those who entered schemes between June 1980 and July 1981, only 31 per cent entered employment as they completed them (Bedeman and Courtenay 1982). YOP did, though, have an impact on the young unemployed themselves. The evidence suggests that, in the early years, YOP was successful in first 'blaming' and then 'remedying' the victims (Stafford 1981, Atkinson and Rees 1982). In this the 'social and life skills' elements, which found a place in all YOP programmes, played a critical part. Much of this was done through further education colleges. Staff were, of course, in no position to do anything about the lack of jobs for the young unemployed. They were, therefore, inevitably bound to concentrate on trying to groom the *particular* young people under their charge, despite the knowledge that this would do little to change the fortunes of young people *in general*. Ann Stafford comments:

Given the structural limitations of the teaching situation, teachers can only act in an individualistic and pragmatic way ... Faced with twelve jobless young people, the immediate task is to increase their [young people's] employability. This leads inevitably to a reinforcement and perpetuation of an individualistic explanation for unemployment ... in unexpected ways and often in ways quite foreign to their well meaning intentions.

(Stafford 1981: 62)

Despite its unpopularity with many young people YOP survived through the volatile years of the late 1970s and early 1980s, a period which also saw the election of the first Thatcher government. By that time the *pattern* of training provision had been set.

By 1982 many YOP trainees had begun to vote with their feet, believing their contemporaries – rather than the commercials – that YOP was 'slave labour' and exploitation leading to the dole, rather than being a training bridge between school and a permanent job (Hughes 1984, Coles 1986). But YOP could not be abandoned without finding something to fill the gap. An MSC consultative paper, *A New Training Initiative*, in May 1981 urged:

As a country, we must now set ourselves the aim of achieving urgent and radical changes in our training arrangements if our industry and commerce and our workforce – both young and old – are to be adequately equipped to face the future.

(White Paper 1981: para 23)

A Youth Task Group was set up with the responsibility to report by April 1982. This described a scheme aimed at 460,000 16- to 17-year-olds (about 25 per cent of the age cohort). They were to be guaranteed a place on a twelve-month training scheme and offered 'an intergrated programme of training, work experience and relevant education' (White Paper 1981: para. 4.10). This was to be piloted in 1982–3 and come on 'full stream' in Autumn 1983. It did – just – make its deadlines, with many key personnel receiving guidelines, manuals and recruits in reverse order. In 1983 a quarter of the age group reaching the age of 16 was recruited to YTS. Training, under YTS, was described as 'high quality', but the nine components largely provided the old mix: work experience, training in particular work skills and 'personal effectiveness training'. Still youth unemployment continued to grow and by 1985, when YTS2 had been introduced, 25 per cent of the age group were being offered a two-year period of training (Jones *et al.* 1988). By then a large and competitive youth training industry had been established, but in 1985 the rules of the game had begun to change.

THE CHANGING SHAPE OF THE YOUTH TRAINING INDUSTRY

In the seven years between 1978 and 1985 'youth training' expanded by more than five-fold. Simultaneously with the growth in numbers there was an increase in the duration of training, from twelve-week courses in the mid–1970s, to a twenty-four-month programme under YTS2. The youth training industry is now so large and complex that a multitude of individuals and organizations are dependent upon it for their livelihood. New staff and new layers of organization have sprung up to cope with youth training. Many large companies have youth training sections to act as managing agents for their trainees. [...] Elsewhere special companies have sprung up to provide the organization and delivery of youth training to clusters of smaller firms. This continues to be big business. Money can be made (and lost) by the efficient (parsimonious) management of MSC/TA income for YTS. [...]

In introducing two-year YTS, starting in 1985, the MSC attempted to build upon the fact that all the above organizations were beholden to them. It began to tighten its control. Training was restricted to those agencies which attained the status of 'Approved Training Organization' fulfilling requirements laid down by the MSC (Baddely 1985). [...] An 'incumbancy payment system' was introduced which served to make financial planning difficult. These changes had an adverse impact on schemes and training providers in the public sector (Broomhead and Coles 1988).

What also has to be recognized is that the expansion of youth training was expedient and 'from the bottom up' and initially devised for the largely unqualified 'bottom' 10 per cent of the age cohort (Atkinson and Rees 1982). But YTS2 is being delivered to a client group of very mixed abilities. The unqualified remain one segment, but trainees also include within their ranks school-leavers with five or more O-levels or their equivalent (Jones *et al.* 1988).

But did this apparent massive expansion change the nature of youth training? The training component of YTS was flexible and many private sector employers, especially large employers, merely took the subsidy and carried on recruiting and training in the way in which they would have done had government schemes never been invented (Roberts *et al.* 1986). But if large companies and the training boards have been allowed to pick up the subsidies, demand their own terms and largely ignore the diktats from the MSC/TA, this is certainly not true of local authorities, colleges of further education and the charities. This is the very partnership which has been involved in youth unemployment measures from the beginning, but from being welcome partners in 1978 they became, after 1985, a destabilized fringe (Broomhead and Coles 1988).

As demographic changes begin to bite further into the size of the 16-year-old cohort in the 1990s, what then? The public sector vanguard of the training industry, conjured up in the 1970s to deal with youth unemployment, may be left without a client group. If, as Roberts has argued, the private sector has responded to youth training by 'taking the money and running', largely as it always has done, the public sector, under pressure from the change of rules in 1985, has had to run much faster, to stand still (Roberts *et al.* 1986). As youth unemployment began to wane after 1985, its client group was beginning to be recruited by private sector schemes as all sections of the training industry trawled down-market. In the training field it is, therefore, very difficult to reach a single, simple assessment which describes the role played by the MSC. It has changed its tactics from year to year, mainly in response to unemployment levels. But it is clear that government is increasingly convinced that *private industry* can supply the *most* appropriate training.

VOCATIONALIZING EDUCATION

On 18 October 1976, Prime Minister James Callaghan made his now famous address to Ruskin College. In it he made it clear that education was no longer to be regarded as an end in itself. It was to be evaluated according to how well it prepared young people for the world of work. The (so-called) Great Debate which followed this speech brought few immediate consequences. The Thatcher government, however, used both 'carrot' and 'stick' politics to make education bend to the preceived needs of industry. [. . .]

The non-advanced further education (NAFE) story

Of all the White Papers on Education and Training of the 1980s it was *Training for Jobs*, published in January 1984, which proclaimed 'vocationalism' in the bluntest of terms. It started with simple dictums:

1. Britain lives by the skill of its people. A well trained work force is an essential condition of our economic survival.
2. But training is not an end in itself . . . . Training must therefore be firmly work-oriented and lead to jobs.

By paragraph 8 it had reached the point where it was prepared to make assertions which caused consternation, even in the mildest of Conservative controlled local education authorities:

8. Training is an investment. It must be seen to pay for itself . . . . Thus decisions as to who is trained, when and in what skills are best taken by employers.

We have already seen that this practice was already largely taking place in YTS and was to be further encouraged with the rule changes for YTS2 in 1985. But *Training for Jobs* did not just deal with YTS. It turned its attention to 'vocational education' undertaken in colleges of further education:

43. If the important developments described in this White Paper are to be carried through successfully, public sector provision for training and vocational education must become more responsive to employment needs at national and local level. The public sector needs a greater incentive to relate the courses it provides more closely to the needs of the customer and in the most cost effective way . . .

It should perhaps be noted that the 'customer' being referred to here was not the student, but the potential employer of trained labour. The paper continued:

45. For this purpose we have decided to give the Commission important new responsibilities by enabling it to purchase a more significant pro-portion of work-related non-advanced further education provided by local education authorities.
46. . . . The intention is therefore that the Commission should by 1986–87 account for about one quarter of the total provision in this area.

This led to a bitter quarrel between central and local government. Tory Shires were (not for the last time) outraged at this interference in edu-cational provision. [. . .] Starting in 1986 local education authorities had to apply to the MSC for funds to run the Further Education system (25 per cent of the total budget), where previously such finance came to them automatically through the Rate Support Grant. In applying for funding, they had to do so in terms laid down by the MSC/TA. This means that the TA define the terms through which educational accounting should take place, and the legitimacy of the criteria used in educational planning. It is no good teachers and lecturers simply dreaming up interesting new courses, no matter how popular or fascinating their content may be. Such courses can only be mounted if a college can demonstrate that it will meet the needs of local industry (MSC/LAA Policy Group 1986). Because of the asymmetrical power relationship between educationalists and the MSC/TA, the whole culture of educational thinking has been forced to change (Broomhead and Coles 1988).

THE ADVENT OF ENTERPRISE

Where Callaghan's Ruskin Speech in 1976 and the Holland Report of 1977 can be regarded as critical milestones in the development and institutionalization of 'new vocationalism', the promotion of a 'culture of enterprise' has much less clear-cut origins. Yet the promotion of such a culture is now busily under way across almost the full range of training and educational institutions. [. . .] It became one of the key axes of change in the late 1980s. Rather than present a full review of the range of initiatives here we will first briefly outline the development of enterprise in just two contrasting institutional areas: the Youth Training Scheme and institutions of higher education.

Enterprise in YTS

One of the major changes in YTS in the late 1980s was the attempt to graft 'enterprise training' on to the scheme. In announcing the initiative, the minister, John Lee, argued that this was not simply an extra component to be added to the YTS aims and objectives. He heralded it as 'one of the most exciting initiatives undertaken by the MSC', one which was to be given 'high priority' and which would 'mark an important change in the thrust of training for young and old alike across all parts of our industrial and commercial life'. The outline of 'enterprise culture' and its significance was achieved by reference to its opposite 'the culture of dependency'.

> In an Enterprise culture people create opportunities rather than wait for someone else to act. They have skills to generate wealth and resources rather than be dependent upon others . . . We want young people to gain the habits of looking for opportunities and not obstacles while they are in YTS. Habits which will stand them in good stead throughout their working lives.
> (Regional MSC Conferences on 'Enterprise in YTS': published script)

These sentiments have become distilled into the six key elements of 'enterprise training' in YTS:

1 displaying initiative;
2 making decisions;
3 managing resources;
4 displaying drive and determination;
5 influencing others;
6 monitoring progress.

But 'enterprise' in YTS is not merely a new agenda for training. It is intended to be a new modality through which training is delivered. The trainer is to become a 'facilitator' rather than teacher; learning is to be 'active' rather than passive; and the process is to be closely integrated into systems of 'assessment' and 'profiling'. Trainees under 'enterprise training' are encouraged to develop 'self diagnoses', 'action plans' and 'self-appraisal' of what they gain from their training. The whole package is to be geared to nationally agreed systems of assessment and the 'action plans' and certificates of 'modules of competence' filed away as a permanent record in a NROVA (National Record of Vocational Achievement) file. NROVA certification is set to become the norm across all institutions of training and education, so that soon even university applicants will expect admission tutors to scrutinize the contents of their NROVA portfolio rather than merely count A-level grades.

Enterprise in higher education (EHE)

After the 1987 General Election, it became clear that the government was intent upon transforming higher education. The Enterprise in Higher Education (EHE) initiative was launched in December 1987 by the Secretary of State for Employment with the support of the Secretaries of State for Education and Science, Trade and Industry, Scotland and Wales. [. . .] Institutions of HE are being offered up to £1m over five years to bring 'enterprise' into the undergraduate curricula. Over 100 institutions submitted bids for EHE money and in 1988 the first eleven institutions had projects under way. [. . .]

The rhetoric through which EHE is being promoted has a familiar ring. Adaptability to a rapidly changing world is to be encouraged amongst all students. They are to be taught 'how to learn' and 'how to apply a body of knowledge' rather than merely absorb an established body of facts and theories. Learning is to become a more active process, with more use of educational technology and practical project work. Many educationalists welcome these required elements of EHE as virtues they would wish to pursue anyway. But EHE promotes these, not as educational values in their own right, but as necessary to the development of skills demanded by industry. The 1989 review of the initiative states clearly that its aim is to use higher education as a vehicle for social engineering *in the interests of employers*:

> The workplace of today and tomorrow requires employees who are resourceful and flexible and who can adapt quickly to changes in the nature of their skills and knowledge. They will need to be able to innovate, recognise and create opportunities, work as a team, take risks and respond to challenges, communicate effectively and be computer literate. These attributes are the core skills of an enterprising person and lie at the heart of enterprising culture . . . The cornerstone of the initiative apart from enterprise itself is partnership. EHE makes possible a substantial and productive role for employers and practitioners so that they can become involved in the work of institutions, particularly in curriculum design, delivery and assessment.
>
> (Training Agency 1989: 3, 4)

[. . .]

ENTERPRISE IN CLEVELAND: 'UNEMPLOYMENT REMAINS THE MAJOR ISSUE'

So far we have traced the growth of 'vocationalism' and the advent of 'enterprise' at a national level. Our framework for analysis, however, stresses that national blueprints are often significantly modified as they are implemented at a local level. We now turn to a brief description of the philosophy and practices of 'enterprise' in an area of high unemployment: Cleveland. At a national level we will argue that, whilst 'vocationalism' initiatives were propelled along by high rates of unemployment, 'enterprise' intitiatives are designed to take hold in an era, and in a context, in which unemployment is not the most pressing concern. Cleveland, then, represents a context in which there is a particularly heightened tension between the two philosophies of 'vocationalism' and 'enterprise'.

In two successive White Papers on Employment in 1988 the government triumphantly pointed to significant reductions in unemployment [. . .] (White Papers 1988a and 1988b). Cleveland County Council, however, in *its* 1988 review of the state of the local economy, concluded 'unemployment remains the major issue in Cleveland' (Cleveland County Council, Research and Development Unit 1988). Cleveland, perhaps more than any other area, has experienced the most dramatic consequences of economic recession and industrial restructuring. A once thriving local economy, traditionally dependent on steel and chemical production, has more recently become famous for having the highest levels of unemployment in mainland Britain. [. . .]

The situation of school-leavers and young people in Middlesbrough and Cleveland is particularly grim. Despite falls, nationally and locally, in the total number of unemployed, the proportion of school-leavers entering full-time employment in Cleveland was the lowest ever recorded in 1988 (approximately 6 per cent). [. . .] Over 70 per cent of the 1987 school-leavers joined YTS, but unfortunately this did not prove to be the much vaunted 'bridge to full-time work'. YTS progression statistics indicate that, in Cleveland, the majority of YTS trainees complete their scheme only to move from scheme to unemployment. Only 17 per cent enter employment from YTS on recent estimations (Cleveland County Council Careers Service 1988).

The economic collapse of Teesside over the last twenty years has, therefore, severely disrupted the movement of young people from school to work. Nor do falls in the local *overall* unemployment rates seem to have widened opportunities for youth employment. Reductions in national unemployment rates disguise the continuing impact youth unemployment has for transitions in this local labour market. [. . .] Cleveland has become a, if not *the*, centre for the development and testing of the Thatcher government's strategy of encouraging 'enterprise'.

In reviewing 'enterprise' in Cleveland we will not focus on EHE or 'enterprise in YTS' but on the development of a separate 'enterprise industry'. A plethora of organizations has sprung up, phoenix-like, from the ashes of Cleveland's economic decline, to deliver the new gospel of enterprise to the young adults of the county. At the last count there were over eighty agencies and organizations concerned with youth enterprise in Cleveland. These provide enterprise training for school pupils (pre- and post-16), for trainees on YTS, for the unemployed in Employment Training and for the self-employed on the Enterprise Allowance Scheme.

The organizations delivering or 'facilitating' enterprise training can be seen as composing a continuum. At one extreme there are important agencies offering advice, counselling and guidance toward co-operative and community based enterprise projects. Typical of such provision is the CREATE organization which operates according to a *broad* definition of 'enterprise'. Here enterprise is understood as: 'making things happen. It refers to the willingness and ability of people to be self determining and flexible, influencing, shaping and taking control over their own lives in any sphere, be that social, personal, economic or political' (CREATE publicity material).

If this is the 'left' end of the enterprise continuum, then the majority of structures, agencies and schemes lie to the 'right'. These may vary in terms of size, and the particular 'client group' they deal with, but they are united by two common factors. First, they receive financial backing, at least in part, from the public purse. Second, they promote a much *narrower* version of enterprise. This equates 'enterprise' with self-employment. Through a variety of administrative bodies and schemes, but through the Enterprise Allowance Scheme (EAS) in particular, young people are encouraged to leave the 'dependency' of unemployment and to become 'their own boss'. This self-employment model of 'enterprise' is delivered in training courses lasting anything from one day to eight weeks; the topics for the training agenda being the basics of capitalist business development: marketing strategies, profit margins, and cash-flows, etc. There is little room within this conception of 'enterprise culture' for less competitive, less individualistic, but more co-operative or collective views of enterprise as a solution to unemployment.

Cleveland Youth Business Centre (CYBC), as its name suggests, is a typical example of this approach to enterprise. Its multimillion pound budget has been supported by the Training Agency, an 'Inner City Task Force' (the North Central Middlesbrough Task Force), local government and the private sector. It aims to provide: 'a valuable, one stop shop, for all young entrepreneurs providing essential, continuous support and advice to develop a viable business from the seed of an idea' (CYBC publicity material). Effectively, what this means is a three-stage process offering 'counselling', 'training', 'starter unit space' and 'backup services' for those prepared to enter self-employment. At the first stage, the intending young entrepreneurs are advised about their business ideas. Second, they are offered specific training courses in business skills. Third, the CYBC offers offices and work-space, at subsidized rates, through which enterprises can operate. This is further supplemented by ongoing support including advice on marketing, bookkeeping, the availability of grants and loans, etc. [. . .]

A particular problem in assessing the impact of 'enterprise' and self-employment in Cleveland is 'multiple auditing'. Many of the organizations promoting 'enterprise' have to operate within a culture of TA monitoring. This demands quantification of 'success' and justifies continuation of funding on a 'payment by results' basis. Thus a particular, 'successful' individual entrepreneur is likely to be counted several times by different organizations as evidence of *their* success, even if contact with the client has been minimal. But the reliance on quantification of outcome has another important effect. If the narrow version of 'enterprise' is employed then, despite 'multiple auditing', there are clear and measurable outcomes – business 'start up' and business 'survival rates'. If, however, the wider philosophy and practice of enterprise is promoted then 'outcome' is a much more nebulous concept. Organizations like CREATE work with a much broader measure of 'success' as 'positive outcome'. This *may* eventually be self-employment, or a completed community project (such as organizing a social outing), but equally a 'positive outcome' of enterprise activities could mean increased feelings of self-efficacy and self-worth among unemployed clients. Clearly this makes it much more difficult to measure 'success' and justify the existence of organizations employing the broader definition of 'enterprise' to funding bodies.

The maze of organizations which has grown in Cleveland during the mid-1980s to deliver the 'enterprise culture' is directly and indirectly dependent upon Training Agency funding. Organizations have quickly been formed and immediately asked to deliver new schemes for changing client groups at short notice. The TA, like the MSC before it, is always in a hurry. Since September 1988, for instance, consortia with acronyms such as HANDS (Help and Development Support), FACE (Facility for Access to Creative Enterprise) as well as CYBC have been enticed to develop short, intensive 'enterprise training programmes' to mesh with Employment Training (ET) requirements. Some of these have been 'feeder' courses for 'enterprise rehearsal' (whereby a client can establish and run a business for a year under the auspices of an umbrella organization, like CYBC, which takes overall responsibility for such projects). Yet these are being managed without any clear concept of 'progression' beyond the end of the eight-week course, and it is unclear what outcomes are possible if ET trainees then decide *not* to start their own businesses.

Furthermore, many of those employed to deliver these initiatives are themselves often in an insecure and vulnerable position. Many have gained their new found status as 'prophets of enterprise' only through previous involvement with the TA through the Community Programme. Others, particularly those in senior positions, are 'secondees' from local industry. But initial multimillion-pound budgets are now being exhausted, and personnel are faced with having to seek out new means of keeping their organizations afloat. The funding of 'enterprise' initiatives, *and their own jobs*, is only short term. [. . .]

CONCLUSIONS

In the introduction we suggested that an assessment of the change from a culture of 'vocationalism' to a culture of 'enterprise' was best accomplished by employing a five-point framework and it is to this that we now return.

First, the literature on 'vocationalism', to which we referred earlier, suggests that it is a concern to make education and training accountable to the needs of industry which unites a range of schemes and initiatives. [. . .] Also of significance is that these are 'bottom up' innovations in which the budget and size of the initiative was largely determined by youth unemployment and that their major impact was in 'remedying' the unemployed (Stafford 1981, Raffe 1984). 'Enterprise' projects, however, have a wider constituency. To be sure, many projects can still be seen as throwing money at the unemployment problem, as was demonstrated by the case of Cleveland. But 'enterprise culture' is now being directed at all sectors of education and training, the unemployed *and* the employed. In education, too, 'enterprise' is being cultivated in all schools and is designed to reach the very pinnacles of the universities' ivory towers. This shift from 'vocationalism for some' to 'enterprise for all' is, we suggest, an important change of direction.

Second, an examination of the pattern of institutional relationships being promoted by 'vocationalism' and 'enterprise' also indicates some marked similarities. [. . .] 'Enterprise' is being piloted under a vague brief with 'wedge funding'. The results of pilots are intended to spread throughout institutions and plans for 'embedding' are now an important part of enterprise contracts. The TA is still a major means through which schemes are promoted and funded. But following the abolition of the Training Commission there are signs that the Training Agency itself may not be master of its own house for much longer. Rather, in the administration of training, TECs, made up of local representatives of business and commerce, are going to be in charge, with TA staff servicing TECs on secondment. Early signs indicate that the large budgets given to TECs (approximately £47 million, for instance, in Cleveland), have ensured that major employers *are* willing to take on and take over the control of training. Indeed, they have already indicated that they want to exercise even more power and control than was envisaged by the White Paper (*Times Educational Supplement*, 21 July 1989). The funding councils controlling higher education are similarly dominated by captains of industry. Together these developments give much more *direct* influence to industry to call the tune in future reforms of education and training.

Third, the rhetorics of 'vocationalism' and 'enterprise' also display important differences. 'Vocationalism' was concerned with changing attitudes to work and industry. 'Enterprise' is concerned to facilitate and promote initiative, a flexible and constructive approach to problem solving, adaptability in using resources and self-monitoring and self-reliance. This may, of course, be no more than a change in linguistic packaging. More significant is the fact that institutional and personal economic survival is sometimes dependent on being prepared to frame tenders and contracts in 'TA-speak'. In many cases, as with YTS, this may be little more than playing language games in order to fund what the institution would wish to commit itself to anyway – a practice which Americans call 'boondoggle'. But because TA contracts are legal commitments, some still regard them as hostages to fortune.

Fourth, we have argued here and elsewhere that the key to understanding the direction and speed of change is to be found in the economic context in which it occurs (Coles 1988). This we see as the most fundamental difference between the promotion of 'vocationalism' and 'enterprise'. The government is repeatedly heralding [. . .] that the real need is now to break down the 'barriers to employment', for example by remedying inadequacies in training provision (White Paper 1988b). Existing and anticipated skill shortages, the White Paper argues, result from failures to recognize 'investment in people' (unemployed *and* in work) as sufficiently important.

This appears to recognize the fifth point in our analytical framework. The White Paper argues that decisions as to who needs to be trained must be devolved to industrialists *at a local level* – where people work and are trained (para. 4.8). It is for this reason that TECs will become the most significant institutions in the 1990s in determining the direction of change.

There are many long standing critics of government training policy who might be expected to welcome, at least in part, these sentiments. Sociological studies of labour markets have, over the past decade, stressed the importance of *local* labour market conditions in determining the fortunes of young people (Ryrie 1983, Ashton and Maguire 1986, Roberts Dench and Richardson 1987, Coles 1988, MacDonald 1988b). But there does appear to be a contradiction between this recognition of the importance of local factors and the continued promotion of major *national* initiatives. Employment Training claims to match the 'workers without jobs' to 'the jobs without workers', without recognition of the geography which divides the two halves of the equation. Similarly, as the discussion of the 'enterprise culture' in Cleveland suggested, 'enterprise' which *in general* may represent a shift in focus in training policy from the *unemployed* to the *employed*, is being heavily funded, in at least this area, as an unemployment measure.

It is this image of the Training Agency scurrying around promoting such apparent contradictions and anomalies in government thinking which has led some critics to label it as an 'adhocracy' – 'an organization capable of sophisticated innovation deploy[ing] teams of experts in ad hoc projects' (Coffield 1984: 29). But 'ad hocary' is sometimes seen as a virtue in enterprise culture, indicating a willingness to be flexible and adaptable in managing resources rather than being tied down by strict rules, regulations and procedures. But whilst this may be regarded as a virtue by government, the Department of Employment and the Training Agency, the constant unpredictability of funding remains the basis for continuing uncertainty and insecurity in Cleveland's precarious 'enterprise industry'.

NOTE

Part of this chapter draws on work conducted under a project funded by the ESRC 16–19 Initiatve on Youth and Enterprise in Cleveland. The research is being carried out by Robert MacDonald and Frank Coffield at the University of Durham. The views expressed here are, however, entirely those of the authors.

ACKNOWLEDGEMENT

We would like to thank Mary Maynard for her helpful comments on drafts of this chapter.

REFERENCES

Ainley, P. (1988) *From School to YTS: Education and Training in England and Wales 1944–1987*, Milton Keynes: Open University Press.
Ashton, D. N. and Maguire, M. J. (1986) *Young Adults in the Labour Market*, Research Paper No. 55, London: Department of Employment.
Atkinson, P. and Rees, T. L. (eds) (1982) *Youth Unemployment and State Intervention*, London: Routledge & Kegan Paul.
Baddely, S. (1985) 'Criteria for approved training organizations', *Youth Training News*, no. 25, Sheffield, Manpower Services Commission.
Bates, I., Clark, J., Cohen, P., Moore, R. and Willis, P. (1984) *Schooling for the Dole*, London: Macmillan.
Bedeman, T. and Courtenay, G. (1982) *One in Three: The Second National Survey of Young People on YOP*, Research and Development Series, No. 3, Sheffield, Manpower Services Commission.
Broomhead, S. and Coles, B. (1988) 'Youth unemployment and the growth of "new further education" ', in B. Coles (ed.) *Young Careers*, Milton Keynes: Open University Press.

Brown, P. and Ashton, D. N. (eds) (1987) *Education, Unemployment and Labour Markets*, Basingstoke: Falmer Press.

Cleveland County Council Careers Service (1988) *Report of the Principal Careers Officer to Careers and Youth Employment Sub-Committee*, October.

Cleveland County Council, Research and Development Unit (1988) *Cleveland 1988–1992: An Economic, Demographic and Social Review*.

Coffield, F. (1984) 'Is there work after the MSC?', *New Society*, pp. 29–30.

Coles, B. (1986) 'School leaver, job seeker, dole reaper: young and unemployed in rural England', in S. Allen, *et al.* (eds) *The Experience of Unemployment*, London, Macmillan.

—— (1988) 'The rise of youth unemployment and the growth of new vocationalism', in B. Coles (ed.), *Young Careers*, Milton Keynes: Open University Press.

Department of Employment (1977) *Young People and Work*, London: HMSO.

Finn, D. (1986) 'YTS: the jewel in the crown of the MSC', in C. Benn and J. Fairley (eds), *Challenging the MSC*, London: Pluto.

Hughes, J. M. (ed.) (1984) *The Best Years*, Aberdeen: Aberdeen University Press.

Jones, B. *et al.* (1988) 'Finding a post-16 route', in B. Coles (ed.), *Young Careers* Milton Keynes: Open University Press.

MacDonald, R. F. (1988a) 'Schooling, training, working and claiming: youth and unemployment in local rural labour markets', Unpublished Ph.D. Thesis, University of York.

—— (1988b) 'Out of town, out of work: research on the post-16 experience in two rural areas', in B. Coles (ed.) *Young Careers*, Milton Keynes: Open University Press.

MSC/LAA Policy Group (1986) *Work Related NAFE: A Guidance Handbook*, London: MSC.

Pollard, A., Purvis, J. and Walford, G. (eds) (1988) *Education, Training and the New Vocationalism*, Milton Keynes: Open University Press.

Raffe, D. (1984) 'YOP and the future of YTS', in D. Raffe (ed.), *Fourteen to Eighteen*, Aberdeen: Aberdeen University Press.

—— (ed.) (1988) *Education and the Youth Labour Market*, Basingstoke: Falmer Press.

—— and Courtenay, G. (1988) '16–18 on both sides of the border: a comparison of Scotland, England and Wales', in D. Raffe (ed.), *Education and the Youth Labour Market*, Basingstoke: Falmer Press.

Rees, T. (1986) 'Education for enterprise: the state and alternative employment for young people', *Journal of Educational Policy*, 3, 1, 9–22.

Roberts, K., Dench, S. and Richardson, D. (1986) 'Firms' uses of the Youth Training Scheme', *Policy Studies*, 6.

——, Dench, S. and Richardson, D. (1987) *The Changing Structure of the Youth Labour Market*, Department of Employment Research Paper No. 59, London: DOE.

—— *et al.* (1988) 'Youth-unemployment in the 1980s' in B. Coles (ed.), *Young Careers*, Milton Keynes: Open University Press.

Ryrie, A. C. (1983) *On Leaving School: A Study of Schooling, Guidance and Opportunity*, Edinburgh: Scottish Council for Research in Education.

Stafford, A. (1981) 'Learning not to labour', *Capital and Class*, 15, pp. 55–77.

Times Educational Supplement (1989) 'CBI advocates more power for local employers' (edited by Mark Jackson), 21 July.

Training Agency (1989) *Enterprise in Higher Education: Key Features of the Enterprise in Higher Education Proposals, 1988–89*, Sheffield: Moorfoot.

White Paper (1981) *A New Training Initiative: A Programme for Action* (Cmnd 8455), London: HMSO.
—— (1988a) *Training for Employment* (Cmnd 316), London: HMSO.
—— (1988b) *Employment in the 1990s* (Cmnd 540), London: HMSO.

Chapter 11

The inevitable future?

Post-Fordism in work and learning

Richard Edwards

Source: This chapter is a reworked version of an article which appeared in *Open Learning*, vol. 6, no. 2, 1991 and was first published as an occasional paper by the Centre for Youth and Adult Studies, The Open University, in 1990.

INTRODUCTION

The United Kingdom economy has undergone major changes since the 1970s. Large parts of manufacturing industry have been lost. There has been a growth in service sector employment. Full-time male participation in the work-force has decreased. Full- and particularly part-time female employment has increased (Hughes 1991). Alongside, and as part of, these changes have been major alterations in the provision of education and training for adults. These processes are still at work and increasingly there have been attempts to chart their significance. During the 1980s, this was most noticeable from the Left in the work of the magazine, *Marxism Today*, and the attempt to chart 'New Times', a restructuring of the economy on post-Fordist rather than Fordist principles, made possible by the availability of information technology and associated breakdown of the consensual 'certainties' of the post-Second World War era. As two of the prime exponents of this thesis put it,

> the 'New Times' argument is that the world has changed, not just incrementally but qualitatively, that Britain and other advanced capitalist societies are increasingly characterised by diversity, differentiation and fragmentation, rather than homogeneity, standardisation and the economies and organisations of scale which characterised modern mass society.
>
> (Hall and Jacques 1989: 11)

This chapter outlines the principles of Fordism and post-Fordism and asks how far there is a similar shift in the principles for the delivery of education and training. The basis for this interest is a concern that the 'progressive' discourse and practice of adult learning, access and opportunity has grown at the same time as resurgent right-wing economic liberalism. Possible conflicting interests are walking hand in hand as partners. Why is this?

Drawing on the forms of analysis suggested by the work of Michel Foucault (1978, 1980), I want to suggest that post-Fordism and its corollaries in the education and training of adults are part of a strategic range of discourses which attempt to 'normalize' a particular view of the future of economic and social life which is, in fact, contingent and challengeable. (I am using discourses in the sense of institutionalized language use of education and training by which we bring forth and make sense of the material world, as part of attempts to control and change it.)

While the position outlined may look similar to a Marxist analysis of the hegemony of the capitalist class in securing its interests through the ideological subordination of the majority working class, the theoretical basis is, in fact, different. In the classic Marxist position, the power operating in the social formation is ultimately grounded in the economic power of the dominant class. In Foucault's analysis this is not the case. Power is exercised in every moment of social life and the way we behave as subjects. In this, power is productive as well as repressive.

> What makes power hold good, what makes it accepted, is simply the fact that it doesn't only weigh on us as a force that says no, but that it traverses and produces things, it induces pleasure, forms knowledge, produces discourse. It needs to considered as a productive network which runs through the whole social body, much more than as a negative instance whose function is repression.
>
> (Foucault 1980: 119)

There is no ultimate foundation which provides the basis for total human emancipation, for example the overthrow of capitalism. Power is omnipresent in human social formations.

The suggestion will be that discourses about post-Fordism are further attempts at 'disciplining' persons into particular forms of social subjecthood, of exercising power over persons. These forms of power facilitate the management and administration of order within the social formation which is compatible with the continuing inequalities of power relations.

FROM FORDISM TO POST-FORDISM

The shift from Fordism to post-Fordism as the dominant organizing principle in the economy has been put forward very clearly in an article by Murray (1989). Murray suggests that Fordism (epitomized in the producton lines introduced by Henry Ford) was the dominant principle of manufacture and distribution in the period from the late nineteenth century to the post-war boom years of the 1950s and 1960s.

With Fordism, one had standardized products manufactured by mass

production plants with special purpose machinery, epitomized in the Char-
lie Chaplin film, *Modern Times*. The classic image is of the production
line with the product going past the work-force, each of whom undertook
a task which was subject to the scientific management techniques of
Taylorism. Standardized products were consumed in the mass market, in
which there was little scope for consumer choice unless you were wealthy
enough to participate at the luxury end of the market.

Fordist organizations were governed by hierarchical bureaucracies, in
which the planning was done by specialists and handed down to workers
and consumers alike. This was a result of and led to authoritarian relations,
pyramidal organizational structures, centralized planning and exclusive job
descriptions.

We therefore have a picture of large bureaucratic, top-down organizations producing goods and services for the masses – the factory and the
Welfare State. Nor is this picture restricted to capitalist economies. Similar
principles can be seen to have operated in the economic changes of the
Soviet Union and Eastern European states under what was until recently
'actually existing socialism', as well as in the economic development of
many 'Third World' countries.

However, Murray suggests that Fordism is no longer the dominant set
of principles governing the economy. He argues that an alternative strand
has developed, made possible by advances in technology and particularly
information technology. This has shifted the emphasis in the economy
from manufacturing for a mass market to the provision of services – shops,
offices, leisure – for particular market segments. The principles governing
this change result in and from post-Fordism.

Technological advances have increased the availability of information
and the speed at which it can be collected, analysed and transmitted. This
has enabled shops to introduce 'just in time' systems of ordering to meet
the specific market needs at any particular time. Increases in demand for
certain goods and decreases for others can be used in the ordering of
supplies from manufacturers. Shops no longer keep large stocks of a
narrow range of items. They have small stocks of a large range of items.
Shops respond to the consumer demands of particular market segments.
Products have a shorter life-span and there is a greater need for innovation
and design. Life-style becomes a dominant motif in the marketing of
specific goods to specific market segments. The mass market is supposedly
dead, replaced by consumer choice and power.

The argument is that technology has given greater power to the consumer and that power is expressed in the diversity of goods required from
the market. Inevitably, this has had an impact upon manufacturing. If
manufacturers have to produce a greater range of goods and be responsive
to specific demands, the mass production line and standardized product
are no longer applicable. The decimation of British manufacturing capacity

in the early 1980s can be seen as the attempted removal of Fordist principles from the British economy, something which appears to have been
repeated in the recession of the early 1990s.

New principles of post-Fordism are being introduced into manufacturing. These principles involve flexible systems of manufacturing, customized
design for specific segments of the market and an emphasis on quality
control. The manufacturing plant in which all aspects of production are
sustained under one roof is replaced by a new form of organization in
which all non-essential work is sub-contracted to other organizations.
Post-Fordism polarizes organizations. There is an increase in the number
of smaller organizations who act as sub-contractors for a smaller core of
large organizations. They are the birds on the rhino's back, which can be
shaken off when necessary without any damage to the rhino.

The economic necessity for greater flexibility and innovation are resulting in and from new organizational forms. These entail the breakdown
of job demarcations and pyramidal bureaucracies. Multi-skilled, flexible
workers are seen as the key to these changes, wherein, as demands change,
so workers are able to drop old tasks and take up new ones. To make
this happen there is thus the need for continuous training, for the support
and development of lifelong learners and the workplace to be actively
constructed as a learning organization.

Given the above analysis, it is therefore unsurprising that these shifts
in the economy can also be seen to be supported at ideological and policy
level by government in three crucial areas. First, there is the emphasis
placed on the need for a more highly skilled and multi-skilled, flexible
work-force. To compete in the global economy Britain will need to ensure
that it has the personnel with the relevant skills to do so and the capacity
to transfer those skills as demands change. Thus, for example, during the
late 1980s, the design frameworks for both the Youth Training Scheme
and Employment Training for the unemployed stressed the ability to
transfer skills as an outcome of participation. Second, there is the development of competence-based National Vocational Qualifications (NVQs),
the competences for which are being specified by employer-dominated
Lead Bodies. If the workplace is to be a learning organization, the provision for assessment and accreditation at work will motivate people to
continue their learning. It also gives employers greater control over the
training their employees undertake. Third, there is the support and funding
of open learning programmes and projects to facilitate the training of
employees without them having to attend colleges, or, at most, for the
very specific training that is required for and by them; the short-lived
Open Tech, the Open College, Training Agency (now TEED) Work
Related Development Fund projects.

Each of these can be argued to be supporting a shift in emphasis in the
economy from Fordism to post-Fordism. How far this shift, if it is

occurring, should be embraced or contested is for further discussion (see Hirst 1989, Westwood 1990, Allman and Wallis 1990, and Sivanandan 1990 for differing positions on 'New Times' and post-Fordism). Key to any answers are the questions of how much and what forms of power are manifested in the choice of consumers. In this, straightforward judgements of progress or regression are not readily apparent, which is itself a part of 'New Times' analysis. However, before examining more critically the post-Fordist thesis – how far it is reflecting actual changes or attempting to normalize a certain direction of economic change – I want briefly to examine the possible impact of these principles on changes in the education and training of adults.

POST-FORDISM IN EDUCATION AND TRAINING

I have suggested that certain changes in education and training have supported the development of post-Fordism in the economy, particularly the increased role for employers, the introduction of NVQs, and support for open learning. This presents a picture of education and training being harnessed to better support economic development, a not unfamiliar argument.

These moves have found expression in concerns over what has been termed 'new vocationalism' and the increasing control of post-compulsory education and training handed to employers. This has taken place both directly and indirectly. For instance, in increased numbers of private training organizations, the development of Training and Enterprise Councils in England and Wales and Local Enterprise Councils in Scotland, and increasing employer representation on the governing bodies of Further Education Colleges (Edwards 1990).

The development of open learning opportunities has been associated in educational circles with increasing access, by making education and training more flexible and responsive to student need. It is argued that open learning has become popular among employers because it allows employees to train in their own time without having to be released from work. It therefore appears to be a more cost-effective form of training. Open-learning techniques also mean that employees are isolated from employees in other workplaces, undermining the material possibilities for discussions of shared concerns beyond the immediate sphere of their training. This suggests that 'progressive' notions of open learning, grounded in increasing and widening access, have been appropriated and narrowed by government and employers for the new vocationalism.

While I would support much of the above, I believe it is based on the fallacy that open learning is simply a 'progressive' branch of education and training, something which needs to be contested. Rather than constructing open learning as the progressive innocent appropriated, I want to suggest that we examine it in the context of the shift from Fordism to post-Fordism I have outlined above. In this context, open learning can be constructed as the post-Fordist approach to education and training, contesting as the Fordism of traditional institutional providers of learning opportunities. It therefore loses the 'innocence' that its supporters suggest it has.

In this shift, organizations are having to become far more flexible in order that learners have access to opportunities relevant to their needs when, where and how they want them. The transmission of learning, of bolting on a particular canon or skills to people as they progress down the production line of education and training, is in the process of being replaced by individual learning programmes tied to the needs of particular individuals, mixing elements of formal, non-formal and informal learning. Associated with these changes are accreditation of prior learning, credit accumulation and transfer and modularization of the curriculum. The standard products of education and training are being replaced by a wider range of goods for particular segments of the market in which the learner is the consumer with consumer choice. Open learning provides the theoretical perspective and legitimation of this post-Fordist shift.

I have deliberately used the terms of Fordism and post-Fordism in setting up this argument, rather than the more familiar ones within the canon of open learning of student-centredness, individual learning needs, and self-directed learning. This is to suggest that the professional boundaries of discourse about open learning, education and training are a limiting factor in our self-understanding and that the practices – discursive and non-discursive, presentational and actual – of educators and trainers are part of the processes of power operating within the wider social formation.

If we accept open learning as the direction to be pursued in education and training, the logical conclusion of this analysis is that the sooner post-Fordist principles are embedded in the organization of the delivery of learning, the quicker the goals will be achieved. In this context, the Open University is in an ambiguous position, as it is essentially a Fordist institution, but discursively committed to the principles of open learning (Campion 1990). Trends in the post-compulsory sector suggest that others are moving ahead faster in this process – specifically tailored learning, the growth of consultancy, temporary and part-time employment, a focus on evaluation and performance indicators. All of which is becoming 'normal'. The particular nature of the structures, processes and outcomes being engendered is relatively unstated.

Post-Fordism in its various manifestations, of which discourses on open learning are one, are normalizing these changes, assisting in the maintenance of social order in a period of rapid transformation. However, alternative discourses are possible and available. [. . .]

THE FUTURE UNDER POST-FORDISM

We are surrounded by examples of individuals, organizations, governments setting out their stalls for the future, many features of which are shared. The highly trained work-force, capable of transferring skills as economic demands change, consumer choice, economic change and transformation are common features of what is presented as the inevitable future, if we get things right.

> Over the next twenty years this country will experience profound economic and social changes, largely as a result of the increasingly rapid spread of existing and new technologies. This could lead to unprecedented shifts in economic activity, and to marked changes in the patterns of work and leisure (or non-work), with less working time needed for much more highly skilled work. Quality will have to replace quantity. Adaptability will become essential. The present scale of these changes is small compared with the future effects of the accelerating speed of change which will reach in the next few years into many more sectors of the economy to affect larger sections of the population. The idea of holding the same job for life is becoming increasingly untenable. Those with the greatest capacity to adapt will survive successfully; those least adaptable, nations as well as persons, will fail.
>
> (ACACE 1982: 181)

> People need to develop a 'broader occupational competence ... concerned with adaptability, management of roles, responsibility for standards, creativity and flexibility.
>
> (CBI, quoted in NIACE 1990: 2)

> The need for higher levels of education and skills in the workforce if Britain is to meet the economic challenges of the 1990s is acknowledged by all ... there is the need for an initiative to promote and support the contribution education and training can make in helping adults to move from unemployment to employment and from unskilled to more skilled work.
>
> (NIACE 1990: 1–2)

We are presented with a view of the future – a form of economic Darwinism – as though it is inevitable and we are asked to adapt to that view, or positively support it. The political choices about the economy and social formation that are involved in accepting this view are not raised as such. They are 'realities' within which we have to operate, the foundations upon which policies are built rather than the outcomes of pre-existing power and policy. What will that 'reality' be?

Here I want to draw on the work of Gorz (1989). He argues that, unless there are substantial changes in the ideology, organization and distribution of work, current trends will result in a social formation very different from that suggested by modernizers of the economy through multi-skilling. The post-Fordist future will produce a particular segmentation of the active population:

– 25 per cent will be skilled workers with permanent jobs in large firms protected by collective wage agreements;
– 25 per cent will be peripheral workers with insecure, unskilled and badly paid jobs, whose work schedules vary according to the wishes of their employers and the fluctuations of the market;
– 50 per cent will be semi-unemployed, unemployed, or marginalised workers, doing occasional or seasonal work or 'odd jobs'.

(Gorz 1989: 225)

In other words, the flexibility and skills needed among the work-force will vary hugely on the basis of the differential positions we occupy in the post-Fordist economy. The highly educated, multi-skilled flexible workers of the future will be the minority experience; the core work-force governed by the practices of human resource management. The bulk of the work-force, by contrast, will be consigned to marginalized positions in low skill areas, insecure in their employment.

We have already witnessed the beginnings of this trend in Britain with the growth in employment in low paid, part-time service sector jobs during the 1980s. These trends have been experienced elsewhere.

In the United States, which is often taken as a model, of the thirteen to fifteen million new jobs created in the last ten years, the majority are in the personal-service sector and are very often insecure, badly paid and offer no possibilities of achieving professional qualifications or advancement – jobs as caretakers, nightwatchmen, cleaners, waiters and waitresses, staff in 'fast food' restaurants, nursing assistants, delivery men/women, street sellers, shoeshiners, and so on.

The 'person-to-person' services are, in reality, the jobs of domestic or personal servants in their modernized and socialized guise . . . As in the colonies in the past and many Third World countries today, a growing mass of people in the industrialised countries has been reduced to fighting each other for the 'privilege' of selling their personal services to those who still maintain a decent income.

(Gorz 1989: 226)

What will be the different results for people if this pattern of future work does occur? It appears that the 25 per cent core workers will be provided with job security and training in exchange for increasing flexibility in working practices. The other 75 per cent will need to be flexible to cope with the insecurity of their situation of unemployment and underemployment. This has disturbing echoes of the philosophy that you make the rich work harder by giving them more, while the poor work harder if you give them less, and the associated tax and welfare policies that become familiar in Britain in the 1980s. Elsewhere, such trends have been identified as part of a 'housewifization of labour', a 'systematic utilization of the sexual division of labour to cheapen both male and female labour (Hart 1992: 20).

The market for education and training will itself be very differentiated, although given the key rubric of flexibility it is unsurprising that open learning is to the fore. For the core workers, education and training will need to be available to cope with the changing demands of the market, to be able to provide relevant opportunities, as and when they are required. For the rest of the work-force, it will be there to support the movement of people in and out of employment, or to keep them occupied by providing a 'revolving door'. How real these opportunities are or whether they are taken up is not the point. Open learning is there to maintain the appearance of opportunity. It marginalizes the issue that, in the marketplace of education and training, it is those with the largest capital in terms of previous experience of learning who are the biggest and most likely buyers.

Discourses about the multi-skilled flexible work-force of the future are therefore misleading in terms of the implications of post-Fordism for the future of work. The minority experience is being constructed as the norm. What these discourses do attempt is to normalize a contestable position. They shift the burden of responsibility for people who are not part of the core onto us as individuals. Being part of the core is the goal, as it is 'normal' to be a high-skilled worker. People can strive for this goal, but if they do not achieve it, it is because they lack the skills. Education and training opportunities are available to them through open learning, as and when they need them, so the responsibility for not participating in the core of the economy lies with them.

Once again, this echoes the policies and discourses about unemployment during the 1980s in which responsibility for unemployment is placed on individuals because they are deemed as not having the necessary skills for the jobs available. Structural unemployment and the policies supporting it are marginalized within the sphere of public discourse and debate. Similarly with post-Fordism. There are not, and will not be, the employment opportunities available for all to be core workers, yet in establishing that as the norm there is the suggestion that all can participate if they have the right skills (Campion 1990).

This is not a neutral process. It is the attempt to maintain discipline and order, to manage people and issues, in a period of uncertain change (Edwards 1991).

CONCLUSION: POWER AND POST-FORDISM

Discourses are tactical elements or blocks operating in the field of force relations; there can exist different and even contradictory discourses within the same strategy; they can, on the contrary, circulate without changing their form from one strategy to another, opposing strategy.

(Foucault 1978: 101–2)

What I have been suggesting is that discourses are not simply neutral descriptions of 'reality', they are also productive and integral to the exercise of power in social formations which in itself cannot be reduced to any single moment (i.e. the state, economic relations, etc.). Discourses are therefore strategic to the ongoing and continuous power struggles in the social formation.

The fact that discourses are not generally articulated in this way is itself a manifestation of power, as 'neutral' descriptions of 'reality' have a power in themselves in making the contingent appear unchallengeable. Within this context, discourses about open learning can be articulated as another aspect of post-Fordism, strategically ranged to normalize a view of the future of work – based in structural unemployment and underemployment – as not only inevitable, but also preferable. As a result of these discourses and the practices they reflect and reproduce, persons will be disciplined into certain forms of behaviour and more readily managed within a social formation of structural inequality. The fact that there could be alternatives is itself excluded by the ways in which the debates are constructed (see Hake and Meijer 1990). We may discuss how best to produce the flexible worker of the future, but who that person will be is left unquestioned.

If left unchallenged, root and branch, the 'paradise' of post-Fordism is for the few. For the vast majority it will be, yet again, 'paradise' unobtainable. In this context, supporters of open learning, among others, need to carefully consider their discursive and non-discursive practices. There is power in discourses about open learning, but perhaps not the power many would like to think.

REFERENCES

Advisory Council for Adult and Continuing Education (ACACE) (1982) *Continuing Education: From Policies to Practice*, Leicester: ACACE.

Allman, P. and Wallis, J. (1990) '1992 and New Times: a critical reading', in SCUTREA, Proceedings of the Twentieth Annual Conference *Towards 1992 . . . Education of Adults in the New Europe*, University of Sheffield, pp. 234–45.

Campion, M. (1990) 'Post-Fordism and research in distance education', in T. Evans, (ed.), *Research in Distance Education 1*, Deakin University, pp. 59–71.

Edwards, R. (1990) 'Where is the Department of Employment taking us? Further education in the 1990s', in *Adults Learning*, 1 (9), 253–4.

—— (1991) 'Winners and losers in the education and training of adults', in

P. Raggatt and L. Unwin (eds), *Change and Intervention: Vocational Education and Training*, London: Falmer Press, pp. 107–27.

Foucault, M. (1978) *The History of Sexuality* (Vol. 1), London: Penguin.

—— (1980) *Power/Knowledge*, Brighton: Harvester Press.

Gorz, A. (1989) *Critique of Economic Reason*, London: Verso.

Hake, B. and Meijer, J. (1990) 'Adult basic education and the labour market in the Netherlands: some contradictions in development in the 1990s', in SCUTREA, Proceedings of the Twentieth Annual Conference *Towards 1992 . . . Education of Adults in the New Europe* University of Sheffield, pp. 122–7.

Hall, S. and Jacques, M. (1989) 'Introduction', in S. Hall and M. Jacques (eds), *New Times: The Changing Face of Politics in the 1990s*, London: Lawrence & Wishart, pp. 11–20.

Hart, M. U. (1992) *Working and Educating for Life: Feminist and International Perspectives on Adult Education*, London: Routledge.

Hirst, P. (1989) 'After Henry', in S. Hall and M. Jacques, (eds), *New Times: The Changing Face of Politics in the 1990s*, London: Lawrence & Wishart, pp. 321–9.

Hughes, J. (1991) 'A critical overview of labour market trends, employment and unemployment', in K. Forrester and K. Ward (eds), *Unemployment, Education and Training: Case Studies from North America and Europe*, Sacramento: Caddo Gap Press, pp. 13–32.

Murray, R. (1989) 'Fordism and post-Fordism', in S. Hall and M. Jacques (eds), *New Times: The Changing Face of Politics in the 1990s*, London: Lawrence & Wishart, pp. 38–53.

National Institute of Adult Continuing Education (NIACE) (1990), *People, Learning and Jobs: A New Initiative*, Leicester: NIACE.

Sivanandan, A. (1990) 'All that melts into air is solid: the hokum of New Times', in *Race and Class*, 31, 3, pp. 1–30.

Westwood, S. (1990) 'Adult education and New Times', in SCUTREA Proceedings of the Twentieth Annual Conference *Towards 1992 . . . Education of Adults in the New Europe*, University of Sheffield, pp. 14–19.

Part 3

Social movements and change in education and training

Chapter 12

Community education
Towards a theoretical analysis

Ian Martin

Source: This is an edited version of a chapter in G. Allen, J. Bastiani and I. Martin (eds), *Community Education: An Agenda for Educational Reform*, London, Routledge, 1990.

INTRODUCTION

> It is commonplace that the characteristic virtue of Englishmen is their power of sustained practical activity, and their characteristic vice a reluctance to test the quality of that activity by reference to principles.
>
> R. H. Tawney, *The Acquisitive Society*

On the whole, the development of community education in Britain reflects the kind of conscientious but essentially unreflective pragmatism which Tawney, in the opening paragraph of *The Acquisitive Society* (1921), identifies as a fundamental attribute of our national character; predictably, this has had both positive and negative consequences. On the one hand, localized and *ad hoc* development has produced a rich diversity of practice. This has now evolved into a substantial and significant movement of educational ideas an activity which cuts across geographical, social and professional boundaries in a unique way. On the other hand, a price has been paid in terms of lack of conceptual clarity and theoretical coherence. Consequently, 'community education' has a credibility problem.

[. . .] The inherent ambiguity of the term provides a convenient cover for all manner of expedient reinterpretation. This may, for example, take the form of the 'rationalization' of services in a way that suggests to some youth and community workers and adult educators that community education is little more than a euphemism for cost cutting. Alternatively, it can apparently offer an instant rationale for doing something, almost anything, about a whole series of pressing new problems and demands: falling rolls and the cost-effective use of plant, the educational management of unemployment and so-called 'education for leisure', parent politics, pupil disaffection, etc, [. . .]

Community education therefore appears to be a bewilderingly broad church, and the problem of definition becomes more acute in direct proportion to the currency of the term. No wonder the correspondent of the *Times Educational Supplement*, reporting a conference of the Community Education Association, remained puzzled by what she described as the ideological 'tussles 'twixt tweeds and leathers' that she witnessed in discussion groups (Caudrey 1985: 10).

The basic question to which this chapter is addressed is how to set about making sense of an educational movement which seems to tolerate, perhaps even to encourage, such a confusing variety of interests, interpretations and applications. It deliberately considers community education in general terms, at a macro level, in order to reflect the generic and amorphous nature of contemporary practice. [. . .] It is offered here primarily as a stimulus to discussion and debate so that we can begin to apply theory in a more systematic and critical way to practice in community education.

The essence of the argument is that it is possible to locate various distinctive patterns in the historical development of community education and that these differ significantly in ideological terms. It is suggested that the hidden agenda of implicit values in community may provide a useful starting point for analysis and evaluation. At the same time, it helps to clarify the continuing debate about definition. [. . .]

Community educators have been slow to theorize about their practice and to probe its coherence. In this sense, we may have become the unwitting victims of our own pragmatism. Much of the literature is descriptive and uncritical. It tends to be somewhat anecdotal and rather bland, or narrowly utilitarian. It is true that some useful and perceptive work is emerging on specific institutional/agency contexts of practice, e.g. Skrimshire (1981), Hargreaves (1982) and Sayer (1985) on secondary school-based community education, and Lovett *et al.* (1983), Brookfield (1983). Fletcher (1980) and Kirkwood (1978) on community adult education. These, however, are deliberately focused accounts which make no attempt to tackle the generic and inter-disciplinary nature of the contemporary community education movement as a whole.

FUNCTIONAL AMBIGUITY

The inherent ambiguity of the idea of 'community' is one of the reasons why a clearer analysis of community education is required. We would do well to cultivate some of Raymond Williams's scepticism about the cosy connotations of a word which has become a conveniently vague label in social policy:

Community can be the warmly persuasive word to describe an existing set of relationships, or the warmly persuasive word to describe an alternative set of relationships. What is most important, perhaps, is that unlike all other terms of social organization (state, nation, society, etc.) it seems never to be used unfavourably, and never to be given any positive opposing or distinguishing term.

(Williams 1976: 66)

We should start by recognizing some of the implications of functional ambiguity (bad sense). 'Community' is a notoriously slippery and contested concept – so much so that some commentators have advocated abandoning it once and for all (see Stacey 1969, Dennis 1968 and, more recently, Hargreaves 1985). Much has been written both asserting and challenging its continuing relevance. For community educators, however, the definition of 'community' is crucial because it implies a critical choice between an essentially hierarchical, socially regressive and static model of social relations and once that is progressive, emancipatory and dynamic. In this respect, as Raymond Plant (1974) argues, the ideological and evaluative dimensions of the community concept are much more important than its descriptive relevance. Unfortunately, however, community educators seldom have time – they also perhaps lack the inclination? – to 'explore a meaning' before they 'espouse a cause' (Plant 1974: 4). 'Community' has become a ubiquitous label partly because it affords those who pedal it the luxury of not being pinned down too precisely.

A brief consideration of how the prefix 'community' is used in official policy initiatives demonstrates not only its ambiguity but also its ambivalence. [. . .] In recent years it has been applied to a dubious assortment of localized, relatively cheap and expediently *ad hoc* responses to fundamentally structural problems (e.g. community programmes for the unemployed, community development for the urban poor, community service for the offender). [. . .] Too often the 'community' label is exploited as a smokescreen to fudge some of the key issues both about power, accountability and resource allocation at national, regional and local levels and about the critical distinction between 'personal troubles of milieu' and 'public issues of social structure' (Wright Mills 1970: 14).

So the basic point for community educators must be about recognizing the negative implications of a functional ambiguity that allows so much of the debris of social and economic policy to be swept under the carpet of 'community'. The warning of John Benington, at the time Director of the Hillfields Community Development Project in Coventry, remains pertinent:

Sociologists in search of the meaning of 'community' have so far come up with ninety-four different definitions. Their diffidence has not prevented politicians and professionals from using it as a kind of 'aerosol' word to be sprayed on to deteriorating institutions to deodorize and humanize them.

(Benington 1974: 260)

In view of this, it is not surprising that some erstwhile enthusiasts of community-based approaches to education have deliberately retreated from the conceptual bog of 'community' to the firmer and clearer ground of 'class' (e.g. see Jackson and Ashcroft 1972).

Nevertheless, it is central to the argument of this chapter that the idea of 'community' as applied to education can also be functional in a positive way. According to David Hargreaves, the essence of community education is the 'blurring of boundaries between educational establishments and their surrounding communities, as well as between teachers and students, and work and leisure' (Caudrey 1985: 10). In this sense, community education stands for a particular quality of relationships among the communities of collective interest and need, not only within the education system but also between educational agencies and their publics in the outside world. [. . .]

Functional ambiguity (good sense) allows community education to be understood as inclusive rather than exclusive. For several reasons, however, it will always be a difficult term to grasp conceptually. First, it challenges the relevance of many of the traditional demarcation lines, specialisms and categorizations of education to the interests and needs of people 'out there in the community'. Second, good practice is, almost by definition, the product of what Eric Midwinter calls 'local diagnosis'. Third, the generic character of community education is both a reflection of, and a response to, continuous change in the community, i.e. the reality of the world that exists outside the traditional closed shops of the education system. It is now widely recognized, for instance, that education should be understood as much more than simply the traditional 'front-end model' of schooling. The logic of 'learnimg through life', however, is not only the progressive deschooling of education but also that it must increasingly become the business of everyone: students, parents and the wider public of the 'learning society' as well as professional educators. But if community education is essentially about 'breaking down barriers' between learning and living (Wilson 1980), it must also be about promoting new and more democratic forms of educational access, accountability and control. In short, community education should be about power. This in turn implies more flexible definitions of 'what counts as knowledge' in curriculum and of educational roles and relationships. If all this is to happen, the functional ambiguity of community education must be exploited in a purposeful and constructive way to promote active collaboration between different communities of educational interest.

THEORY AND PRACTICE

[. . .] It is often said, and even more often forgotten, that 'there is nothing as practical as good theory'. But if we are to apply ideas with any rigour to the confusing variety of contemporary practice in community education, it is necessary to complement the descriptive and anecdotal with more critical and analytical accounts. In particular, it is important to clarify the different patterns of historical development in the evolution of community education and to assess the extent to which these reflect distinct philosophies about the relationship between education and community.

To what extent, for example, is the idea of 'community' still meaningful, and how can the definition of this peculiarly elusive concept both help and hinder our thinking about education and social change? Presumably, 'community' meant something very different in the rural Cambridgeshire of Henry Morris in the 1920s and 1930s than it did in the inner cities of the Educational Priority Areas and Community Development Projects of the late 1960s and early 1970s. It may be time to jettison once and for all the idea of the community (singular) as some kind of organic and consensual social entity and accept instead that it makes more sense to talk about communities (plural), whose identities may both reflect common patterns of interest as well as residence and also come into conflict with one another. Indeed, given the divisive and pervasive reality of mass unemployment, relative deprivation and racial disadvantage, it may well be more appropriate to speak of building local communities of endurance, resistance and struggle (see Jenkins 1985) than to try to reconstruct a broken consensus.

The remainder of this chapter considers two basic questions about the relationship between theory and practice in community education. First, to what extent is it possible to detect any underlying thematic coherence in the work of community educators which transcends the particularities of context? Second, how can the historical development of community education be disaggregated so as to formulate analytical models which clarify the range and diversity of interpretation in practice? It is also briefly indicated how this kind of theoretical analysis can be used to stimulate further thinking about new variations on the community education theme.

BACK TO BASICS

Intrinsically, community education is a relatively meaningless term. It now has widespread currency but lacks any generally acknowledged definition. This is partly because until quite recently the application of the term of developments in education tended to be retrospective rather than prescriptive.

Nevertheless, it is suggested that the combination of 'community' with 'education' at the very least implies a readiness to renegotiate – perhaps even to reverse – some of the traditional role relationships between the 'us' and 'them' of the educational process, e.g. teacher and student, professional and lay person, producer and consumer. In this sense, 'community' represents the changing world outside the institutional cocoon of the professional worker, and 'community education' is about evolving more open, participatory and democratic relationships between educators and their constituencies. The reciprocal quality of these relationships is crucial; community educators claim to work with people – not for them, let alone on them. Community education should be about partnership and solidarity rather than paternalism or manipulation. This fundamental elements of role redefinition and reversal has wide-ranging implications for the nature of educative relationships, the context of learning and the potential for the redistribution of educational opportunity (both vertically within the individual's lifetime and horizontally across the social structure).

The logic of such rethinking is often expressed in a basic commitment to the concept of 'lifelong learning'. Both the Community Education Association and the Scottish Council for Community Education, for instance, identify forms and varied contexts throughout life, as the starting point for their interpretations of community education. Its essential purpose is therefore to translate the rhetoric of 'lifelong learning' into educational reality. School is only the beginning of a continuous experience of 'learning to be', i.e. to become more fully human (Faure *et al.* 1972), or what Henry Morris called the 'art of living'. It should be emphasized that this is a radical and fundamentally iconoclastic perspective because it implies sustained educational engagement with the social reality of people's lives in the community. It therefore challenges not only dominant assumptions about the form and age-graded organization of the 'front-end' schooling but also the relevance of the narrow professional specialisms we have constructed to service our trained perceptions of other people's social and educational 'needs'. Time is on the side of community education in this respect. The technical demands of economic change and the social demands of increased leisure and demographic factors, for instance, will inevitably precipitate a radical convergence of traditional professional monopolies in educational and social service provision.

It is therefore significant that the Community Education Association, which claims to represent the community education movement nationally, confers primacy on 'lifelong learning' in its attempt to define common ground among practitioners. The other key themes [...] follow on from the recognition that 'Learning takes place in many and varied contexts throughout the individual's life.' This tenet provides a basic rationale for the Association's view of community education as both a practical and a philosophical commitment to:

- Developing strategies of social and educational redistribution which can help to create a more just and equitable society.
- Promoting closer coordination and collaboration between local agencies in both the statutory and voluntary sectors.
- Supporting local initiatives in community development which seek to give people more power and control over their own lives.
- Encouraging more open and democratic access to the human and material resources of the educational system.
- Redefining our notions of curriculum and learning process in such a way that education both 'generates individual autonomy and facilitates social cooperation'.

(Hargreaves 1985)

This kind of thematic approach is useful to the extent that it helps to identify a degree of commonality among community educators. The question is, of course, how such rhetoric is translated into reality. How are all these good intentions interpreted, prioritized and implemented in practical situations which are often complicated by competing needs and conflicting interests, different institutional expectations and constraints, and limited resources? [. . .]

A tentative theoretical analysis

[. . .] This chapter reflects several years' experience of working with very mixed groups of in-service students and the demand imposed by them to make sense of community education in ways which reflect their own particular interests and concerns. Once discussion moves beyond generalities, what is striking is the extent of disagreement – and this is more than simply a crude polarization of, for example, conservative teachers in 'tweeds' and radical community workers in 'leathers'. It is important therefore to stress that in our experience differences of interpretation are not just a function of particular contexts of practice: they are personal and philosophical as well as professional and institutional.

Recently three groups of students were asked to prepare brief statements beginning with the words, 'Community education is about . . .'. The results of this exercise were both interesting and problematic:

1 Community education is about the accessibility of education to everyone so that people can achieve a fuller and more rewarding life. People need to be involved in controlling more of their lives, making decisions through discussion and debate.
2 Community education is about modifying the existing education system to the benefit of those who are considered disadvantaged or deprived. Its aim is to give people who 'miss out' a better deal.
3 Community education is about acting in solidarity with those people in

society who have least power, enabling them to analyse their situation and to achieve political change. Power to the People!

How are we to explain the coexistence of such different perceptions of the nature and purpose of community education?

Dave Clark suggests that a review of current practice in community education reveals a continuum of five levels of interpretation ranging from the purely pragmatic to the overtly political (Clark 1985). These can be summarized as in Table 12.1.

Table 12.1 Review of current practice

Model	Purpose	Community educator's role	Query
1 Dual use	Cost-effective use of plant	Administrator/ manager	No more than common sense?
2 Community service	Meeting local needs	Multi-purpose provider	Educational rationale?
3 Networking	Sharing/exchange of local educational resources	Network agent	Control and direction?
4 Awareness raising	Analysis of key current issues	Enabler/catalyst	Nature of praxis?
5 Ideological approach	Political education and social action	Advocate/ change agent	Institutional tolerance?

Source: After Clark (1985).

Table 12.1 is a useful contribution to the continuing debate about definition because it demonstrates the difficulty of reaching any kind of meaningful consensus when the whole gamut of practice is considered. It also raises important questions about how far formal education institutions, especially schools, can accommodate the more radical versions of community education. Although Clark appears to confuse the issue by labelling the fifth model 'ideological', the sense of his argument is that all interpretations of community education (whatever their claims to neutrality or pragmatism) are value-based. Each is intrinsically ideological because each reflects a particular set of implicit values. The more unstated or taken for granted these are, the more systematically they need to be examined. It is now a truism that a policy of 'not taking sides' is in itself an ideological statement in favour of the *status quo* (see, for example, Sheppard 1983).

However, it is not clear from this account how and why community education has come to be defined in such different ways. This demands further investigation of the growth and anatomy of community education.
[. . .]

Study of the history and the literature of community education reveals distinctive elements in its development, originating in particular social and political circumstances. Furthermore, historical enquiry leads naturally to ideological analysis because it inevitably raises questions of context, purpose and value. It can therefore be used to explore some of the hidden agendas that inform the practice of community education. But this necessarily involves a conscious effort to get under the surface of the implicit ideologies beneath. This may be neither obvious nor easy. Although few would now seriously argue that education can be regarded as a neutral process, we are often expected to act as if it were. [...] It is no coincidence that some of the most cogent critiques of community education focus on its apparent coyness – or is it naivety? – about the values it stands for (see, for example, Merson and Campbell 1975, Lawson 1977).

At present, therefore, there is still a dearth of value-based or ideological analysis of community education as a generic and inter-disciplinary field. Keith Watson's distinction between what he identifies as 'evolutionary' and 'revolutionary' models in the development of community schooling provides a useful starting point (Watson 1980). [...] However, it is too narrowly school-based to apply to the wider spectrum of community education as a whole. [...]

The typology presented below is the product of mutual confusion I have shared and enjoyed with several groups of in-service student collaborators. It was originally developed as a conceptual framework to guide reading, promote inter-disciplinary study and suggest in a tentative way some of the reasons for contested interpretations. It is essentially an attempt to fill what Titmuss (1974) calls the 'conceptual value vacuum'. By organizing historically derived material in ideological terms.

A survey of twentieth-century developments appears to reveal three major strands in the evolution of community education in Britain. First, the secondary school-based village/community college movement pioneered by Henry Morris in Cambridgeshire (e.g. see Rée 1973, 1985); second, the trend towards community primary schooling in some urban areas following the Plowden Report (1967) and experimentation in the Educational Priority Areas (e.g. see Midwinter 1972, 1975; Halsey 1972); third, innovative work in adult education and community development undertaken in some of the Home Office sponsored Community Development Projects in the late 1960s and early 1970s (see, for example, Lovett 1975, Lovett et al. 1983). It is suggested that each of these were formative interventions in the historical development of community education and that all of them are still reflected in current practice. For the purpose of analysis they are significant because they imply quite different value assumptions and therefore premises about the relationship between education and community. [...] It is these implicit 'ideological concepts' that are used to construct a value-based analysis.

It should be emphasized that the typology is intended to represent a spectrum of qualitatively different ideologies of community education, not some kind of crude historical or chronological continuum starting from the 'primeval soup of Cambridgeshire' (O'Hagan 1985). In fact, contrary to the received wisdom of the mainstream community education movement, it can be argued that in a strictly historical sense the consensual 'village college' tradition is the relative newcomer. Both the other models can be shown to have deeper, if now somewhat obscure, roots. For example, the 'reformist' and 'radical' models connect respectively with the original university settlements and early youth clubs, and with the working-class self-education movement which is strongly associated with the emergence of indigenous, pre-Marxist socialism (see Simon 1974, Johnson 1979). In this respect, the typology as it is presented here can be misconstrued because reference is restricted to twentieth-century developments in what has only quite recently come to be known as 'community education'. [...]

It must, of course, be emphasized that these models (Table 12.2) are abstractions. Their aim is explanatory and heuristic. Such 'ideal-types' are exploratory rather than definitive, analytical rather than descriptive. Their value is therefore instrumental to the extent that they help to confer critical distance and disentangle the complex and often contradictory nature of reality. [...]

In this account key historical currents in the development of community education are identified and defined ideologically, essentially in terms of the assumed concepts of community they imply. It is this hidden subtext of social and, ultimately, political values which makes each model distinctive and coherent in social and educational terms. The point about the ideas and concepts behind these key interventions is precisely that they were largely unconscious, or certainly not articulate in any explicit way, at the time. Looking back, however, we are able to use the advantage of hindsight to contextualize, differentiate and compare the 'brute facts' of history. But this requires a conscious effort to 'expand the mental grid which decides what will fall into our field of perception' (Smith 1983: 44).

Although there has been considerable dilution and cross-fertilization in practice, each model is distinguished by particular and characteristic contexts of community education at the local level in different ways, and combine both to enrich and confuse the national scene. All three models have left their mark on the contemporary movement and claim their adherents among practitioners. The 'universalists' are particularly concerned to sustain and reinterpret Henry Morris's vision of education as a 'cradle to grave' process that is relevant to all aspects of communal life and can be promoted through open-access and integrated local provision. On the other hand, the 'reformist' position, originally associated with the now somewhat discredited rationale of 'compensatory education',

Table 12.2 Models of community education

Implicit model of society/community	Universal model	Reformist model	Radical model
Implicit model of society/community	Consensus	Pluralism	Conflict
Premise	Homogeneity and basic harmony of interests	Heterogeneity and inter-group competition	Class structure, inequality and powerlessness
Strategy	Universal non-selective provisor for all age/social groups	Selective intervention to assist disadvantaged people and deprived areas	Issue-based education, equal opportunities and social action
Initial focus	Secondary school/community college	Primary school/home/neighbourhood	Local working-class action groups
Key influences	Henry Morris	Eric Midwinter, A. H. Halsey	Tom Lovett, Paulo Freire and deschoolers
Twentieth-century origins	Cambridgeshire and Leicestershire village/community colleges	Plowden Report (1967) and Educational Priority Areas	Community Development Projects, innovative adult education and community work
Dominant themes	Lifelong learning Integrated provision Openness and access Decompartmentalization Rationalization Co-ordination Voluntarism Neutrality Co-operation	Positive discrimination Decentralization Participation Social relevance Home-school links Preschooling/play Informal adult education Self-help Partnership	Redistribution/equal opportunities Community action power Redefinition of priorities Local control Political education Learning networks Structural analysis Solidarity and collaboration
Organization	Top-down (professional leadership) Formal Programme Institution Reactive		Bottom-up (local leadership) Informal Process Locality Proactive

continues to reflect the concern of many community educators to discrimi-
nate positively on behalf of those who are regarded as socially and
educationally 'disadvantaged' in society. However, the negative notion of
'cultural deprivation' built into early versions of compensatory intervention is rejected in favour of a positive definition of the educational
potential of home, neighbourhood and local culture. The emphasis is
therefore on active educational partnership at the local level, the important
of which is now widely recognized at all levels of this compulsory education system. Finally, the 'radicals' continue to use the relative autonomy
enjoyed in some forms of non-traditional adult education and community
work to develop with local people political education and social action
focused on concrete issues and concerns in the community. Although the
idea of education as a means of redistributing power remains an important
theme in the thinking of many community educators, in practice this
kind of work is vulnerable to its own subversive logic and marginality.
Nevertheless, it represents a significant reaffirmation of a venerable and
largely autonomous tradition.

In reality, of course, most community education takes place in the
blurred areas between the theoretical models. In this sense, they are neither
mutually exclusive nor exhaustive. Given their ideological differences,
however, cross-fertilization will produce a degree of tension or incompati-
bility of the kind that is often evident in practice. The applied value of
ideological analysis is that it can help to explain this and to clarify the
dilemmas of choice which frequently confront practitioners. [...]

There are, of course, limitations and pitfalls in any such attempt to
make sense of the development of practice in a theoretical way. Ideological
analysis, for instance, can be misinterpreted as propaganda. It must therefore be stressed that the purpose of the typology is not prescriptive –
even though it does demonstrate that practice is always political in terms
of choices and priorities. Nor does it pretend to offer blueprints for action.
In reality, institutional expectations and constraints may well predetermine
the community educator's scope. On the other hand, multi-purpose posts,
such as that of school-based 'community tutor', often involve conflicting
demands and these need to be clarified theoretically before they can be
confronted practically. Finally, the historical derivation of the typology
may restrict its relevance to the full range and diversity of current developments in community education. Part of the educative purpose of such
models, however, is to probe their inadequacies and construct alternatives.
If this analysis provides an initial focus for applying theory to practice, it
is also meant to be a starting point for further thinking. As indicated
below, a group of feminist students has recently used it in precisely this
way.

GENERATING FURTHER THINKING

The dynamic and always problematic relationship between education and the changing reality of life in the community should be at the heart of community education. [. . .] New versions of community education deliberately seek to reflect the changing and often grim reality of people's lived experience and to engage purposefully with it. Education must now, for example, be about the social, economic and political implications of new patterns not only of education, work and leisure [. . .] but also of demography, race relations, family life and gender roles (in both the domestic and public spheres). If community education is to remain relevant to the experience and expectations of people in the community, it is essential that it is continually redefined and reconstructed to reflect the changing reality of their lives. It may therefore be useful to give one example which illustrates how new theoretical perspectives are being generated in an attempt to articulate and examine current trends in practice.

In recent years some feminists have taken an interest in community education because, they argue, women constitute a particular community of interest in terms of their social experience. It is therefore important that feminist community educators should develop their own theories of practice (see, for example, Thompson 1983). The feminist perspective has recently been used by a group of students to extend and at the same time challenge the original typology. The model of community education they have derived from a feminist premise is quite distinctive (Dodd *et al.* 1985) (see Table 12.3).

The purpose of this extension of the original typology is to articulate a distinctively feminist understanding of community education reflecting the interests and experience of particular students, and in the process to stimulate discussion and debate about a significant trend in contemporary practice (e.g. separatist experimentation in schooling and youth work, women's studies and health groups, positive discrimination/action in adult education, women's aid, self-help initiatives). The main point here, however, is that although the ideological premises of the master [*sic*] typology have been rejected, the analytical framework is retained and used to generate a new, theoretical perspective on a specific current development in community education. This helps to ensure a degree of equivalence and thus to facilitate comparison. Presented in this way, the feminist argument may at least be given more serious and systematic consideration than it often receives in general discussion. We all have something to learn from the unique insights and methods that feminists are bringing to the theory and practice of community education.

A group of black students is now working on a similar project. Again, what matters is that they see community education as an opportunity to express a particular view of education and to control the learning process

Table 12.3 Radical feminist model of activity

Implicit model of society/ community	Radical feminist
Premise	Gender-related inequality
	Oppression of women
Strategy	Positive discrimination/action
	Gender role analysis
	Separate provision
	Reconstruction of female knowledge and reality
Initial focus	Girls'/women's groups
	Women's studies
	Feminist education
Key influences	'Discounted' women in history
	Mary Wollstonecraft
	Virginia Woolf
	Jane Thompson
Twentieth-cent. origins	Suffragette movement
	World Wars I and II
	Modern birth control
	'Sexual revolution'
Dominant themes	Separatism/collectivism
	Control/autonomy
	Nature of oppression
	Family, education and work
	Personal politics
	Nature of learning process
	Excavation and analysis of women in history
	Redefinition; female continuity, identity and knowledge

in a way that reflects the distinctive history, experience and aspirations of the black community.

Community education must be responsive to this process of continual extension and reconstruction if it is to remain relevant to change in society and changing definitions of 'community'. Perhaps the acid test of this relevance is the extent to which we regard the development of alternative interpretations as legitimate contributions to the continuing debate about definition.

CONCLUSION

[. . .] Too often discussion about the meaning of community education takes place in a theoretical vacuum. The argument presented in this chapter is that it can be more firmly located historically and ideologically [. . .]. It provides a frame of reference for reflexive thinking, dialogue and constructive disagreement.

It is, however, no more than a tentative and provisional statement of some of the apparent connections and contradictions in community education. Its primary purpose is to stimulate discussion and further thinking and to encourage the elaboration of alternative analyses which reflect the continually changing contexts of practice. The ultimate test of the value of such abstract models may be that they enable us to theorize about practice with enough confidence to abandon them and construct alternatives.

REFERENCES

Benington, J. (1974) 'Strategies for change at the local level: some reflections', in D. Jones and M. Mayo, *Community Work One*, London: Routledge & Kegan Paul.

Brookfield, S. (1983) 'Community adult education: a conceptual analysis', in *Adult Education Quarterly* 33 (3), Adult Education Association of the USA, Washington.

Caudrey, A. (1985) 'Community tussles 'twixt tweeds and leathers', in *Times Educational Supplement*, 5 April.

Clark, D. (1985) 'Definitions defined', in Community Education Development Centre, *Network*, 5, 1 January.

Dennis, N. (1968) 'The popularity of the neighbourhood community idea', in R. E. Pahl (ed.), *Readings in Urban Sociology*, Oxford: Pergamon.

Dodd, G., Harrison, B. and Martin, I. (1985) 'Community education: a feminist perspective', in *Journal of Community Education*, 4, 3 December.

Faure, E. *et al.* (1972) *Learning To Be: The World of Education Today and Tomorrow*, UNESCO.

Fletcher, C. (1980) 'The theory of community education and its relation to adult education', in J. Thompson (ed.), *Adult Education for a Change*, London: Hutchinson.

Halsey, A. H. (ed.) (1972) *Educational Priority*, London: HMSO.

Hargreaves, D. (1982) *The Challenge for the Comprehensive School*, London: Routledge & Kegan Paul.

—— (1985) in S. Ranson and J. Tomlinson (eds), *The Government of Education*, London: George Allen & Unwin.

Jackson, K. and Ashcroft, R. (1972) 'Adult education, deprivation and community development: a critique', Paper no. 7, Conference on Social Deprivation and Change in Education, University of York.

Jenkins, D. (1985) 'A theology for the liberation of tomorrow's Britain', (Report of 1985 Hibbert Lecture, BBC Radio 4) in *Guardian*, 15 April.

Johnson, R. (1979) 'Really useful knowledge': radical education and working-class culture, 1790–1848', in J. Clarke, C. Critcher and R. Johnson (eds), *Working-Class Culture: Studies in History and Theory*, London: Hutchinson.

Kirkwood, C. (1978) 'Adult education and the concept of community', in *Adult Education*, 51.

Lawson, K. (1977) 'Community education: a critical assessment', in *Adult Education*, 50, 1.

Lovett, T. (1975) *Adult Education, Community Development and the Working Class*, Ward Lock.

——, Clarke, C. and Kilmurray, A. (1983) *Adult Education and Community Action*, London: Croom Helm.

Merson, M. and Campbell, R. (1975) 'Community education: instruction for inequality', in M. Golby, *et al.* (eds), *Curriculum Design*, Croom Helm/Open University.

Midwinter, E. (1972) *Priority Education*, London: Penguin.

—— (1975) *Education and the Community*, George Allen & Unwin.

O'Hagan, B. (1985) 'The contradictions of universalism', in Community Education Development Centre, *Network* 5, 7 July.

Plant, R. (1974) *Community and Ideology: An Essay in Social Philosophy*, London: Routledge & Kegan Paul.

Rée, H. (1973) *Educator Extraordinary*, London: Longman.

—— (1985) *The Henry Morris Collection*, Cambridge: Cambridge University Press.

Sayer, J. (1985) *What Future for Secondary Schools?*, Basingstoke: Falmer Press.

Sheppard, D. (1983) *Bias to the Poor*, Sevenoaks: Hodder & Stoughton.

Simon, B. (1974) *The Two Nations: The Educational Structure, 1780–1870*, London: Lawrence & Wishart.

Skrimshire, A. (1981) 'Community schools and the education of the "social individual" ', in *Oxford Review of Education* 7.

Smith, A. (1983) *Passion for the Inner City*, London: Sheed & Ward.

Stacey, M. (1969), 'The myth of community studies', in *British Journal of Sociology*, 20 (2).

Tawney, R. (1921) *The Acquisitive Society*, G. Bell & Sons.

Thompson, J. (1983) *Learning Liberation: Women's Response to Men's Education*, Croom Helm.

Titmuss, R. (1974) *Social Policy: An Introduction*, George Allen & Unwin.

Watson, K. (1980) 'The growth of community education in the United Kingdom', in *International Review of Education* XXVI, UNESCO.

Williams, R. (1976) *Key-words*, London: Fontana.

Wilson, S. (1980) 'School and community', in C. Fletcher and N. Thompson (eds), *Issues in Community Education*, Basingstoke: Falmer Press.

Wright Mills, C. (1970) *The Sociological Imagination*, London: Penguin.

Chapter 13

Adult education and community action

Tom Lovett

Source: Jane Thompson (ed.), *Adult Education For a Change*, London, Hutchinson, 1980, pp. 155–73.

The role of adult education in community action has aroused a great deal of debate and discussion amongst socially committed adult educators.[1] On the one hand are those adult educators who see in it an exciting posibility to extend the concept of adult learning, to make it more relevant to the interests, needs and problems of the working class and to open up educational resources to the latter so that they can make the maximum use of the opportunities it offers them.[2] On the other hand are those who feel that 'adult educationists should be wary when they are offered the resplendent new garments of community development, intended to transform their perception of themselves and their possibilities as they sally forth as community adult educators'.[3] The latter argue that the concept of 'community' should not be taken too seriously and that the role of adult education in the community development/community action process is more limited than the enthusiasts might have us believe.[4] Theirs is a more sceptical, cautious analysis; highly critical of the political naivety of the former and a more explicitly Marxist analysis, locating the origins of local community problems in the larger economic and social inequalities of a class society.

In the first model the role of adult education in community action is seen as one of providing the working class with an effective educational service so that they can take full advantage of the educational system *and* make the best use of their individual talents and abilities. Adult education is viewed as a general, comprehensive, community adult education 'service' meeting a variety of needs and interests amongst the working class, encouraging personal growth and development, and supporting greater community awareness and involvement. It provides for the general educational interests and needs of individuals (for example, informal group work, O-levels, languages, keep fit, etc.) in working-class communities and offers educational assistance to groups engaged in local community action. This was the approach of the adult education work in the Educational Priority Area Project in Liverpool.[5]

The second model has been closely associated with the work of Keith Jackson and his colleagues from the Liverpool Institute of Extension Studies in Vauxhall in the early 1970s. Throughout the literature on this work there is a consistent emphasis on the need to engage the residents in relevant education of a high standard which makes no concessions to informal community discussion methods or the 'learning through doing' approach. Working-class activists are to 'be given the chance to come to terms with a subject skill or field of knowledge so that they can understand its internal rules, become an expert as far as possible.[6] This is regarded as an essential educational contribution to social action.

The distinction between these two positions presents a number of problems for those involved in adult education with working-class men and women. On the one hand there is an emphasis in many adult education institutions and organizations on community education, or social and political education. [. . .] However, the practical implications are rarely understood or appreciated. [. . .] On the other hand the radical critique characteristic of the Vauxhall approach, and the educational emphasis arising from it – whilst important – is, I believe, unnecessarily limited in scope and in many respects does less than justice to the complexity of the situation on the ground and the opportunities available for linking adult education constructively to social/community action whilst avoiding the danger of both educational elitism and 'informal' education.

In my own view the relationship between adult education and community development is neither the grand opportunity seen by the optimists nor the more restricted role outlined in the sceptics' approach. I believe adult education *has* an important role to play in community action, that it is not necessarily a restricted one and that the concept of community should be taken seriously. However, before elaborating on this I want to look at two historically important initiatives outside our tradition of socially committed adult education. Both were attempts to link adult education more closely to movements for social and political change. Both were committed to, and intensely involved in, the process itself drawing no fine distinctions between action and education. One was the Antigonish Movement at the University of St Francis Xavier in Nova Scotia, Canada. The other was the Highlander Folk School in Tennessee, USA.

THE ANTIGONISH MOVEMENT

As with the Liverpool Institute experience, the Antigonish Movement was university based and initiated. It was also situated in a very economically depressed area. In this case a mainly rural, depopulated region on the eastern seaboard of Canada. It also emphasized the importance of the economic aspect of local community problems. However, the work took place in the 1920s and 1930s and it was initiated and directed by two Catholic priests, initially by Father Jimmy Tompkins and later by Father Moses Coady.

It was a programme of adult education, self-help and co-operative development which became world famous. It was far from being non-directive and, in fact, the leading figure in it, Coady, was a charismatic personality who passionately believed in the role of adult education as an agent for social change in society. To him adult education was an aggressive agent of change, a mass movement of reform.[7] [. . .]

Generally speaking there were two phases to the movement. One in the 1920s when Tompkins put a great deal of pioneering effort into persuading local people to tackle the social and economic problems in the community. And the second in the 1930s when, as a result of Tomkins's efforts, the University of St Francis Xavier opened an extension department with Coady as Director. During this period there was more emphasis on training and education but both men regarded the whole process as essentially educational and drew no fine distinctions between action and education. The methods used ranged widely – for example, mass meetings, study clubs, radio listening groups, short courses, kitchen meetings, conferences, leadership schools and training courses.

The mass meeting was the place where the educators preached their message. They took the initiative because, although Coady believed that education should be concerned with the everyday problems facing people in the region, he did not believe in just responding to 'felt needs'. He put more emphasis on the creation of awareness explaining that 'a fish doesn't know he lives in water until he is taken out of it.'[8] He did not believe that the educator should avoid unfamiliar words and language.

After the mass meeting people were organized into study clubs or discussion groups. This was regarded as the key educational technique in the Antigonish Movement: 'the foundation of the people's programme for adult learning'.[9] Everyday problems were discussed and success depended on intelligent local leaders and proper study materials. The study clubs quickly advanced to direct action. A variation of the study club was the radio listening group which enabled the movement to reach a larger number of people with relevant learning material. This basic work was complemented by the more intensive work at conferences, short courses and training schemes on the university campus. It was in fact a comprehensive and extensive programme of adult education and social action which owed a great deal, not only to the charismatic quality of Coady's leadership and Tompkins's pioneering fieldwork but also to the basic philosophy behind the movement. This was simple and straightforward, understood and accepted by the network of voluntary workers (many of them clerics!) which formed the backbone of the movement. The basic principles were:

(i) The needs of the individual must have primacy.
(ii) Social reform must come through education.
(iii) Education must begin with the economic situation.
(iv) Education must be through group action.
(v) Effective social reform involves fundamental changes in social and economic institutions.
(vi) The ultimate objective of the movement is a full and abundant life for everyone in the community.[10]

It was a populist movement with a vision of a new society. Although it was strongly anti-Communist it was nevertheless influenced by, and imbued with, certain co-operative and Christian socialist principles based on a critical analysis of the existing social order. It stressed the need not only for working people to build their own, alternative, co-operative society but for full participation in all the major institutions in society.

Although most of the literature on the movement is uncritical, and not particularly analytical, there are suggestions that this very public and active commitment to social change produced tensions between the movement and the local political and educational establishment. For instance in 1938, at the height of the movement, a university report stated that, 'It will be difficult for the University to continue to carry the burden of the Extension Department'[11] – apparently the latter was considered expendable!

When Coady died in 1959 the movement appears effectively to have died with him and it became institutionalized and enshrined in the establishment of a Coady International Institute. Little of the work remains and a recent analysis of the movement states:

> In Canso and Little Dover 50 years after Father Jimmy started his work there the people are still struggling with poverty and deprivation. Women working in the fish plant in the early 70s made $14 a night before taxes. In their efforts to organize the people here got help from Father Gerry Rodgers of the Extension Department of St Francis Xavier University, the living embodiment of the Antigonish Way. But he's a very lonely man.[12]

Antigonish believed that radical change would come about through education, public participation and the establishment of alternative institutions, that is co-ops and credit unions, not explicit political action. It was not a revolutionary movement and it has been argued that it damped down radical political agitation, directed the attention of the workers from striving for a new social and political order and, 'removed the need for the political system to perform efficiently and to meet the needs of the people instead of the elite. It may have prevented its collapse'.[13]

Nevertheless, although the Antigonish Movement lacked any explicit class analysis or radical political philosophy it did succeed in engaging large numbers of workers in relevant education linked to social action with methods and techniques which even today would be regarded as too radical for many educational institutions. It drew no barriers between social action and adult education and was engaged on a number of fronts linking one to the other. Despite its limitations it is a good example of how such work can be developed from a committed adult education base.

HIGHLANDER

The Highlander Folk School in the USA was established in the 1930s by Myles Horton. Like Antigonish, it was situated in one of the most socially and economically depressed regions in North America, a mixture of mining and agricultrual communities in Tennessee. Like Antigonish its founder and leading figure throughout its early history was strongly imbued with Christian/socialist principles and deeply influenced by the Danish Folk High School Movement.[14] The latter was regarded by both as a prime example of how an educational movement could be linked effectively to movements for social change and the development of a sense of national pride and identity. Highlander also had a simple philosophy which was, however, based on a more explicit class analysis.

Highlander's basic philosophy is summed up well in the following extract from a letter written by Horton in 1933 shortly after the school was established:

> Our task is to make class-conscious workers who envision their roles in society and to furnish motivation as well as technicians for the achievement of this goal ... We have found that a very effective way to help students to understand the present social order is to throw them into conflict situations where the real nature of our society is projected in all its ugliness. To be effective, such exposure must be preceded, accompanied by and followed by efforts to help the observer appreciate and digest what he has seen. This keeps education from getting unrealistic. While this process is going on, students need to be given an inkling of the new society. Perhaps this can be done best by having our communal living at the school come into this picture as an important education factor.[15]

However, although committed to a revolution to alter basic political and economic relationships, Highlander was not ideologically rigid.[16] Like Antigonish the emphasis was on working with people on real issues and problems and emphasizing the importance of co-operation and acting in unison.

Unlike Antigonish, however, Highlander was an independent educational establishment with a more explicitly socialist philosophy and its approach was radically different. It did not *initiate* programmes of social action, like Antigonish. Instead, it concentrated on identifying and working closely with emerging social movements thrown up by the times and people, providing them with practical advice and assistance on the ground as well as educational support in the form of workshops at Highlander. The latter generally fell into two distinct categories. As the particular movement gathered force the workshops were broad and loose in range, usually without a specific topic. As the movements gained momentum more concrete information was requested and greater use was made of experts.

In the 1930s Highlander played an active role in the bitter struggle to organize trade unions in Tennessee, not by providing classes and courses, but by being actively involved on the picket line and in the mass demonstrations and providing information and opportunities for discussions on strategies and tactics. Horton was arrested during one of the most bitter campaigns in a mining town called Wilder and charged with: 'coming here and getting information and going back and teaching it'.[17] It was the first of many such arrests. The strike had a powerful effect on the Highlander staff who were involved in it. They were themselves ideologically committed but realized that to accomplish their goals workers themselves would have to state their own beliefs and that Highlander had not only to serve the people but be of the people.

During the 1930s work with the unions meant this sort of active commitment and involvement, complemented by conferences and residential workshops at Highlander and study groups out in the local community. As the unions became more organized these increasingly developed into union training schools and Highlander became somewhat disillusioned by union conservation. [...]

However, Highlander had always seen its work as a long-term process adapting to new movements and circumstances and, during the 1950s and 1960s, it turned its attention, increasingly, to the problems of black workers. It played an important supportive role in the growth of the Citzenship Schools (designed to assist illiterate negroes to read and write so that they could pass the voting test) and in the civil rights movement. As a result of this, and its earlier work with the trade unions, Highlander was labelled a Communist training school by the racialist and reactionary forces in the south. Eventually in 1961 the State of Tennessee seized the school's property and revoked its charter. The idea and the institution were, however, quickly reorganized and rechartered under its present name, Highlander Research and Education Centre Inc.

Since 1964 Highlander had concentrated on the problems of poverty and inequality in Tennessee – still one of the most depressed regions in the USA. However, it has also attempted to unite the various depressed minorities throughout the United States. For example, in 1970 it held a workshop attended by militant blacks, Puerto Ricans, Indians from six nations, Mexican Americans and people from the Appalachians which, although it highlighted the antagonisms between the various groups, illustrated the fact that none of them were free to determine their own destiny and all were poor. This was one of numerous attempts by Horton and others to assist the growth of a bottom-up radical coalition in the USA.

Highlander's original purpose, educating for a revolution that would basically change economic and political power relationships to the advantage of the poor and powerless, has clearly not been achieved. That was obviously an impossible task for one Folk School! However, Highlander's educational methods and techniques are now used in various grassroots initiatives throughout the USA and there is evidence that a radical coalition is emerging.[18] Highlander has played a pioneering role in encouraging that process.

NORTHERN IRELAND

Much of the recent British debate about the theory and practice of adult education in the field of community development and community action finds an echo in the two North American examples discussed above. Many of the 'new' concepts and methods in community development and community education (and the related theories of radical educators like Freire), were understood and practised at Highlander and Antigonish over 40 years ago. As is so often the case in adult education it is not a matter of new theories and concepts but new arrangements responding to different circumstances and influenced by prevailing social/political and economic theories.

In some respects the situation facing Highlander and Antigonish was less complicated, more clear cut, than the situation facing radical committed adult educators today. The inequalities and the injustices were starker, more obvious, and the choices facing the educators concerned clearer than those facing their counterparts today. Maybe this accounts for their faith in the power of adult education; their simple message; their vision of the new society; their open, public sense of social commitment, dedication and active involvement in building that new society. They both paid a price for their radical commitment, however. Antigonish is now a lost dream. Highlander survived better probably because of its cranky independence, its non-institutional base, its ability to adapt to new movements and most important, its radical critique.

In terms of their *educational* contribution both took a broad view and did not seek to define too precisely what shape that contribution should take. They utilized a variety of methods and techniques ranging from the informal to the formal depending on the time, place and circumstances. Highlander placed more emphasis on educating leaders for emerging social movements whilst Antigonish sought to create and shape a 'movement' providing educational support at a variety of levels. Both, however, used real issues and problems as material for an educational process which – although it did not ignore the need for hard information and training – placed more emphasis on the development of the will, the imagination and creative human relationships than analytical skills. Highlander in particular stressed the important educational role of music and songs and other aspects of local culture in its work.

In their respective ideologies and strategies they reflect the two aspects of the contemporary debate about community development, community action and adult education mentioned earlier. On the one hand, Antigonish placed its faith in the creation of alternative social and economic institutions and structures at local, community level. On the other hand, Highlander placed its faith in providing educational support for emerging social movements which would fundamentally alter existing political and economic structures. [. . .] Generally speaking the former adopted a community development strategy with an emphasis on the creation of alternatives, whilst the latter adopted a community action strategy with an emphasis on conflict and radical political change. [. . .]

In Northern Ireland, at the Institute of Continuing Education, Highlander and Antigonish have been important influences, along with English initiatives, in deciding the educational strategies and methods the Community Action Research and Education project should adopt. Religion plays a large part in people's lives as it did in Nova Scotia and Tennessee. Many of the settlers in Tennessee were Ulster Irish and the music of that area has roots in Irish culture. Northern Ireland is a mixture of rural and urban communities and farming is still one of the most important industries in the province. There is still a traffic in evangelical ministers between Tennessee and Ulster. No wonder Northern Ireland has been described as Britian's Tennessee!

However, I do not want to push these comparisons too far. Northern Ireland is part of the economic and political structure of the United Kingdom – one of the most economically depressed regions in that economy with a long history of unemployment and poverty. It is a region which has not only gone through the pangs and torments of civil and military conflict but one which has witnessed great changes in its economic and social structure as a result of industrial decline, urbanization and redevelopment. [. . .][19]

A recent analysis suggests that it has a higher level of poverty than any other part of the United Kingdom.[20] It is a divided community. Its tragedy is that the conflict has often assumed the proportions of a civil war between Catholic and Protestant working class.

However, despite the conflict and the divisions between the working class, the social and economic changes referred to above have resulted in the growth of numerous community organizations throughout Northern

Ireland in both Catholic and Protestant areas.[21] They have found common ground in the midst of communal conflict. This is the constituency we have decided to work and identify with, viewing it as the only hope for a united working-class movement which, through this common struggle, might find a solution to its larger political problems and divisions. In doing so we have had no option but to take the concept of 'community' seriously since it was one which is used by the people themselves to describe their work and to articulate their hopes and ideals. Thus 'community' is not a concept imposed from above but one which springs from the grass roots and is held sincerely and passionately by very articulate community leaders.

Our base is an institutional one. In numerous public documents reference was made to the 'large-scale development of community oriented education'. This means putting 'educational resources at the disposal of the community'[22] to help in resolving the social and economic problems of the area. Such public statements of intent and purpose are always suspect until they are matched with practice. It's doubtful if the implications were understood or appreciated at the time. However, since it was a new institution with new staff, able to develop their own roles without any prior commitments to fulfil, it was possible to take these statements of intent seriously and to develop work in the community in the knowledge that it was official policy and a priority for the institution. Of course it soon became obvious that people had different views about what community should be served. Our emphasis on working-class communities and organizations has always been something of a minority interest and priority, but at least we have been able to pursue it, unencumbered initially by other responsibilities, free to develop and define our role. However, this proved to be a difficult situation and, until money was provided from outside sources, it was an uphill struggle.

Like Antigonish and Highlander we have over the years since then sought to support, and identify with, the two sections of the working class in their common struggles and to provide what resources and assistance we can, making a point of stressing the extent of university resources and our commitment to making them available.

This has not proved easy. On the one hand our practical interpretation of 'putting education resources at the disposal of the community' – which often meant simply using Institute premises for meetings and discussions about all sorts of social, economic and political problems facing working-class communities (they were one of the few neutral premises available) – was viewed with some suspicion by the Institute and meant that they had to be 'dressed up' as classes or seminars. On the other hand community activists were, and still are, suspicious of academics and their intentions. This is something which can only be resolved at a personal level, over time, by active involvement and it remains a 'personal' rather than an institutional solution to the problem.

Our work like Highlander has, generally speaking, fallen into two phases. During the first phase, when the community movement was gathering strength, we were involved in various local initiatives, such as setting up resource centres, organizing conferences on broad topics and issues and assisting in the creation of a province-wide federation. In the second phase we became more actively involved in running workshops and seminars on more specific topics and issues, providing opportunities to learn certain skills and obtain items of information.[23] At present we are engaged in producing radio discussion programmes,[24] organizing local study groups throughout Northern Ireland;[25] assisting in a programme of linked weekends for community activists; running a research workshop for local activists interested in the Derry economy; organizing a two-year extra-mural certificate in community studies in which we hope to link theory and practice, using materials arising out of the work here, as well as experiences and analysis from abroad.

In all this work we have taken a sympathetic but critical approach to the prevailing community ideology and the strategies arising from it. We have encouraged active discussion and debate about the latter and the role of socialists within it. This has taken the form of seminars and workshops at which a variety of activists presented their written views and opinions for discussion and debate. We have found, like Antigonish and Highlander, that the people we are involved with are suspicious of what they regard as the cold clinical 'academic' approach. They tend to emphasize the practical, the affective, the imaginative, the need to create new structures out of new relationships. [...]

In some respects our task is both easier and harder than it is elsewhere in the UK. We do not have a strong Socialist/Labour/Trade Union tradition, although that can on occasions be a hindrance rather than a help! The changes of the last decade in Northern Ireland have, comparatively speaking, radicalized some sections of the working class here – including some sections of the Protestant working class.[26] This provides opportunities to engage in a dialogue about what shape a new society should take and the role of socialism in it. Our task is more difficult not only because of the divisions within community groups about their role but the divisions between them about the future of the state.[27] Many on both sides associate socialism with planning, bureaucracy and lack of freedom. That is what they know of socialist dream. The struggle of the working class to achieve that dream is not, with some exceptions, seen as part of their heritage. We have thus placed some emphasis on finding ways of illustrating the common culture and problems of the Northern Irish working class, for example, through the radio discussion programmes, which are a sort of oral social history and material which helps to illustrate the similarities with working-class problems elsewhere in the UK and relates this to earlier working-class struggles – to develop in fact a sense of working-class history and culture. In all this work we have sought to combine the affective and the analytical, using aspects of the local culture as well as art, music and literature to help people articulate their dreams and aspirations, to investigate the major themes in their lives and to provide opportunities for serious analytical study and the acquisition of skills and information.

Freire sees this process in stages, that is, an initial stage of 'investigation' by the educator; a second stage in which learning material is produced which uses cultural artefacts familiar to the people, to explore major themes in their lives as reflected in the issues and problems they face. In the third stage, this material is discussed in cultural circles. [...] In the fourth stage Freire stresses the need to use specialists, like economists and sociologists, to assist in the more detailed analysis of the themes discovered in the third stage.[28]

We have found Freire's analysis and classification of this process helpful. However, his emphasis on *stages* does an injustice to the complexity of the evolving situation on the ground where different people, and different groups, are at various stages at the same time. We for example are involved on a number of fronts simultaneously, providing 'courses' for leading activists, whilst also involved in more informal work in workshops, seminars, study groups as well as practical action on the ground.

We are also aware that a simple 'economic' analysis and explanation of community problems does an injustice to the complexity of the 'themes' shaping and changing people's lives here. We have sought therefore, not only to insert an economic perspective into the community debate, but also to include the political, the social and the cultural. Thus one of our radio discussion series was on religious stereotypes and another on changes in family and community life.

We feel, like Ralph Miliband,[29] that the search for a modern interpretation of the socialist dream, especially in the situation we find ourselves in here, entails a long search – a continuing dialogue which of necessity encompasses a wide variety of groups and individuals who are experiencing tremendous changes in their everyday lives and relationships. [...]

We hope in this way to assist in the creation of a radical social movement which will, of necessity, bring together people belonging to different groups and parties as well as individuals who belong to none. Like Miliband we visualize that some form of loose federation or alliance will be necessary and that it will attempt to articulate the 'themes' and visions implied in various aspects of the community struggle as well as to offer a radical critique of the existing order. Thus we have not concentrated specifically on community organizations but, through workshops and conferences, brought together activists from community groups, women's organizations, trade unions and those concerned with creating alternative institutions at local level. We have also assisted in organizing conferences on political options in Northern Ireland and the problem of human rights. All of this work has brought together not only Catholics and Protestants, but also supporters of various para-military groups in a debate which offers some hope for the future.

However, we realize there are dangers in overemphasizing the need to establish links with organizations like the trade union movement. It can result in a form of educational elitism which, while providing classes in political economy and work on research, only reaches a tiny proportion of the working-class population. The need is to marry this form of social action with community action on the ground. Attempts by those involved in the latter to establish community control or work towards community 'development' should not be dismissed as they often are by those on the left. They have historical parallels in the history of the working class, that is the building up of local working-class organizations and informal social structures whilst engaged in wider social and political action.

They are two sides of the same coin and it is just not true to argue that all problems and issues facing the working class can *only* be resolved by mass movements for social and political change. The search for 'quality' in human relationships and convivial local institutions, a feature of the work of many local people involved in community development, tends to be ignored by political activists or dismissed as irrelevant. The mass movements' struggle is, however, long-term, and new relationships and new structures at local level can be created which at least will illustrate what the new society might look like. It was done in the past in the most adverse conditions. It can be done today.

We have no illusions about that process but we believe radical educators must play a role in it whilst providing support for a social movement. It is doubtful if such a role will, or could be, undertaken by the formal adult educational system. [. . .] What is required is a new educational 'movement' based on existing independent initiatives – like the local resource centres. [. . .]

Our hope lies in the possibility of establishing a residential centre which would link in to the network of local resource centres to provide research and educational facilities, concentrating on weekend, and week-long workshops, with staff employed in the centre and in the field. It would be clear about its purpose and methods as the creation of the radical working-class movement, in which adult education would assist in encouraging a dialogue and analysis, not only about community action, but about wider social and political problems. Such a dialogue would seek to go beyond narrow Republican and Unionist stereotypes to a realization of the heritage and culture shared by both communities, an appreciation of the strengths in their different traditions, and the opportunities available to create a new future based on their common efforts and aspirations. That is the challenge for adult educators here in Northern Ireland. A smiliar challenge and opportunity faces all committed adult educators involved in community action.

REFERENCES

1 Harrison, J., 'Community work and adult education', *Studies in Adult Education*, 6 (1), April 1974; Lawson, K. H., 'Community education – a critical assessment', in *Adult Education*, 50 (1), May 1977.
2 Lovett, T., *Adult Education, Community Development and the Working Class*, Ward Lock, 1975.
3 Jackson, K., 'The marginality of community development – implications for adult education', *International Review of Community Development*, Summer 1973.
4 Ibid.
5 Lovett, *Adult Education, Community Development and the Working-Class.*
6 Jackson, 'The marginality of community development', p. 27.
7 Coady, M., *Masters of Our Destiny*, New York: Harper & Bros., 1939.
8 Laidlaw, A. F., *The Man from Margaree – Writings and Speeches of M. M. Coady*, Toronto: McClelland & Stewart Ltd, 1971, p. 57.
9 Laidlaw, A. F., *The Campus and the Community – The Global Impact of the Antigonish Movement*, Montreal: Harvard House Ltd, 1961, p. 116.
10 Ibid., p. 97.
11 Ibid., p. 90.
12 Lotz, J., 'The Antigonish Movement', in *Understanding Canada: Regional and Community Development in a New Nation*, Toronto: N.C. Press Ltd, 1977, Ch. 10, p. 113.
13 Ibid., p. 112.
14 Adams, F., 'Highlander folk school: getting information, going back and teaching it', *Harvard Educational Review*, 42 (4), November 1972.
15 Ibid., p. 516.
16 Adams, F. and Horton, M., *Unearthing Seeds of Fire – The Idea of Highlander*, N. Carolina: J. F. Blair, 1975, p. 206.
17 Ibid., p. 33.
18 Perlman, J., 'Grassrooting the system', *Social Policy*, New York: Alan Gartner, September/October, 1976.
19 For an analysis of these changes and how they have affected a Protestant working-class community in Belfast, see R. Weiner, *The Rape and Plunder of the Shankill, Community Action: The Belfast Experience*, Belfast, Notaems Press, 1975.
20 Evason, E., 'Poverty: the facts in N. Ireland', *Poverty Pamphlet*, no. 27, Child Poverty Action Group, 1976.
21 Lovett, T. and Percival, R., 'Politics, conflict and community action in N. Ireland', in P. Curno (ed.), *Political Issues and Community Work*, London, Routledge & Kegan Paul, 1978.
22 1973 Brochure – New University of Ulster, Institute of Continuing Education, Londonderry.
23 Lovett, T., 'Adult education and community action – the N. Ireland experience', in C. Fletcher (ed.), *Community Education '77*, University of Nottingham, Department of Adult Education, 1977.

24 Lovett, T., 'Community education and local radio', in M. Pungate, P. Henderson and L. Smith (eds), *Collective Action – A Selection of Commmunity Work Case Studies*, Community Projects Foundation and Association of Community Workers, 1979.
25 Mackay, L. and Lovett, T., 'Community based study groups – N. Ireland case study', *Adult Education* 51 (1), May 1978.
26 Weiner, *The Rape and Plunder of the Shankill.*
27 Lovett and Percival, 'Politics, conflict and community action in N. Ireland'.
28 Freire, Paulo, *Pedagogy of the Oppressed*, Harmondsworth, Penguin, 1972.
29 Miliband, R., 'The future of Socialism in England', *The Socialist Register*, 1977.

Chapter 14

Dangerous knowledge

Canadian workers' education in the decades of discord

Michael R. Welton

Source: This chapter is an edited version of an article which appeared in *Studies in the Education of Adults*, vol. 25, no. 1, 1991.

Labour history is a thriving academic enterprise in Canada; the study of workers' education is not. None the less, adult educational historians are turning some attention to recovering the educational dimensions of workers' culture and politics,[1] and several prominent labour historians[2] have, in focusing on workers' attempts to create an oppositional culture, opened up important questions. How do workers in particular times and places come to understand themselves, their work, their social institution, competing ideologies? How do they acquire a set of competencies? How do they not only adapt to, but act transformingly in, societies presenting formidable barriers to autonomous workers' education? When we examine processes of industrial conflict and change through the learning lens, we can see that the battles are always intellectual and practical. Particular forms of social and political action proceed from an idea that alternatives to capitalism are necessary and possible. Before persons can change their behaviour and their society, they must first be enlightened as to that possibility. Collective enlightenment (the transformation of collective self-understanding and identity) is the learning catalyst, empowering actors to engage in, within limits, transformative action in the world. The struggles of workers in the turbulent decades under scrutiny can be viewed as a contest between supporters of conflicting visions of what constitutes valid enlightenment, empowerment, and transformative action. Thus, given the importance of ideas in generating action, and the importance of education in the creation and promotion of these ideas, education must always be considered in attempts to understand the larger processes of social conflict and change.[3] To understand and perhaps explain the wonderful complexities of workers' education, we need to situate workers' education in multiple contexts and discursive fields, examine the sites workers create for reflection (the organization of enlightenment), the critical themes they examine, and the outcomes of learning processes (the organization of action).

We are all aware of the notorious difficulties in delineating the bound-aries of workers' education. For my purposes, the boundaries of workers' education ought to be drawn such that we can study both the 'schools of labour' and 'labour's schools'. Simply defined, the schools of labour are the socially organized workplaces, embedded in networks of economic, social, and political control. Important technical, social, political and ideo-logical experiential learning is occurring in the workplace [...] and perhaps the strike is the most important learning occasion directly linked to the work site. Labour's schools are those spaces workers themselves, their leaders, or sympathetic pedagogues open up for reflection on the meaning of their work and culture. Labour's schools take many forms: (a) 'educational moments' woven into particular social practices such as the assembly meeting (the Knights of Labour saw these as 'schools of instruction') or political party activity; (b) specific educational forms created by the workers themselves (journals, newspapers, forums, and so on); and (c) educational forms provided for workers by agencies and institutions outside the workers' own organization (WEA, university extension programmes).

In this chapter I am particularly interested in what I take to be a rather fascinating puzzle. In our ordinary language use in the field of adult education, we do, indeed, distinguish adult from workers' education (and wonder about some of the issues at the interface), and often talk about the emergence of 'adult education' in, say, the 1920s.[4] There are several ways of understanding this. While we all admit that adult learning is present at all times and places, we must reject the idea that 'adult edu-cation' has an essence that only need be represented in appropriate, value-neutral scientific language. [...] Adult education is made visible, given a body, only when it is constituted by a 'discursive field' (ideas, texts, theories, use of language). But this constituting process is not a unitary, totalizing act. Competing discourses jostle and struggle with one another over the control of the constituting process. In unsettling times of histori-cal transition (Canada from the late nineteenth to early twentieth century was shifting to a monopoly form of capitalist production and relations) oppositional forms of adult learning erupt in a multiplicity of sites precipit-ating the struggle to constitute 'adult education'. [...]

Discursive practices are, of course, related in complex ways to nondis-cursive practices (social systems, class and gender divisions, economic needs, institutions). Particular discursive practices are intimately bound up with social power and control. Knowledge/power cannot be thought apart.[5] This insight demands that we pay attention to the way adult education discourse sets the limits on what counts as authentic educational practice, and perhaps more important, social and political action. Adult educational discourses might be read as a very important way that our society organizes its power relations.

My strategy in this chapter (which examines working class culture, 1896–1922) is, first, to characterize the political economy and the labour movement's sense of collective identity, and then to examine the educational thought and initiatives occurring within the workers' movement and those agencies outside the movement itself. [...] My conclusion is that some adult educators have, as one of their jobs, the quelling of the insurrections of subjugated knowledges. Others, it seems, have the task of participating in the insurrection itself.

WORKING-CLASS CULTURE 1896–1922

From the late nineteenth century until the end of the First World War, Canada was a nation being transformed. As the monopoly form of capitalism emerged – a ragged process of uneven economic development and labour market segmentation – new mines, mills, factories, and railway camps dotted the country. Three million new Canadians came into the country to work in the new industries and produce the 'prairie gold' as the Canadian west opened up for agricultural development and settlement. To Canadianize the immigrant became, for some educators, the 'one great commanding problem' of the time.[6] People flooded into the cities altering the balance between city and rural dweller. Canadians were now confronted with another 'learning challenge' – how to cope with urban life and how to preserve the rural way of life. Industrialization immigration, urbanization – these were the critical societal learning challenges for Canadians.

Historians have characterized the relationship between capital and labour in this period as especially conflictual and turbulent.[7] Workplace restructuring and transformation confronted Canadian workers with a diverse set of problems. In south-central Ontario, for instance, skilled workers resisted the introduction of Taylorist technological changes.[8] More characteristic, however, were the strikes initiated by 'less skilled' workers in the coalfields of Cape Breton, Nova Scotia, and BC, the west coast fishing industry, and the Quebec textile industry. Strikes in these industries were often violently repressed. Perhaps one of the most evocative metaphors for this period can be drawn from Cape Breton. Protesting their wretched conditions in community and work site, over 3,000 striking UMWA miners planned a giant parade in Glace Bay, July 1909. After listening to some speeches at the parade grounds, they marched, led by their leaders. Things went smoothly until they reached Cadegan's Bank, which separates the towns of Glace Bay and Dominion. As they crossed the bridge, the leaders were shocked to find a machine gun mounted on the steps of the Roman Catholic Church of Immaculate Conception, the army poised nearby, ready to fire.[9]

Canadian workers did, indeed, reflect on the critical themes that swashbuckling corporate capitalism was placing on the 'curriculum.' A multi-plicity of labour's schools ('pure and simple' international craft unionism, labourism, Christian socialism, syndicalism, revolutionary Marxism) competed for an audience fragmented by region, nature of the industry, ethnicity and gender. But for a brief historic moment in Canadian working-class history, the Winnipeg General Strike of 1919, an eclectic radicalism infused with new social principles – the exuberence of wartime radicalism, international working-class advance – created a climate in which proletarian victory seemed possible. Education, we have said, must always be considered in attempts to understand the larger process of social conflict and change. We now provide a synoptic look at workers' education in Winnipeg from 1912 to 1921, with a side glance to Cape Breton, before turning to an analysis of conflicting discursive fields within 'adult education' during this period.

What sites did the resilient Winnipeg workers create for the 'organization of enlightenment?' What critical themes did they examine? What were the learning outcomes? The most eclectic of the workers' educational projects in Winnipeg was the People's Forum. Originating with social gospel/social work activities in the city's legendary north end in 1910, the originators of the Forum included people who, during the war years, would become convinced of the need to create a fundamentally different society – a co-operative commonwealth. [. . .]

Operating independently of the Winnipeg school system until 1914, the People's Forum held regular Sunday meetings in local theatres until it floundered in 1917, largely because of the commitment of many of its leaders to radical political activities. Throughout the turbulent years from 1912 to 1917, *The Voice*, a workers' paper which criticized capitalist abuses from an essentially Christian ethical position, carried weekly reports of events at the People's Forum in Winnipeg, and in a host of others in surrounding communities. The workers' press announced lectures and meetings and often carried verbatim lecture texts. The People's Forum, evidence suggests, encouraged participatory engagement, discussion always following lectures. The workers' press did not provide equal coverage of the lectures of other educational forums – the YMCA and the University of Manitoba.

Judging from the reports in *The Voice*, the Forum debated a wide range of critical themes. Speakers called for increased political involvement because 'our system of government . . . places great power in the hands of a few men', and numerous speakers addressed the issue of militarism, the need for social reconstruction and the need to teach children in their own language. The latter theme signals the presence of an active ethnic presence in Winnipeg's north end. The anti-militarist theme offended some school board members, and forced the Forum committee into some compromises. [. . .]

By the autumn of 1917, the leadership of the Forum had dispersed, but workers' educational activities continued unabated. Rejecting the People's Forum's affiliation with the public school system and 'bourgeois reformism', the Winnipeg Trades and Labour Council (WTLC) announced in September 1917 a series of Sunday afternoon lectures, featuring socialist and progressive speakers. This lecture series lasted only one season. But in 1918 the nondenominational Labour Church had begun, and included a programme of Sunday afternoon lectures, featuring the 'radical wing' of the People's Forum (J. S. Woodsworth, Fred Dixon, Salem Bland and William Ivens, the Labour Church's instigator). The People's Forum and the Labour Church, bridged by the WTLC lecture series, form a continuum of educational activity. Together, Maciejko claims, they formed a 'consistent and concerted programme of workers' education initiated by the radicals and sustained by popular support'.[10] By the end of 1918, it seems safe to conclude, Winnipeg workers had been enlightened to the point where they believed that alternatives to capitalism were necessary and possible.

As working-class militancy quickened in 1918 and 1919, provoking great fear among the middle and upper classes, the educational campaign among workers intensified. Organized in March 1919 after the epochal Western Labour Conference, the One Big Union (OBU) sought to unify all workers in a single union which could achieve its purposes, economic or political, through general strikes. It would embody proletarian solidarity. The revolutionary syndicalism, though alienating highly skilled craft unions, caught the imagination of many Canadian workers for a flickering historical moment.[11] The linkage between the OBU and the Labour Church was strengthened when more conservative unionists took over the WTLC and the *Western Labour News*. [...]

Perhaps the most significant development in Winnipeg in September 1919 was the Labour Church and OBU's call for the formation of a Labour College for Winnipeg after the bitter defeat of the General Strike of May and June. A parallel initiative, several years later, occurred in Nova Scotia – particularly among the radical coal miners, who were very interested in workers' education. The workers wanted a permanent provincial Labour College that would draw on the expertise of teachers and college professors.[12] Nova Scotia workers would not get what they wanted, and would have to wait until St Francis Xavier University provided educational services for workers in the late 1920s and 1930s. But St Francis had its own agenda, and one major item was to quell the insurrection of community knowledge and political action in industrial Cape Breton.[13]

The OBU, itself, was also active in organizing classes and lectures. Of all the classes conducted by the OBU, those in economics were the most popular. From the beginning, the educational classes of the OBU were considered to be preliminary to the establishment of a Labour College in

Winnipeg. With this dream in mind, Winnipeg workers wrote to the firebrand Scottish radical John McLean of the Glasgow Labour College, and also to the Rand School of Social Science. The international labour movement – at least its more militant wing – clearly thought they needed a permanent school to nurture their brand of oppositional consciousness. But a Canadian Labour College would not materialize until the 1960s, and then only under the watchful eye of reformist trade union bureaucrats running the Canadian Labour Congress.

Workers' education, however, was not confined to the Forum, the Labour Church and the OBU. Radical political parties – an integral if fractious part of the configuration of labour's schools – were also involved in the movement in Winnipeg. The Socialist party of Canada (SPC), tracing its origins to Winnipeg in 1890 but having its deepest roots amongst the hardrock miners of BC's mountains, rigorously and dogmatically schooled its resolute vanguard in Marxist axioms. Animated by a chiliastic vision of capitalism's inevitable end, the SPC saw the education of the proletariat as its ultimate political function. Reform for SPCers was 'powder sprinkled over the festering sores of that organism called human society'.[14] They were convinced that workers needed only to learn Marx's analysis of capitalism and they would become revolutionaries. By 1910 the SPC was conducting study classes in economics (the curriculum focused on the need to abolish the wage system), and in Canadian history and English for immigrants. Like the Forum meetings, SPC classes were noted for audience participation. Undeniably, however, the sectarianism and impossibilism of the SPC (it eschewed, in principle if not always in practice, working with trade unions) was unattractive to many British-born Winnipeg members of the radical movement. Still, there can be no doubt that SPC leaders' analysis of a class-polarized society resonated deeply amongst many workers in the tense years at the end of the First World War.

Other small but not insignificant socialist parties like the Social Democratic Party (SDP) – which split from the SPC in 1911 – also arranged some evening classes during the 1912–13 session. The SDP's brand of socialism, its tone and tactics, was more palatable to the broad-based Winnipeg left. The SDP juggled its Marxist principles and its commitment to work unceasingly for reforms, an approach that brought it considerable support, including that of eastern European immigrants. But its adult educational work was accomplished primarily through the People's Forum, and some of its members worked with the youth wing. Other parties – the Dominion Labour Party and the Independent Labour Party – engaged only sporadically in regular educational programmes under their direct auspices. Their members were, however, involved in the educational programmes of the People's Forum, OBU, and Labour Church, testifying to the importance placed on adult education by those actively seeking to restructure society in accordance with some variation of socialist principles.

What emerges from this synopsis of the educational activities of radical workers in Winnipeg, says Maciejko, is not a 'picture of random or purposeless activity, but a pattern with direction and consistency'.[15] According to Allen Mills, J. S. Woodsworth believed that: 'The making of socialists . . . was an intellectual activity, requiring for its success a constant appeal to the spoken and written word. Socialism would arrive . . . through voluntary action that derived from the power of clear, methodological, and rational argument itself.'[16] Many radical workers shared Woodsworth's faith in the power of intellectual activity as integral to the 'organization of action.' There was widespread recognition that education was essential to the change process itself. Even H. G. Fester, chair of the Ontario section of the WEA and committed to the WEA's programme of 'organized classes', recognized that radical organizations deserved a place in the 'scheme of workers' education'. Though labelling the radicals' educational work as purely propagandist, Fester admitted that their numerous publications and educational activities had awakened some minds out of lethargy.[17] From this knowledge of the power of ideas in the political battle came the proposal to place on the entrance of the OBU's Plebs Hall the inscription: 'Read, Study and Investigate, for in the application of the meaning of these words, we conquer'.[18]

But the workers' movement, in Winnipeg and elsewhere in Canada, did not conquer Canadian society. In May and June 1919, approximately 25,000 men and women struck in sympathy with the embattled workers of the city's building and metal trades; in other cities of Canada, workers staged massive support strikes. These political actions, which had social and political learning outcomes, testify, one might suggest, to the success of the teachings of labour's schools. Yet, the strike was crushed, leaders associated with the OBU and several others were jailed (the OBU collapsed in 1920), the fragility of utopian hopes was revealed, and the basic reformism of the labour movement was exposed. Labour radicalism called forth its dialectical opposite, reaction from the dominant order: The Citizens' Committee of 1,000 moved to suppress the strikers, special police raided labour halls and strike leaders' homes, and 'foreign Bolsheviks' were jailed. Viewed through the workers' learning lens, we could hypothesize that the Winnipeg General Strike taught the workers how dangerous their knowledge was, the enormous difficulty of achieving a collective identity, and the fierce resistance to transformative action regarding basic power relations in the society. The General Strike of 1919 led, like the collapse of the Knights of Labour in an earlier decade, into a new period of profound disillusion within working-class experience.[19]

WORKERS' EDUCATION AND COMPETING DISCURSIVE FIELDS

Our picture of the adult education discursive field in the first two decades of the twentieth century is not yet complete. Writing two years after the Winnipeg General Strike, Father Jimmy Tompkins captured something of the sentiment present amongst thoughtful univeristy educators when he declared in his pamphlet, *Knowledge for the People*:

> Old ways of thinking have been broken up and a new spirit today can no more be doubted than we were permitted to doubt, during the years between 1914 and 1917, that we were at war. Nowhere is this new spirit more in evidence than in the field of Education. No other idea has so gripped the people of the whole world as the desire for more knowledge, better intellectual training, and better organised effort in their various callings. It has gripped them *en masse* and without regard to condition, class or circumstances. Men and women everywhere are clamouring for the equal opportunity that education and intellectual training give.[20]

Significantly, Tompkins pointed approvingly to developments within the global university extension movement and the WEA; he did not mention any of the forms of adult education present within the workers' movement itself. What Tompkins's ringing proclamation [...] veils is precisely how the universities and other emergent adult education forms (like Frontier College) understood the social crisis and what constituted legitimate educational practice. If labour radicalism – the outcome of informal and nonformal social and political learning processes – confronted the coercive apparatus of the state, these same workers also faced an ideological opposition which would, directly or indirectly, contest their educational practice.

The Canadian university extension movement emerged in the first two decades of the twentieth century. It, too, recognized the potential of adult education in resolving the social conflict. Although Queen's University organized some tutorial classes in 1889, the University of Alberta Extension Department, created in 1912, was really the first in the field. The University of Toronto organized its Extension Department in 1920. It provides a useful focal point, since it sponsored the first WEA tutorial classes *for* workers and is considered Canada's most prestigious centre of higher learning.

In a three-page document simply entitled 'University Extension', written in 1922, the University of Toronto presented its understanding of the nature and purpose of adult education. This seemingly innocuous document provides crucial insights into the way the university, as the socially and historically designated space for legitimate knowledge production and dissemination, was constructing adult education. From the opening line, this text is pervaded by a profound sense of danger and crisis. 'At this moment,' the anonymous author(s) declared, there is a 'crisis in the whole world of education.' How was the crisis perceived? Public schools and the technical training provided by universities had left out the 'most important part' of education. Neither had developed the 'power of thinking' or 'useful criticism', but more significantly, neither had built up a 'thoughtful, comprehending human spirit'.[21] The latter task was most urgent.

The crisis in education, for the text's author(s), only reflected a much deeper crisis – that of a class-polarized society. The author(s) contended that what now existed in Canada were two more or less unrelated standards of thinking and speaking. Canada was a severed society, speaking two warring ideological languages. 'There is an immense danger to a country in the existence of two languages, the language of the cultivated and the language of the street, neither of which is really comprehensible to the other.' The choice of the street/cultivated metaphor is significant. The languages of social transformation – products of workers' own learning and experience – are consigned to the street, the realm of the undisciplined, the untrained, the untutored, and the rebellious. Indeed, one catches in the text's identification of adult education with 'formalized' instruction by 'trained' tutors [. . .] the notion that only knowledge cultivated by the professor/gardener is legitimate. For the author(s) contend that 'if it could be brought about that more or less the same proportion of every class could be found in the tanks of thoughtful cultivated people, an immense stride would have been made in the abolition of class differences'.[22]

It is imperative that the university extend its 'higher culture' to those classes previously neglected. Because the 'whole basis of national unity rests upon the theory of the nation being an aggregation of persons who, on the whole, think alike, and it is very difficult for two sets of people to think alike who speak more or less different languages and think in different categories', a 'large expansion' of adult education is called for. Incorporating the workers into this higher culture is intimately bound up with the extension metaphor: to extend means to control. The fundamental motivation for extending adult education is not, as suggested by Tompkins and 'University Extension', to provide what the workers want (they demand, we just respond), but to promote social harmony between capital and labour. This is to be accomplished through the idealist project of creating a standardized, uniform, monologic culture. But this monologic voice can only speak its values by repressing workers' polyphonous voices. Adult education, as constructed by university extension, had given itself an impossible task [. . .] of equalizing the classes without abolishing class domination.

Why was the WEA successfully established in Toronto at the end of
the First World War? To be sure, some working men had asked the
University of Toronto to co-operate in establishing an organization similar
to the British WEA. But working-class people were not the main impetus
behind the founding of the WEA in Toronto. All of the key players [. . .]
believed that the foundations of democracy were under siege in a crassly
materialistic age. Clearly alarmed by the Russian Revolution, the Winnipeg
General Strike, and the OBU, and startled by the enormously increased
strike activity, rapid growth of trade unionism, and expansion of labour
political action in Ontario, these middle-class academics 'sought to use the
Association as a means to curb the spread of radicalism'.[23]

In an essay, 'The education of the working man', published in the
prestigious *Queen's Quarterly* in 1919, W. L. Grant spoke gravely of the
'flood of ideas' sweeping over the 'civilised world'.[24] Nineteenth-century
laissez-faire individualism had collapsed and only the 'cash nexus' seemed
to be holding the society together. How could democracy endure? The
working class wanted, in his view, a 'new *concordat* between Capital and
Labour and the State'. They wanted to be owners alike in industry and
politics. But only those who were 'educated' were fit to take part in
guiding the destinies of the state. Uneducated working people and citizens,
Grant believed, leapt uncritically at every new idea. 'Ideas without education' were 'very dangerous fodder. Ideas without education mean the
triumph of the half-baked; and the results of the triumph of the half-
baked are manifest to the world in Russia today.' Education, as construed
by Grant, had to subjugate alternative knowledge forms produced in
learning sites outside the control of those with disciplined and cultivated
minds. If the 'broad sunlight of education' were to be spread over the
workers' maisma 'of incoherent ideas,' then adult education had to be
organized. And the university would be the centre, 'the splendid fertilising
nucleus.' Grant's constitution of adult education is neither innocent nor
value-free. The call for 'organized' (formal) adult education under the
disciplinary eye of the trained tutor must, necessarily, exclude and delegit-
imate 'unorganized' (nonformal/informal) learning. This tactic on the conceptual level is integral to the political struggle to ensure that the 'perverted
vision' of Bolshevism (now a symbol for dangerous learning) does not
'widen itself to take in the whole country'. Grant, celebrated the British
WEA – its historic links with Oxford – precisely because of its moderation.
'The WEA,' Grant opined, 'is thus the educational side of the Labour
Movement; a great school of Political Science for the working classes.'
But the WEA, in Canada as in Britain, was only one of labour's schools,
a good antidote to class struggle.[25]

All the educators who supported the WEA insisted that the teaching be
done by university professors. 'It is the University, after all,' declared
Glazebrook, 'that contains the treasury of knowledge and the training in

method that are required.'[26] This would be a matter of some controversy. Writing to Grant on 13 October 1921, classics professor W. S. Milner thought that the 'success of the WEA as an educational ideal was seriously imperilled'.[27] The controversy, one of many to dog the WEA's path until its demise in the late 1940s, was over union activist James Ballantyne's desire to teach a course in Marxian economics. Though not denying the right of the university to deal with Marx, Milner thought it both unwise and absurd to exercise this right. How could the university support a teacher from the workers' own ranks? Despairing and disconsolate, Milner took his stand for the 'culture of mind and spirit'. The 'unhappy truth', as he saw it, was that the WEA had 'fallen into the hands of Labour that is more anxious for power than for culture, and that the spiritual force of the movement is on the ebb'.

The WEA was, in fact, contested terrain throughout its history.[28] Conflicting visions of adult education – its purpose and process – would be articulated by multiple voices. In the early years of the Association, a number of working men [...] believed that workers with more knowledge could help to improve the existing political and social system. They hoped it would be improved through a workers' educational movement that increased workers' understanding of political and social issues. These worker-activists shared the academics' faith that truth could be examined in an unbiased way – the grand vision of the British WEA tutorial movement.[29]

All agreed, too, that a technical education was not enough, and that workers needed access to a broader knowledge. Significantly, however, other workers emphasized the need for social justice and attacked the limitations of education in a class society and insisted on the social and collective purpose of the WEA. The redoubtable Winnipeg labour movement shared this latter conviction. In 1915 they had met with University of Manitoba Professor J. A. Dale to discuss the formation of a chapter of the WEA. From the start they were suspicious. The University of Manitoba, the committee claimed, was for the rich and provided only 'scraps of knowledge' for workers. After the meeting the Winnipeg Trades and Labour Congress (TLC) decided not to support the WEA because they had to deal with professors who were in the grip of capitalist ideology.[30] The WEA was unable to establish itself in Winnipeg until 1938. This mutual suspicion between the labour movement and the universities is one of the important sub-texts in the history of Canadian, as well as global, workers' education.

In discussing this disparity of views, Radforth and Sangster observe:

Common language such as 'education for citizenship' masked some very significant differences between the aims of the educationalists and those of the labor activists. The class differences of the two groups do much to explain the divergent meanings behind their words. On the one hand, the educationalists saw the WEA as, in part, an experiment in social control. They sought to use their positions as academics and intellectuals to maintain existing power relations in society. On the other hand, the labor activists hoped to further the cause of labor and to help redress the imbalance of power in society. These fundamental differences existed within the Association from the start. Inevitably, as time progressed, the underlying tensions would surface.[31]

In March 1922 the *Canadian Forum* noted that throughout Canada workers were 'suspicious' of both the WEA and Frontier College. What was at the root of worker suspicion of Frontier College? Alfred Fitzpatrick, a disillusioned Presbyterian minister, organized the Reading Camp Association in 1899 (it would become Frontier College in 1919). For Fitzpatrick, the *laissez-faire* state of the late nineteenth and early twentieth centuries had neglected the men working in isolated and wretched railway, lumbering and mining camps (the 'bunkhouse men'). Through silence and lack of intervention, the Canadian state legitimated the exploitation of the campmen's labour and their maintenance as uneducated wage-slaves. Nor did the trade unions pay any attention to these men. Continually calling on the state to intervene in deploying resources for neglected adult learners, Fitzpatrick would be repeatedly rebuffed, despite his powerful moral argument that the state derived its funds from frontier industries.

In his text, *The University in Overalls*, Fitzpatrick described the origins of Frontier College as an educational mission to the bunkhouse men. Fitzpatrick's adult educational discourse is a unique mix of radical and conservative elements. He was appalled at the elitism of Canadian universities and criticized them for their ivory-tower separation from the real world of the hand. 'Classes,' he declared, 'must be held, not only in the schools and universities, but in the shops, on the works, in the camps and fields and settlements of the frontier.'[32] The University of Toronto could hardly find the resources to run a few tutorial classes! In an eloquent chapter, 'Education and the Frontier Camps,' Fitzpatrick argued that the urban-based middle class had appropriated the labour of those toiling and sweating in the mines and camps. Their wealth production, he said, had endowed the resources used by the middle and upper class in the cities. Fitzpatrick castigated the philanthropists who endowed the colleges and ignored the 'living and housing conditions of their own workers in the camp and mills'. The task of educationalists was nothing less than 'to devise ways and means of taking the school and colleges to the frontier'.[33] The men of the camps needed justice, not charity.

Fitzpatrick's educational vision is rooted in the social regenerative assumptions of late Victorian society. He argued that education was for all men [sic], and not for a priviliged class alone. Appropriating Marx's notion of humanization through labour, but not his radical politics, Fitzpatrick – the early twentieth-century social gospeller – thought the solution to structurally rooted problems lay with the redemption of the individual through empathetic provision of basic adult education (literacy and citizenship training). This is a paternalistic and moralistic vision. Yet, Fitzpatrick stood outside the establishment, unlike the patrons of the Mechanics' Institutes and supporters of the Toronto WEA, with the voiceless and the mute. His discourse was patronizing but spoken with a deeply humanistic accent. His social-gospel ideology moved him towards the neglected while simultaneously constraining his educational practice, repressing more overtly political education for social transformation and a nonconformist conception of citizenship.

But there can be no doubt that, like W. L. Grant and other early university supporters of the WEA, Fitzpatrick feared the 'Bolsheviks'. When strikes swept the camps in 1919, he contended that the labourer-teachers' activities would determine whether the camps would produce 'Lenins or Lincolns'.[34] Working under the banner, 'Welfare–Instruction–Canadianising–Leadership', the labourer-teachers' objectives were: (a) to educate the worker and give him a fighting chance, (b) to educate and citizenize [sic] the immigrant, and (c) to meet the 'Red agitator' on his own ground. Fitzpatrick emerged from the social dislocation and political ferment of the war more convinced than ever that the labourer-teacher could exercise a moral-redemptive influence on the 'dangerous foreigners'.[35]

Fitzpatrick seemed to believe that with a little education, a camp worker would cease his 'evil' habits. He envisioned his Reading Camp instructors as models of 'staunch Canadians', inculcating Anglo-Canadian and Protestant values. Thus, with some education and paternalistic guidance from the 'right' sector of society (he recruited middle-class university students), not only would the campmen's lives be improved, but this achievement would help stabilize the social order. Fitzpatrick, in spite of his humanism, instrumentalized adult education in the interests of social harmony.

Linking Fitzpatrick's commitment to 'Canadianize', the 'Red Scare', and the labour movement, Donald Avery speculates that organizations like Frontier College aggravated the immigrants' sense of their own cultural identification. Shunned or patronized by traditional nativist institutions, alienated immigrant workers turned to groups which sought to transform Canadian society through revolution – the IWW, OBU, and Canadian Communist Party.[36]

Frontier College's educational radicalism and political conservatism represents a distinct form of adult educational discourse in the decades of discord. Fitzpatrick challenged the conventional educational wisdom of the day. Canadian universities were small, inward-looking institutions with rigid academic requirements, and the extension movement (with the possible exception of the University of Alberta) was pathetic and forlorn. While more radical political voices would surely have contested Fitzpatrick's attempt to contain rebellious knowledge, they would have been sympathetic to his call that the workers be offered bread and not stones.

CONCLUDING CRITICAL THEOREMS

1 The struggles of workers in the turbulent decades of discord can be viewed as a contest between supporters of conflicting visions of what constitutes valid enlightenment, enpowerment, and transformative action. A multiplicity of labour's schools offered their vision of the purpose of adult education in a society viewed as essentially conflictual. Outside labour's schools, adult educators offered their vision of adult education in a society viewed as essentially harmonious (though momentarily divided).

2 Adult education does not have an essence; competing discourses struggle with one another for hegemony. Adult education is always both normative and descriptive, and does not mean the same thing to everyone.

3 Particular discursive practices are intimately bound up with social power and control. Adult education discourse sets the limits of what counts as authentic educational practice. This theorem seems borne out in our analysis of how the legitimate and authoritative formal educational institutions (university extension and WEA) attempted to constitute their particular discourse as normative. The success of this manoeuvre to establish discursive hegemony is bound up with the power relations of the society – the ability of the dominant order to block/manage, coercively and conceptually, the autonomous contestatory learning processes erupting in a multiplicity of learning sites (workplace, community, trade union, political party, news paper and so on).

4 While a simplistic social control model of the WEA or university extension is inadequate to grasp the complexities of workers' education, the extension metaphor signals a move on the part of the dominant order to manage and constrain knowledge and action that threatens social order.

REFERENCES

1 Welton, M. R., 'The depths of despondency: the struggle for autonomous workers' education in the Vancouver WEA, 1942–1948', *CASAE History Bulletin*, May 1986; Welton, M. R. (ed.), *Knowledge for the People: The Struggle for Adult Learning in English-Speaking Canada, 1928–1973*, Toronto, OISE Press, 1987.

2 Keeley, G. and Palmer, B. D., *Dreaming of What Might Be: The Knights of Labour in Ontario, 1880–1900*, Cambridge University Press, 1982; Palmer, B.,

Working Class Experience, the Rise and Reconstitution of Canadian Labour, 1800–1980, Toronto, Butterworth, 1983.

3 Fay, B., Critical Social Science: Liberation and its Limits, Ithaca, Cornell University Press, 1987; Maciejko, W. J. 'Read, study and investigate: workers education in Winnipeg, 1912–1921', CASAE History Bulletin, May 1986; Simon, B., 'Can education change society?', in J. D. Wilson (ed.), An Imperfect Past: Education and Society in Canadian History, Vancouver University of British Columbia Centre for the Study of Curriculum and Instruction, 1984.

4 Stewart, D., Adult Learning in America: Eduard Lindeman and his Agenda for Life-long Education, Malabar, Florida, Robert Krieger, 1987.

5 Foucault, M., Power/Knowledge: Selected Interviews and Other Writings, 1972–1977, New York, Pantheon/Random House, 1980.

6 Anderson, J. T. M., The Education of the New Canadian, Toronto, James Dent & Sons, 1918; Fitzpatrick, A., The University in Overalls, Toronto, Frontier College Press, 1920; Woodsworth, J. S., Strangers Within our Gates, Toronto, University of Toronto Press, 1909 (reprinted 1972).

7 Brown, R. and Cook, R., Canada 1896–1921: A Nation Transformed, Toronto, McClelland & Stewart, 1974; Jamieson, S., Times of Trouble: Labour Unrest and Industrial Conflict in Canada, 1900–1966, Ottawa, Information Canada, 1968; Palmer, Working Class Experience.

8 Heron, C. and Storey, R. (eds), On the Job, Confronting the Labour Process, Kingston and Montreal, McGill-Queen's University Press, 1986; Palmer, Working Class Experience.

9 Mellor, J., The Company Store: James Bryson McLachlan and the Cape Breton Coal Miners 1900–1925, Toronto, Doubleday, 1983.

10 Maciejko, 'Read, study and investigate', p. 9.

11 McCormack, A. R., Reformers, Rebels and Revolutionaries: The Western Canada Radical Movement 1899–1919, Toronto, University of Toronto Press, 1977.

12 MacDonald, G., 'Workers' education in Nova Scotia: illuminating/learning/history', CASAE History Bulletin, May 1986.

13 Coady, Moses, Masters of their Own Destiny, New York, Harper & Row, 1939.

14 McCormack, Reformers, Rebels and Revolutionaries, p. 54.

15 Maciejko, 'Read, study and investigate', p.13.

16 Mills, A., 'Cooperation and community in the thought of J. S. Woodsworth', Labour/Le Travail 14, 1984, pp. 103–120, p. 105.

17 Fester, H. G., 'Workers' education in Canada', Proceedings of the [US] National Conference of Social Work, 1924.

18 Central Labour Council of the One Big Union [OBU], 'Executive Minutes', 6 January 1920.

19 Palmer, Working Class Experience.

20 Tompkins, J., Knowledge for the People, Antigonish, Nova Scotia (private publication), 1921, p. 3.

21 'University Extension', University of Toronto Extension Papers, 1922, File 1, Box Print Materials, University of Toronto Archives, no pagination.

22 'University Extension'.

23 Radforth, I. and Sangster, J., 'The struggle for autonomous workers' education: the Workers' Educational Association in Ontario, 1917–1951', in Welton (ed.), Knowledge for the People, pp. 73–96, p. 75.

24 Grant, W. L., 'The education of the working man', Queen's Quarterly, October 1919, p. 160.

25 Fieldhouse, R., 'The 1908 report: antidote to class struggle', in S. Harrop (ed.), *Oxford and Working-Class Education*, University of Nottingham, Department of Adult Education, 1987, pp. 30–47.

26 Glazebrook, R., 'Memorandum to Educational Commission, 1921', *W. L. Grant Papers*, Box 2, Public Archives of Canada.

27 Milner, W. S., 'Letter to W. L. Grant, 13 October 1921', *W. L. Grant Papers*, Box 2, Public Archives of Canada.

28 Radforth and Sangster, 'The struggle for autonomous workers' education'; Welton, 'The depths of despondency'.

29 Fieldhouse, R., 'The problems of objectivity, social purpose and ideological commitment in English university adult education', in R. Taylor, K. Rockhill and R. Fieldhouse, *University Adult Education in England and the USA*, London, Croom Helm, 1985, pp. 29–51.

30 'University Tutorial Classes', 1915.

31 Radforth and Sangster, 'The struggle for autonomous workers' education', p. 78.

32 Fitzpatrick, *The University in Overalls*, p. ix.

33 Fitzpatrick, *The University in Overalls*, p. 42.

34 Cook, G., 'Educational justice for the campmen: Alfred Fitzpatrick and the foundation of Frontier College, 1899–1922', in Welton (ed), *Knowledge for the People*, pp. 35–51, p. 47.

35 Avery, D., *'Dangerous Foreigners': European Immigrant Workers and Labour Radicalism in Canada, 1896–1932*, Toronto, McClelland & Stewart, 1979.

36 Avery, *'Dangerous Frontiers'*.

Chapter 15

Popular education for women
A study of four organizations

Rosemary Deem

Source: This is a revised version of a paper given at the fifth Westhill Sociology of Education Conference in January 1982.

INTRODUCTION: WOMEN'S POPULAR EDUCATION

Richard Johnson defines popular education as that which:

> means starting from the problems, experiences and social position of excluded majorities, from the position of the working people, women and black people. It means recognizing the elements of realism in popular attitudes to schooling, including the rejection of schooling... It means working up these lived experiences and insights until they fashion a real alternative.
>
> (Johnson 1981a: 813)

This chapter examines a form of education for adults which starts from the problems, experiences and social position of an excluded majority: women. Such education is not schooling, not compulsory, not organized primarily by the state, and is almost entirely conducted in single-sex groups. The education so provided can be considered 'popular' because women have organized it for themselves, albeit with some help from outside agencies. Furthermore this kind of education recognizes, although not necessarily for the purposes of achieving radical change, that women share certain interests and hold a common position in society, particularly in the home, the family and community, hence building on women's 'lived experiences'. In order to achieve such education, women have had to struggle hard against ideologies of gender stereotyping and patterns of male dominance and power which try to confine women to the private sphere of the home and the family, away from the public sphere of employment and formal political power.

The organizations with which this chapter is concerned are influenced strongly by gender and by patriarchal relations and ideology. They open up a small public space for women outside the home (see Stacey and Price

1981) but are located outside, although not unregulated by, the state, in what Gramsci termed 'civil society' (Gramsci: 1971: 56). Civil society may be understood as those aspects of society and social action which occur outside the sphere of the state (e.g. households or voluntary organizations).

The four women's organizations considered here are not merely of importance for the reasons given above. They are also important in that they transmit knowledge, develop skills and provide education largely outside the formal education system. The categories 'schooling' and 'education' are often collapsed by writers and researchers into one, so that what happens to women (or men), after they leave full-time school or full-time higher/further education, has been little considered by many educational theorists. Yet some of the same theories used to analyse schooling are equally relevant to adult education outside the formal system. For example, it has been argued by Shaw (1980) and by Spender and Sarah (1980) that single-sex schooling helps women to reject gender stereotypes and male dominance and make curriculum choices that are traditionally not taken by females. Yet, as we shall see in this study, single-sex educational groups of adult women are not necessarily either oppositional or feminist (in the sense of having a political commitment to improving women's position in society). Further, if we look at adult education for women, that which is not organized primarily by the state does not necessarily differ much from that which is (this does not refer, of course, to private *schooling*, which is a rather different matter), although there is in some quarters a belief that popular education organized outside the confines of the state *is* likely to be more radical (see CCC's 1981, Johnson 1981a, 1981b).

WOMEN IN GROUPS AS AN EDUCATIVE CONTEXT

This chapter draws on a study conducted during 1980–1 in Milton Keynes, a new city in the south of England. The study involved, amongst other things, an examination of all clubs, organizations and other groups in the city which admitted women as members, and also formal adult education evening and day classes. The research methods used included observation, questionnaires, structured and unstructured interviews, and analysis of documents and pamphlets relating to the groups and organizations studied (for more detailed information about the research, see Deem 1986, 1990). Most of the evening and day classes and a few of the organizations were open to both sexes, although it was noticeable that where women were present they were either in a tiny minority or were numerically dominant in a group. The organizations in which women predominated had a number of striking features, although, of course, not *all* of these apply to *all* the groups:

1 A high educational content in many activities.
2 The use of didactic teaching methods.
3 Teacher-centred, passive learning styles.
4 Indications of deviance by some learners (for instance, talking during the presence of a main speaker or demonstrator about something unrelated). This has some similarities to similar forms of resistance to education found in studies of male working-class boys (Willis 1977), except that the women's attendance is voluntary whereas pupils are compelled to attend.
5 A strong concern with 'keeping order' and a quiet atmosphere.

Women's organizations and clubs have previously been examined by sociologists, for example, in Stacey's classic community studies of Banbury (1960 and 1975). Research on leisure has noted their importance for women (Parry and Johnson 1974, Roberts 1978, Delamont 1980), and the 1973 Russell Report (DES, Committee of Enquiry 1973) on adult education recognized the relevance of voluntary groups in the provision of educational opportunities for adult women. Women's groups, too, are often connected with community and caring activities as observed by Gregory:

> It is likely that women, during periods of having no paid employment have been particularly resourceful in their use of local communities to further ends that seem to them socially desirable. The work of the Women's Institute and voluntary caring organizations demonstrate an aspect of this.
>
> (Gregory 1982)

WHY WOMEN JOIN EDUCATIVE ORGANIZATIONS

A number of possible reasons suggest themselves:

1 That women's male partners are more willing to allow women to attend educational or 'caring' or 'home-making' activities and those where alcohol is not available, than alternative social activities such as dancing, mixed events or pubs (Deem 1982, Green et al. 1990). This, of course, does not affect women who live apart from men, athough as Stanley (1980) points out, cultural expectations about what activities women should engage in affect all women, with 'policing' of many public and social meeting places by men, to ensure that women are either made to feel uncomfortable or keep away altogether. What men, collectively 'allow' women to do has many connections with control over female sexuality, as well as the notion of women as male possessions in a marriage contract. Social class is also a big factor here; in general the evidence suggests that middle-class women have more freedom of manoeuvre than working-class women (Deem 1986, Green et al. 1990).

2 Largely because of the considerations outlined above, but also owing to constraints such as lack of childcare facilities, there *are* relatively few places where women may meet socially with other women in a non-threatening atmosphere. Activities like bingo or women-only sessions at fitness clubs are often popular because of this (Green *et al.* 1990).

3 Women in public places in British society are often expected to behave in circumscribed ways – for example, not gossiping or engaging in frivolous talk; lowering their eyes when talking to men who are not relatives; taking care about dress; not being alone after dark (Stanley 1980). Of course, these expectations are much mediated by social class and ethnicity, and the constraints apply much less to educational contexts and women-only groups than to mixed company.

4 For women who are not engaged in full-time paid employment, women's groups represent a chance to escape from the privacy and isolation of the household, even though the topics considered may sometimes still be oriented towards 'home-making'.

5 Women actually enjoy and seek out the company of other women.

6 Women of all social groups often show an interest in self-education, although they may be less likely than men to embark upon formal classes or training courses (Sargant 1991).

WOMEN'S GROUPS: A CLASSIFICATION

The four groups in Milton Keynes referred to here can be classified according to Raymond Williams's categorization of types organization, or as he terms it, 'cultural formation' (Williams 1981).

1 Specialist organizations which focus on a particular activity or interest, an example of which is the Flower Arranging Club.

2 Alternative organizations, which develop where there is no existing institutional provision – for example, the Women's Institute Branches and Poundhill Women's Club.

3 Oppositional groups, where there is active opposition to established Institutions and the conditions prevailing in these – for example, the Women's Section of the Labour Party.

THE SOCIAL COMPOSITION AND CHARACTERISTICS OF THE FOUR WOMEN'S ORGANIZATIONS

The four groups outlined have a number of common features. They are all single-sex (although the Flower Arranging Club did not actually debar men), meetings are held at regular times in public halls or meeting places (which itself may impose formality on the knowledge transmission process), and all set out to transmit knowledge and/or skills of various kinds to their members. All four have clear sets of objectives which affect their organization, social relations and pedagogy. As Dale says: 'The framing of objectives in *any* particular way has consequences for what can be taught and how it can be taught' (Dale 1981: 75). In addition to these similarities, the four groups also operate in civil society and can be regarded as voluntary organizations or groups. One of the most interesting characteristics of the four organizations under discussion is their almost total distance from the economy and the labour market. Although all four are regulated or influenced to some degree by state institutions, the extent of this and its effects are different in each case.

The Flower Arranging Club and Poundhill Women's Club both met in Milton Keynes Development Corporation or local authority funded premises, which imposed certain restrictions on duration of meetings, required formal officers for groups or some allocation of legal/administrative responsibility to individuals, and imposed some restriction on activities because of fire and safety considerations and local regulations about use of public premises. The WI branches in this study did not receive any grant from the local education authority, as some branches did at the time of the research. However, in 1980–1 when this research was done, the WI National Federation had been receiving a grant from the Department of Education and Science since 1945 for the advancement of women's liberal education (Goodenough 1977), part of which went towards the costs of its permanent educational establishment at Denman College. Past Presidents of the WI and other members have sat on government committees, and the WI (and its urban counterpart, the Townswomen's Guild) is often consulted by government, local authorities and quangos, as well as by the Civil Service, on matters concerning women, home-making and rural life. In its early years the WI was taken under the wing of the Board of Agriculture for a while, and during both World Wars made a major contribution to food production at the invitation of the Ministry of Agriculture. Yet despite this apparent degree of incorporation into the state, individual WI branches remain able to decide their own activities and have never been slow to criticize government and local authority policies, especially those relating to women, family, marriage and children, as well as to many other issues of general interest (Goodenough 1977).

The Labour Party Women's Section had a clear connection to the state through its parent organization's concern with parliamentary democracy and social/economic/political reform as a means of achieving socialist political objectives. However, this particular section was the closest to an autonomous oppositional feminist group of the four considered, and its activities owed little to state regulation. Indeed some of its activities were often directed against the policies of state institutions. Thus, all the groups had a private existence outside the state's sphere of influence. At the same time the groups offered women a toe-hold on the public and political sphere of life, either directly, as in the Labour Party section, or indirectly, when the WI gave evidence to government committees.

Another issue for consideration here then is the extent to which any or all of the groups challenged the *status quo*, whether this was in relation to social disadvantage or any other feature of society. In other words did any of the groups have radical intentions?

The Flower Arranging Club

About half the members were in paid work, some part-time. A considerable number of the remainder were of pensionable age. The rest were full-time housewives and mothers. All the members I encountered on my visits were white. Typical occupations of those in jobs were clerical and secretarial and shop work, with a few from the caring professions. This club did not offer any challenge to the *status quo* and indeed flower arranging in our society is regarded as a stereotypically female activity.

The Women's Institute

The branches found in the research area varied in their class composition but typically fell into the following groups: local middle-class women running small businesses or involved in agriculture on a large scale (that is, not peasant farmers), or having male partners who are managers or who have their own businesses; those working in, or having previously worked in, the professions; working-class women, mostly in clerical, secretarial, shop or cleaning work or in low-paid health or welfare work, and full-time housewives. No black or Asian women were members of the branches I visited. Middle-class women were prominent in most branches. The National Federation of Women's Institutes has been dominated since its inception by middle-class women and by members of landed county families (Goodenough 1977). The WI is ostensibly concerned with transmitting dominant social values, ideology and cultures but nevertheless it can and does present challenges to the *status quo* (for example, the National Federation campaigned vigorously throughout the 1980s for the separate taxation of married women).

Poundhill Women's Club

This club had the most restricted membership of the four, drawing on those living very locally. Most members fell into two categories: secretarial (those in clerical, shop, or technical/professional jobs) and full-time housewives. All but a tiny number were married to men in professional, managerial or technical occupations rather than in manual work. However, unlike the other groups, this club did contain some Asian women.

The less formal structure of this group and the diversity of its discussions meant that it was hard to identify dominant individuals and
projects. The group did not often challenge dominant values, ideologies
or culture. One of its more striking characteristics was the concern of
its members with upward social class mobility, through the purchase of
previously rented Development Corporation housing, particular forms of
dress, values and other aspects of life-style. In so far as the group facilitated
this concern, it was not in a good position to challenge the *status quo*.

Women's Section of the Labour Party

This group was overwhelmingly composed of white women in some way
involved in education, principally as teachers. Of those few currently not
engaged in paid work, the majority had undergone teacher-training in the
past. This group saw its major tasks as providing a support network for
feminist women and challenging the *status quo*, especially in relation to
social class, race and gender.

Despite the variation in social composition, organizational characteristics,
and the extent to which groups reinforced or challenged the *status quo*,
all four appear to contribute to the development of women's culture and
cultural values in our society and do not simply reflect existing culture.

THE PROCESS OF EDUCATIONAL TRANSMISSION IN THE FOUR WOMEN'S GROUPS

I now want to examine the ways in which educational knowledge and
skills are transmitted to each of the four groups. Bernstein suggests that
educational knowledge is realized through three message systems – namely,
curriculum, pedagogy and evaluation – and that two main types of educational knowledge code, or sets of educational principles, underlie the
shaping of these three message systems (Bernstein 1975). The two codes
are the collection code, in which the organization of knowledge has a high
degree of boundary maintenance (for example, between high- and low-
status knowledge or between teacher and taught) and the integrated code
where boundaries are blurred (for example, between areas of knowledge
such as science and English literature, or between teacher and taught). As
with most theoretical work, Bernstein's ideas require some modification
when applied to the research data described here but are nevertheless
helpful in understanding the educational variations among the four groups.

The Flower Arranging Club

The club had formal officers and a committee. It met monthly in the evening, using a public hall. Members paid an annual subscription plus a fee for each meeting. Meetings usually consisted of a demonstration or talk by a visitor plus some 'business' conducted by the committee and opportunities to purchase materials from a stall. Members sat in rows of chairs in the body of the hall. Visiting demonstrators were placed on a platform, formally introduced and thanked, and usually provided an opportunity for questions after completion of the talk or demonstration. The chairman [sic] or secretary tried to keep members quiet if they became too noisy. The curriculum had a narrow range – arranging flowers, choosing and growing suitable flowers, and care and display of household plants. Pedagogy was didactic; members were not encouraged to interrupt a speaker or demonstrator, did not take notes, and could only ask questions when specifically instructed to do so. Those sitting at the back of the hall may have had difficulty in hearing or seeing what was going on at the front of the platform, and one consequence is that such members frequently engaged in their own conversations, not necessarily about flower arranging. Such conversations were apt to grow louder in any quiet parts of the proceedings. There was some informal small group discussion of the talk/demonstration after the demonstration finished. Demonstrators made use of the 'look and see how I do it' method rather than the 'this is how you might do it' method. Members had little chance to discuss their own efforts at flower arranging or their own ideas on the subject within the formal context of the meeting. The Club did however run some special classes separately for beginners. Those who got most from the club in terms of knowledge of flower arranging (as opposed to those who are more interested in sociability with other women) appeared to be those with the most experience of the craft; absolute beginners might enjoy watching a demonstration but probably would not learn how to arrange flowers from that alone.

The Women's Institute

All the branches studied had a president and a formal committee. There was also a complex county and national organization, mostly elected. Members paid an annual subscription, and then for refreshments at each meeting. Meetings were held once a month; some branches met in the afternoon and others in the evening. A public or church hall was normally used. Members sat in the body of the hall, with the president and speaker on a platform. Meetings at the time of the fieldwork in 1980–1 usually took the following form: the singing of 'Jerusalem'; the reading of minutes of the last meeting during which the president would stand on the platform and go through any business such as forthcoming courses, arrangements for markets, visits to other branches, outings, county and national affairs, and fund-raising. Then there was usually a speaker or demonstration, followed by questions, a competition for members (for example, for the best cake or soft toy or piece of embroidery, members having brought these with them) followed by serving of tea. The curriculum was much wider than the Flower Arranging Club, covering a range of rural and domestic crafts, from corn dollies to dressmaking and cookery, as well as discussion of topical issues related to the community, women's rights, and citizenship. Thus a variety of skills and knowledge might be acquired. At the time of the study, courses and classes were also run locally by the county organization and by Denman College.

Pedagogy at branches was observed to be didactic and no questions were encouraged until the speaker had completed the talk or demonstration. Members rarely wrote anything down whilst listening to speakers. Throughout the meetings I attended, presidents kept order, sometimes using a bell. Nevertheless, like any classroom and the Flower Arranging Club, the WI meetings had its deviants who talked in whispers and from time to time burst into louder conversation, this occurring especially in the back few rows. A buzz of talk was almost always audible. Several of the WI presidents whom I met distinguished between 'good' and 'bad' branches, according to the degree of ease or difficulty they experienced in keeping their members in order. Members did have the opportunity to talk informally to the speaker and to each other when tea was served at the end of the meeting.

Poundhill Women's Club

The Club had a chairperson (very unusual terminology in a non-feminist women's group) and a formal committee. Membership was open to any women living on the estate the club was named after and there was a small membership fee. Meetings were held fortnightly in a community room attached to a middle school. There was no connection with any other group and it was started by a group of women new to the area who wanted to get out of their houses and meet other women socially, but at the same time learn something useful. The potential curriculum was very wide, and certainly not confined to domestic concerns; a variety of local people were approached to give talks about hobbies, the community, their job or a craft. Outings and meals out were also arranged, and the group did some fundraising for good causes.

There was no platform in the room used, members sat round in a circle and there was much less formality when a speaker attended than in either of the organizations discussed previously. Members might interrupt a speaker to ask a question and fairly lively discussions often ensued. The speaker was treated as an equal and in consequence pedagogy was much more informal, and the experience of members considered equally valid. There was relatively little concern with keeping order except at the very beginning of a meeting when business and minutes were dealt with. Partly for these reasons and partly because the meetings contained only about 15–25 women (as opposed to over 60 in the WI and Flower Arranging Club) there was no continual 'buzz' of conversation nor any deviant back row. Whereas the Flower Arranging Club and the WI may be seen to operate a form of collection code – with strong divisions between valid and non-valid knowledge, quite strong boundaries between teacher and taught, and a concern with keeping order – the Women's Club appeared to have moved towards a more integrated code, with weak boundaries between different areas of knowledge, little insulation of teacher from taught, and little concern with maintenance of order.

Women's Section of the Labour Party

At the time of the research there was a formal committee because the relationship of the Section to the local constituency Labour Party demanded it. However, in reality, the formal committee was operative only in so far as secretarial work goes, and even this was usually shared among several members. The Section was open to any woman who is a Labour Party member or even those who intended to become one. Meetings were held once a month in the evenings. There was no separate membership subscription (party subscriptions are paid to a local branch, not the Section) and money was raised through a variety of activities when required. Meetings included an agenda and minutes and a discussion, which were usually led by a talk; a different chairperson was elected for each meeting. Members sat in a circle; proceedings were informal. The curriculum covered many political activities and interests, including feminist and socialist theories, direct action, positive action inside and outside the party, and consideration of the members' own roles as women. Speakers were either group members or invited from outside, but were treated no differently from other members and were interrupted and quizzed at any point. Sometimes a particular text was used as a basis for discussion, or sometimes a topical issue. Pedagogy was informal and sometimes almost invisible. Sometimes collaborative written work was used as a basis for discussion. Members took notes if they wished, and most joined in discussions at some length.

This was the only group of the four which was both overtly feminist and whose discussions ranged over the economy, politics, community, domestic life and childcare but also explicitly challenged the *status quo*. There was no concern with keeping order; if several people spoke at once, their topics nearly always related to the main discussion. The existence of an integrated code was much more strongly indicated here than at Poundhill, with very weak classification (as regards boundaries between subjects) and weak framing of knowledge into the roles of 'teacher and 'taught' (Bernstein 1975). This was despite the fact that the group was part of a highly bureaucratic and hierarchical national political party.

In order to highlight the educational features of the four groups, I shall now briefly compare them with a conventional adult education evening class in O-level Sociology, which also formed part of the 1980–1 study.

O-level Sociology evening class

This was a one-year course with an examination at the end, two-and-a-half terms of meeting for two hours once a week, plus homework. There were twenty students, mostly women, paying a termly fee. The tutor was male. Students sat in rows of desks and the tutor talked from the table facing the class. Over half the time was taken up with a lecture, on which students took extensive notes. Discussion was at specified points except when someone had an urgent question or did not understand a point. The tutor spent much of the discussion period trying to wean people away from discussing their everyday experiences and encouraged them to talk 'sociologically'. Most of the class, however, seemed uncertain what this meant.

The few male students dominated the discussion and the tutor's attention.[1] Some women never participated at all unless asked a direct question. Discussion did not flow freely but was constantly referred back to the tutor. The curriculum was determined by the relevant O-level syllabus and the interests of the tutor. Pedagogy was traditional and didactic and there were strong boundaries between teacher and taught as well as between 'common sense' and 'sociology' (the latter imposed by the tutor with some difficulty).

The formality and principles of transmission here were similar to the Flower Arranging Club and the WI but the mixed group appeared to inhibit some women both from participating in the discussion and from talking about other topics with their friends. This is congruent with the arguments and research presented by Spender in her analysis of the reasons why women prefer to talk to women (Spender 1981). It appears too (confirmed by informal discussion with students after the class) that the quality of the learning experience in the class was no different from that found in the Flower Arranging Club and the WI; in all three the women were fairly passive although eager learners. However, whilst the WI and the Flower Arranging Club offered their members a say in what topics were discussed or demonstrated, this option did not exist in the evening class. The comparison suggests that where women's own experiences, problems and social position have some influence on the educational context (that is, the education is popular), even if such education is not necessarily radical or oppositional it does meet a real need amongst women and offers a positive, even if sometimes rather teacher-centred, learning and social experience.

CHALLENGES TO GENDER STEREOTYPING, GENDER DISCRIMINATION, AND WOMEN'S POSITION IN SOCIETY

The one question which remains to be asked about the four groups is the extent to which the groups studied challenge or accept dominant ideas about women's position in our society. If we place the groups on a continuum from non-feminist to feminist, this research project concluded that this was how they fell:

Non-Feminist			*Feminist*
Flower Arranging Club	WI	Poundhill Women's Club	Women's Section of Labour Party

The groups examined here had no clear connection to the organization of the economy (although the WI operates regular produce markets), and only one had any well-defined connections with government or the political sphere more generally. It is also evident that single-sex groups of women, whilst avoiding some of the problems of male domination, do not necessarily challenge gender stereotyping or indirect gender discrimination whether through their activities or through their existence as groups of women. Thus, the activities of the Flower Arranging Club and the WI rested heavily on a sexual division of labour in which women's main activities were principally oriented to the domestic sphere. Just as Stacey and Price (1981: 165), quoting Chamberlain's study of Fenland women (Chamberlain 1975: 135–6), note that 'the Gislea women were clear that women have a special and separate contribution to make to parish affairs', so the women in these two groups saw their activities and their positions in semi-public life as legitimate because these could be linked to women's traditional roles. The other two groups, however, had started to move away from this position, perhaps because their members were younger and had more contact with the contemporary women's movement. The difference lies not only in the capacity of the Labour Women's Section and the Poundhill Club to extend their discussions beyond domestic affairs and sometimes to develop a critical view of women's position in society, but also in their efforts to develop a more open and active mode of teaching and learning than was present in either the Flower Arranging Club or the Women's Institute branches studied.

Yet the Flower Arranging Club and the WI provided much of value to women, including informal as well as formal sociability and educational opportunities, even though some of the skills and knowledge they offered were on occasion old fashioned and sometimes gender-stereotyped, or socially devalued. In some cases the experience of holding positions of authority in organizations like the WI can enable women to enter public life at a more overtly political level, for example as local councillors or magistrates (see Deem 1984, Spender and Sarah 1980 and Shaw 1980). The skills and knowledge acquired can also contribute towards developing a new or revamped form of paid work. The Flower Arranging Club and the WI certainly did not simply reflect the *status quo* even though they did not always overtly challenge it. And whilst such groups may support some aspects of women's inequality, such as the responsibility for domestic work and childcare, these organizations can challenge and help to change other aspects of the role of women, such as the right of women to an independent social life and a place in civil society outside the home.

Conversely, neither the Poundhill Women's Club nor the Labour Party Women's Section, despite a greater apparent challenge to the *status quo*, was able to make any significant impact on many aspects of women's inequality. Thus it was usually women themselves who had to arrange childcare whilst they attended meetings and it was women who usually had to prepare a meal before going out or who had to reorganize their whole day or week in order to be an active member of their group. Despite the encouragement and confidence which the Labour Party Women's Section evidently gave to its members, men still dominated the constituency party, held many of the important offices in the party, and formed most of the successful candidates in local government elections. Thus each group is subject to, and challenges and adapts to, different aspects of the *status quo*.

SOME CONCLUSIONS

It has been suggested in this chapter that sociologists and others interested in the academic study of education may have much to learn by looking at organizational forms other than compulsory schooling. Women's adult education takes place in a variety of settings, transmits several different types of knowledge and a variety of skills and offers different degrees of consent, resistance and adaptation to both class and gender divisions. Although the four groups which have been examined have many similarities, they also display differences in social composition, organizational characteristics and modes of teaching and learning as well as in their curriculum. Not all of them are radical in intention, despite the undoubted popular character of their continued existence. The analysis here also suggests that the demand for single-sex forms of education for women may run into many difficulties and achieve less in terms of overcoming women's inequality than has been suggested by some writers (see Deem 1984, Spender and Sarah 1980 and Shaw 1980). In this connection there is a need to explore in more detail the internal workings of a larger variety of all-female institutions and groups. Education and schooling, as Arnot (1981) points out when discussing the political economy perspective, cannot be analysed in isolation from other social institutions. It is only by examining an assortment of educational contexts that we can hope to fully understand both what women bring to education and what they have the potential to gain from it.

NOTE

1 For a discussion of how men often dominate discussion in mixed-sex groups, see D. Spender (1981).

REFERENCES

Arnot, M. (1981) 'Culture and political economy: dual perspectives in the sociology of women's education', *Educational Analysis* 3 (1).
Bernstein, B. (1975) 'On the classification and framing of educational knowledge', in *Class Codes and Control* (vol. 3, 1st edn), London: Routledge & Kegan Paul.
Centre for Contemporary Cultural Studies (CCCS) (1981) *Unpopular Education*, London: Hutchinson.
Chamberlain, M. (1975) *Fenwomen*, London: Virago/Quartet Books.
Dale, K. (1981) 'From expectations to outcomes in education systems', *Interchange* 2 (2–3).
Deem, R. (1982) 'Women, leisure and inequality', *Journal of Leisure Studies* 1 (1).
—— (ed.) (1984) *Co-education Reconsidered*, Milton Keynes: Open University Press.
—— (1986) *All Work and No Play: The Sociology of Women and Leisure*, Milton Keynes: Open University Press.
—— (1990) 'Women and leisure: a sociological investigation', Unpublished Ph.D thesis, The Open University.
Delamont, S. (1980) *The Sociology of Women*, London: Allen & Unwin.
DES Committee of Enquiry (1973) *Adult Education: A Plan for Development*, London: HMSO.
Goodenough, S. (1977) *Jam and Jerusalem: A Pictorial History of the Women's Institute*, London: Collins.
Gramsci, A. (1971) 'Notes on Italian history', in *Selections from Prison Notebooks* (trans. by Q. Hoare and G. Nowell-Smith), London: Lawrence & Wishart.
Green, E., Hebron, S. and Woodward, D. (1990), *Women's Leisure: What Leisure?*, London: Macmillan.
Gregory, S. (1982) 'Women among others – another view', *Journal of Leisure Studies* 1 (1).
Johnson, R. (1981a) 'Socialism and popular education', *Socialism and Education* 8 (1).
—— (1981b) 'Education and popular politics', *Society, Education and the State*, Milton Keynes: Open University (Unit 1, Course E353).
Parry, N. and Johnson, D. (1974) 'Sexual divisions in life style and leisure',

Unpublished paper given to the British Sociological Association Conference, University of Aberdeen.

Roberts, K. (1978) *Contemporary Society and the Growth of Leisure* Harlow: Longman.

Sargant, N. (1991) *Learning and Leisure*, Leicester: NIACE.

Shaw, J. (1980) 'Education and the individual: schooling for girls, or mixed schooling – a mixed blessing', in R. Deem (ed.), *Schooling for Women's Work*, London: Routledge & Kegan Paul.

Spender, D. (1981) *Man-Made Lanugage*, London: Routledge & Kegan Paul.

—— and Sarah, E. (1980) *Learning to Lose*, London: The Women's Press.

Stacey, M. (1960) *Tradition and Change*, Oxford: Oxford University Press.

—— et al. (1975) *Power, Persistence and Change*, London: Routledge & Kegan Paul.

—— and Price, M. (1981) *Women, Power and Politics*, London: Tavistock.

Stanley, L. (1980) 'The problem of women and leisure: an ideological construction and a radical feminist alternative', *Leisure in the 80s Forum*, Capital Radio, 26–8 September.

Williams, R. (1981) *Culture*, London: Fontana.

Willis, P. (1977) *Learning to Labour*, Aldershot: Saxon House/Gower.

Chapter 16

'Drinking from one pot'
Yemeni unity, at home and overseas

Chris Searle and Abdulgalil Shaif

Source: This is an edited version of an article in *Race and Class*, vol. 32, no. 4, 1991.

Outside of expatriate Yemeni communities, very little is known in Europe or North America about Yemen and its people.

The unification in May 1990 of the two separate Yemeni states, the Yemen Arab Republic in the north and the People's Democratic Republic of the Yemen in the south, created little interest in the establishment press of the West. And yet, this unity was achieved in an era of intense fragmentation of nations and secessionism in many parts of the world, including countries very close to the Yemen. It was also managed voluntarily, without war or rancour, and with each separate state willingly offering up its individual sovereignty.

In this interview, given in July 1990, Abdulgalil Shaif gives a perspective from the heart of the emigrant community on Yemen's anti-imperialist history and its new unity.

Sheffield has a population of 2,000 Yemenis, most of whom are the families of now redundant steelworkers, who arrived in the city during the 1950s and 1960s, and who are organized through two separate community associations that reflected their origins in the two formerly separated Yemens. The unification has been greeted with great joy by Yemenis abroad, and is seen as a powerful stimulus for their own community development in Britain and elsewhere.

Shaif's story is one of a small black community in the gut of a large British ex-industrial city, struggling for social justice in its new setting, as well as striving to maintain and revitalize its links with the homeland: the story of a people who have two homes and two struggles, and a story of two generations keeping faith with each other in the old/new land of post-imperial power.

Chris Searle: What were the main reasons for the movement of Yemenis to Britain, particularly Sheffield, in the 1950s?

Abdulgalil Shaif: The 1950s and 1960s were a period of industrial boom in Britain. As a result, many Yemenis, encouraged by the British, came over here to fill the labour shortage. They were looking for a better standard of living than that which British colonialism was giving them. This created a large influx of Yemenis to Britain at that time.

They left a Yemen that had become very backward in its social and economic conditions under British colonialism. For example, there were only one or two schools in the whole of Yemen to cater for Yemeni young people – and they were occupied by the sons of sheikhs and sultans whom the British were training to handle the colonial bureaucracy, to service their needs and the needs of international capitalism. People lived in very bad and ugly housing. In Aden, the suburbs and slums were overcrowded, as people were migrating into the city and the British naval base in order to work in the port. That was the only work that existed there. So employment was only available in one sector of the economy, working for the colonialists.

But most of the people who migrated to Britain were country-dwellers, from the hinterland outside Aden. [. . .] They also came from North Yemen. [. . .] In the city itself, people were quite satisfied to stay and work in the port and service sectors, as these were the areas where there was work and the colonial economy seemed to be prosperous. These tended to be people with minimum skills who could handle the bureaucracy. But the people who came to Britain generally had no knowledge of reading and writing. They were mostly farm labourers, as most of the Yemen was dominated by farming. These were subsistence farmers growing fruit, citrus and potatoes, living in very backward conditions. They were poor, often hiring themselves out to aristocratic landlords who would pay them as little as possible and expand their lands at the expense of the peasants at the same time. So this also explains why some of the poorest of the farmers migrated to Britain in the 1950s: they had so little land that they found it impossible to make any kind of living from it. And to avoid the constant struggle with the aristocracy – who had British military support – they decided to come and try life in Britain instead, as they were being encouraged by the British to come and fill the gaps in labour here.

They came to Sheffield. They also went to Cardiff, to Birmingham, to Brighouse and Scunthorpe and other parts of Britain, but in the 1950s Sheffield was seen as a boom industrial city. The jobs were here, in British Steel, Firth Brown's and all the other firms. There was the attraction then of finding five or six jobs in one day! That's how the Yemenis found it here. You could move around from one job to another in one or two days. This ease of finding jobs in Sheffield soon spread by word of mouth. People wrote home to their friends and relatives and told them to come.

CS: What kinds of conditions did the Yemenis find here?

AS: They had to take the worst jobs possible, those which had been vacated by British workers in the steel industry. They did the crane driving, they did the truck driving, the hammer stamping, the cleaning up – they did the most menial and dangerous jobs, working at close quarters to the noise and dust all the time. And all these jobs were done in twelve- and sixteen-hour shifts with the very minimum of pay – £10 or £12 a week, which was just enough to keep your family going, with no chance to save any money.

You see, when Yemeni workers came to this country, they came with a dream, a longing. The British and the landed aristocracy in Yemen told them that, by coming over here, they would be able to earn so much money that when they returned, they would be able to build their own castles in Yemen! Yet when they came here, they found that the reality of the situation was very different – it certainly wasn't like picking apples off a tree, as the people used to say. It was a case of having to work damned hard all hours in order to survive. [. . .]

If you want the most concrete evidence of the conditions of the work which they did in Sheffield, you only have to look at their health *now*. Industrial deafness is 90 per cent among the working-class Yemenis. They had to put up with an average noise level of 40 decibels every single working day.

My father suffers with this deafness, so does my uncle and many, many of their friends and relatives. Coupled with this, they also suffered from the consequences of all the dust – with asthma. Some 30 per cent of our community suffer from asthma and this can pass to the children, so it's very worrying. Then there's also skin diseases – dermatitis – also caused by the conditions in which they had to work. All this arose from that period of work. And if you come to the Yemeni Advice Centre, you'll see as people come in – one's lost a leg, one's lost an arm, another's lost a finger – all these problems. There's hardly one Yemeni ex-steelworker who hasn't had an accident at work. [. . .]

CS: What was the relationship of the Yemenis who migrated here to the struggle against imperialism in the Yemen? Did they contribute to it, or did they bypass it by coming to Britain?

AS: They were certainly out of the country during the time of the armed struggle between 1962 and 1967. Yet the struggle was going on well before that, in a different form and context. In the 1950s, there were the *intifadas* in the Hadramout area and elsewhere against the landed aristocracy, waged by the peasants. Some of our people here were certainly involved in these rebellions against those who ruled on behalf of British colonialism, so they also took part in the overall struggle to change the structure and remove the aristocracy. These *intifadas* were crushed by the planes, helicopters and tanks of British imperialism, in a very similar way to how the Israelis tried to crush the Palestinians. They were defeated largely because they lacked leadership. These were spontaneous revolts with no real goal or strategy.

People didn't really know where they wanted to go beyond getting rid of the local sheikh or sultan. There was no party that could interpret the process it was taking on. The 1962–7 struggle was completely different. It had the support of the revolution in the north of the Yemen, and it also had the support of the working class in and around Aden, as well as the peasantry and the intellectuals. It was also inspired by the nationialism of Egypt and the victory of Suez.

There is no doubt that most of the Yemenis here would have joined in that 1962–7 struggle, had they stayed in Yemen. They would have been part and parcel of the revolution. Even so, they made their contribution from here in the form of their solidarity. It was immense. Money was sent over to buy military equipment, to buy ambulances, to pay for propaganda. The Yemeni Workers' Union was formed in Britain, not so much to maintain the culture or support the upbringing of young Yemenis in England but to bring solidarity to the revolution in Yemen, help to organize these remittances and get the money across. Before that, people sometimes didn't send their money back because they earned so little and after their expenses here they had so little left. [...]

The hearts of the people here were with the revolution. They couldn't be involved actively, but they supported it economically and through their solidarity and propaganda. [...] They wanted the British out. Even though they lived in Britain, they wanted the Yemen to be free and independent. And remember, at this time, there was a lot of nationalism and racism here in Britain, and for Yemenis here to take that stand against British imperialism took a lot of courage and commitment.

Our people here were not solidly organized at that time as a community, even though they always saw themselves as one Yemeni people. The first community organization of the Yemenis wasn't established in Sheffield until 1971. Remember that, in September 1962, there was the revolution in the north that ended the monarchy and threw out the Imamic regime. Then, in October 1963, the armed revolution, led by the National Liberation Front, began in the Radfan mountains in the south. This eventually expelled the British in 1967. [...] The two revolutions cannot be divorced from each other. Yemenis believed that, and from here they looked at these events with joy. 'We're going to have unity soon!', they thought, because the principal aim of both these revolutions was to unify Yemen, once independence was secured and the revolutions had succeeded. That has always been the Yemenis' dream, one united Yemen. [. . .] Unfortunately, it didn't turn out that way, as the revolutions took two different paths.

CS: How did the Yemenis in Britain organize to improve their lives?

AS: There were two different forms of struggle for Yemenis in Sheffield, and in the UK as a whole. The first period was from 1955 until 1971, which lacked any form of political organization or leadership. It involved experiencing racism at work, exploitation at work, bad housing, experiencing all aspects of poverty and lack of finance, and experiencing the pain of divided families. This was the period of *experience* rather than struggle, of getting to know and understand the oppression of being black and working class in Britain. They had experienced oppression under the aristocracy in Yemen, now they began to know a different oppression here. It was not so bad, but they knew they were seen as foreigners, as immigrants, and if they started fighting and struggling and shouting straight away, they thought they would be sent back. There was always that fear. Remember, many had received no formal education. They were illiterate and didn't know their rights here in Britain. They didn't know how this country worked. They didn't know the history of working-class struggles here and what they had achieved. They didn't know about trade unions – they had come from a peasant background, remember – and they didn't know about the National Health Service.

But, by 1971, Yemenis here had become a lot more confident. They had seen one and a half million people expel the British and make the revolution succeed in the south of their country. They had seen the people of the north kick out the Imamic regime which had been ruling for hundreds of years, and which had the support of Saudi Arabia and the imperialist powers. So now they felt able to carry the struggle forward here to improve their living conditions and that of the other black and working-class people in Sheffield. [. . .]

The first thing the Yemenis here wanted to do when they organized themselves in 1971 was to support the revolution and learn all about it. They could only learn in Arabic. So the first information [. . .] that they gained in working-class consciousness and organization was not about the struggle here in Britain. It was about how the Yemenis organized the revolution back home. That was what taught them how to organize themselves as working-class people first of all, and then they applied that to their life and experience here in Sheffield. But they didn't learn about working-class struggle and development in Britain. They were divorced from that, and that was a part of the racism they faced. If local working-class organizations had helped to give them an education about organization, about taking power, it would have integrated them into the movement and they would have developed with that. But it didn't happen that way. The British trade unions and working-class organizations didn't bother reaching them, so they took their inspiration from their own struggles in the homeland.

CS: What was the impact of the decline of the steel industry in Sheffield on the Yemeni community here?

AS: In 1978–9, we experienced the first real spate of redundancies in the steel industry. The Yemenis were hit harder by these than any other community in Sheffield, including the black communities. It was a situation of 70–80 per cent unemployment suddenly striking an entire working community. There was terrible demoralization and people were unsure and unclear about what the future held for them. They found themselves suddenly unable financially to help their families back home, and had no prospect of any alternative employment here. They received £2,000–£3,000 redundancy payments – if they were lucky, £5,000 – and it seemed to them that their working lives were over. They either sent this money back home to support their families, or just put it in a bank for when they needed to go to the Yemen or bring someone from their family over here. The uncertainty and insecurity that resulted from all this created the need to organize the community in a way that hadn't happened before. It was an *unemployed* community now, and we had to learn to fight for our rights from the city council, from the Department of Health and Social Security, from central government and all the other institutions, like trade unions and insurance companies. So here were two phases: one, the experience of large-scale unemployment within the heart of the community, and two, the different kind of struggle that had to be launched in order to organize against that.

Circumstances were grim. Unemployment raised issues which weren't there before, issues of loneliness, isolation and depression. People found themselves walking the streets, sitting in cafés, playing cards, unable to retrain because of lack of opportunities, language difficulties and illiteracy – which has always been one of the biggest problems that the community has faced. Of course, if there had been this retraining or the existence of literacy classes, it would have helped in the creation of alternatives, or of a new direction for the community, but there was nothing for our people. For the Yemenis there were no opportunities, no encouragement or understanding for a new and changed future to suit their needs. So the Yemeni community organizations, even as they exist now, were born out of those very real and concrete problems.

The other factor in causing us to begin seriously to organize ourselves was racism. We were beginning to see how corrosive and violent this was, not only in an institutional sense, in the ways in which we were denied jobs through it – so much so that some of our unemployed had to anglicize their names on application forms to stand any chance of getting work – but in the number of racist attacks we faced. This is what really made us come together, and we are now seeing them on the increase again, as if we are reliving them some twenty years later.

In May 1989, an elderly Yemeni, Musa Mohammed, was on a bus with a friend, coming from the Attercliffe mosque, when two youths set upon him, abusing him and ripping off his prayer hat and throwing it out of the window. They beat him and kicked him badly on his face, legs and chest, and two hours later he was dead, having had a heart attack. Six hundred of us came out on the streets after that, and we organized a lot of publicity, and meetings with the leader of the city council and chief constable of South Yorkshire. The police denied it was a racist attack, calling the attackers 'thugs' but not racists. Then there was the attack on the Metro Café in Firth Park. Five masked white youths burst in, while Yemenis were playing cards and drinking coffee. They wore leather clothes and motor-bike helmets, and, screaming 'black bastards', they smashed everything with hammers, chains and knives. I was there. Nobody could move, they were that stunned. So this pattern of violence hasn't abated since those early days of the community organizations, and has always made us much tighter as a community, much more disciplined and vigilant.

It was largely a new generation of Yemenis who built these new structures in the community. They hadn't experienced work in the steel industry like their fathers had done, but they had experienced a state education. They began to identify the problems, because they lived with them within their families. They began to exchange and discuss analyses, insights and strategies, they talked to their mothers, fathers and older people in the community, and together they began to formulate a response to its genuine and most pressing needs. It was this leadership – young, conscious and Sheffield-bred – that developed new links between the generations and infrastructures across the community, that developed these new and vital organizations to fight for this new community of the unemployed. It wasn't the fathers, it was the sons and daughters who began to mobilize the resistance that was necessary. They refused to be obedient, they set out to challenge the system. They weren't like their fathers in this respect. Their parents, despite being hard, working-class people, *had* been obedient, had been reluctant to say no and fight back. They felt that their lives and those of their families would be in danger if they made that challenge. So they didn't challenge the council, the employers, the unions or the government. Their children felt none of these constraints. This was the difference between our two generations. The young Yemenis looked at all these problems and said, on behalf of the entire community: 'We can't continue like this. Our circumstances are bad, they require us to struggle. We need to use the time and energy we have now to organize ourselves as working-class people who are unemployed and who need a better way of life.' It was the result of the conversations we had with our parents about such themes that caused us to build the community organizations that we still have now.

CS: How much of the motivation of this generation of young Yemenis was sparked off by the realization that the school system had failed them? How have you tackled the questions of language and education?

AS: The young Yemenis were born into black working-class families. They could have easily followed in the same footsteps as their parents. In their lives at school they experienced racism, found failure and received a standard of education that was unacceptable to both themselves and their parents. There wasn't encouragement or opportunity. We can't look back and say that the school system served us well. For example, I was advised by my head teacher and other teachers to go on the Youth Training Scheme. I was adamant. I wanted to take A-levels. But they told me my CSEs weren't good enough. It was a chronic system of low expectations for black and working-class children. But I *knew* that, with encouragement and opportunity, I could do well. Even though I knew that when they looked at me, they could only see failure, without seeing or understanding my potential. That was typical, and it is still happening. I knew that if I went on YTS I would end up with the same kind of life and prospects as my father, and I also knew that he didn't come all the way from Yemen to Sheffield for that to happen.[1]

This made our generation want to put a lot of our life and commitment into building up the community organizations. We knew that in the Yemen there was a revolution and people there who would look after us. That link was so important to us. We knew those same comrades would always struggle and persevere to maintain and preserve it, and continue to develop it. But for us, we felt we had almost a revolution to get on with here, for our community. [...] Let's support what is happening back home, but let us also concentrate our minds and energies on what is happening to Yemeni people in England. We understood we couldn't have a revolution here in the same way as back home, but we could ensure that the standard of life for our community improved, being fully realistic and taking account of the circumstances of the system of this country and the city where we lived. We knew that white working-class people wouldn't carry the struggle for us as Yemeni people. We knew that our struggle had to be carried through by ourselves.

During the early 1970s, we had organized, in an *ad hoc* manner, literacy classes in Arabic, run by volunteers. Otherwise, there was very little educational activity. The first issue we identified in the late 1970s was the need to continue, strengthen and develop this literacy work within the community. This was taken very seriously, and was organized without any help or funding from the local education authority. The thinking was that if people learned Arabic, they would be able to read newspapers from back home, write letters and keep in close contact with events and families in the Yemen. They would be able to pass on the Arabic language to their children – and this was seen as essential. It was always feared that our children would grow up without their language – and, therefore, without their culture and identity. Others saw it for different reasons. For example, my father urged me to learn Arabic so that I could explain to him in Arabic what was happening in Britain and how to work the British system of life. He took me with him to the DHSS, he took me with him to the tax office, even to the firm to get his wages – he took me with him, because he thought that someone would say something to him that he wouldn't understand. So we were there as interpreters, as translators, as a support mechanism to our parents. The parents felt proud and secure, having a bilingual child with them.

So the first community language schools developed in the late 1970s. They developed in the context of uninterest and discouragement from the local school system. It ignored our needs. I went to several schools to ask for support and to use their resources to open a community language class, and they said, 'No, if you want to open a class somewhere, go ahead, it's up to you. But we're not taking any notice of this.' I don't know whether it was the schools seeing these classes as competing with them, or whether they frowned on them because they were classes being run and provided by 'unprofessional' people. But, whatever the reasons, the assumptions were racist, that we couldn't run these classes properly, that they were unnecessary, or that these Yemenis are running their own classes today, tomorrow they might open a factory next door! Those sort of stereotypes flourished. The schools didn't see us as a part of the community that is enriching their school. But we saw it that way – that if the children learnt their own community's language, they would bring that bilingualism as a benefit into the mainstream of school life and culture. They would develop much more quickly and deeply at school, and then be able to transmit their concepts and ideas in a much fuller way, thus improving and broadening what was going on at school.

I came through a community language school, and the ideas and skills it sparked in me I passed on to my younger brother and sisters in Arabic, to my cousins in Arabic, to my parents in Arabic, and the whole community has learned from them. If I had been educated in English only, I could never have transferred these things in this way, and they would have been isolated within me and the community would not have benefited. You see, we think education is about sharing, co-operating, learning from each other, passing on insights and exchanging thoughts, developing our community – we need our languages if we are going to do that.

Our first language school started in a hut in a park in Crookes, that we shared with the Caribbean community. It was the first example of co-operation between our two communities. It would take about forty to fifty children. It was far too small and the children would spill out into the park, and we had to teach them there. It was our first feeling of the struggle shared by both communities – they were speaking in Creole and we were learning Arabic. Unfortunately, this co-operation didn't develop – I wish it had done – but these are the kind of shared experiences which we need to discuss and learn from in the future.

Then, in 1985, the Yemeni Community Association began. There had been a change in receptivity and sensitivity within the Sheffield city council. They had started listening to us at last, and this was a very important development as it resulted in some funding for, and the renovation of, this building that we are sitting in now. It was also an important development for the white community, as they recognized us as a community, with specific needs and features. Before that it was as if they had never seen us, we were invisible to them. They didn't realize that Yemenis living here saw Sheffield as their home. We may have had a family and a home in Yemen, but we loved Sheffield too, it was our home also. I, like all Yemenis here, am proud to know this as my home. When I am at home in Yemen, I think of my home in Sheffield. It may be two homes, but so what? We're proud of that. If I can improve links between my home in Yemen and my home in Sheffield, I would love to. If I could help local white people to go to Yemen, I'd love to, that's the beauty of it. I support anything that benefits ordinary people in this country, as well as in Yemen – whether it's the development of their community, their education, housing, health and all other opportunities. This is why the 'Cricket Test'[2] idea of only supporting one particular people or group that Norman Tebbit came out with would be unbelievable for me and all Yemenis. When I'm in Yemen, I miss Sheffield, I want to come back to Sheffield so much. Yet when I'm here, I long for returning to Yemen, particularly now as it is united at last.

Then two years ago we developed our literacy campaign. We had studied, and been inspired by, the literacy campaign in the south of Yemen in the years following independence, which was very successful. Our campaign here in Sheffield came about through a collaborative approach, from both inside the community and sincere people inside the education system. It was a combined struggle by the older people who wanted literacy, the younger people who wanted further education and careers, and workers and administrators in education who were prepared to fight for resources for black communities.

These three elements were linked and organized together. Already, we have had sixty to seventy people involved, and out of these, 20–30 per cent have gone on to courses in further education, and others to various employment schemes. It has also radicalized a community that has always been culturally bound – especially its women. [. . .] We always had cultural issues that sometimes held us back and needed to be tackled, and the literacy campaign came at the right time to help us tackle them. It brought our young women to the forefront of the community. The school system had failed our young women too. It had never reached out to them or their parents, and built links with the communities and families to try to understand them or encourage them, to identify the ways in which they were culturally restricted, or to give advice or the career development that could push their daughters towards new paths in life. My younger sister wanted to be a doctor, but if I had not been around to help and encourage her, she would never have moved towards that aspiration. The school would not have done it. But I am certain that she *will* be a doctor, she has all the attributes, the intelligence, the determination and the patience.

Now the literacy campaign has brought the parents of the young people right into the heart of education. They are being educated by their own sons and daughters. The family and the community have become *one* in this campaign, the youngers and the elders. And the parents have now seen that the young people have the ability to teach, and the young people have recognized this in themselves. So, in a few years time, they can become qualified and come into the state schools as teachers, or take up other professional careers, like doctors and lawyers, and eventually give service back to the community. All these possibilities are visible to them now. And what has been most radical is that the young women involved in the campaign as literacy assistants have been the most dynamic and successful elements. This has helped to remove the stereotype of passivity attached to our women from both within and outside the community.

CS: What about the successful struggle the community has waged around compensation for those whose health was damaged through their work in the steel industry?

AS: As we saw, the health problem within our community was directly related to the work problem, the exploitation of our people and the terrible conditions in the steel firms where they worked. I remember speaking to my father one day and he said to me, 'Are you speaking, or are your lips just moving without speaking?' 'I'm speaking to you,' I said. 'Can't you hear me?' 'No,' he said. So I took it seriously and went to the doctor with him. He said, 'You've lost a lot of your hearing, you'll have to go and see a specialist.' This was typical of hundreds of Yemeni workers in the deafening noise of the steel industry and those who worked in very close proximity to it. Why weren't they provided with muffs, with ear protection?

It wasn't until 1978–9, when the majority of Yemenis were being made redundant, that the employers started providing this. By this time, it was too late for most of our fathers. They had worked for thirty years without any protection at all. I read in the *Guardian* about the problem that white workers in similar jobs were having. So I thought, 'Well, what about the Yemenis?' People were coming to see me at our advice centre about problems with the DHSS, etc., and I suddenly thought to myself, 'Why am I talking so loud to these people?' They were coming right close, putting their ears next to me and asking me to repeat everything I said. So I phoned the occupational health project and they said, 'Well, let's test ten people.' We did, and they were all deaf. So we did a lot more tests, week after week. Then we realized that almost the whole community of ex-steel workers were deaf. So we contacted lawyers and said, 'Can we get our fathers and uncles compensation for this?' They said, of course we could. So we made eventually over a million pounds for people within the community who had suffered industrial deafness. Most of this money has been sent to families back home, to buy tractors for their farms, or to buy themselves houses here. It was seen within the community as a real victory, and a reward for struggling and not giving in.

But it showed another injustice. People who made their compensation claims from insurance companies could get it, but those who claimed through occupational pensions from the DHSS could not get it. There was a time limitation – they had to make their claim within five years of being made redundant. By 1986, when we waged this compensation campaign, that time had passed for most of our ex-workers. The trade unions they belonged to – the Transport and General Workers' Union was the main one – not one of them had informed them about this limitation, so millions of pounds of potential compensation was lost. Over 700 claims were turned down by the DHSS. This was the real evidence of the neglect of the Yemeni workers by trade unions, by other workers and by progressive white organizations generally. It was also further proof of why we had to build and struggle through our own organizations rooted in our own community life.

CS: How did you work to overcome the divisions in the community here in Sheffield, that had been caused by the fact that there were two separate Yemens, with differing state ideologies?

AS: Because the revolution in the south of the Yemen took a different course to that of the north, similar dialectics were set in motion within the Yemeni communities of Britain. The main principle of both revolutions was Yemeni unity, so even though we found ourselves in two different community organizations, we were, in fact, struggling for the same things. Many of us were ashamed to say that we were either from the 'North' or the 'South'. We found that very difficult to come to terms with; we always saw ourselves and our identity as simply Yemeni. We came from the same country with the same culture and language, the same religion, family structure and attitudes. And in Britain, too, we faced the same struggle – for better housing, or for better education for our children, to develop the language schools and literacy. So, although we organized separately, there was always this link, this collaborative approach, this exchange of information and strategy. It was the political agenda, hidden at the back of our heads, that was different, with some of us taking a socialist path of development, some of us taking a more Islamic and traditional approach. This wasn't only in Sheffield, this happened every-where else in Britain where there were Yemenis – two different organiza-tions, two different management committees.

But as soon as the unity talks and negotiations started happening in earnest in Yemen, then they happened in our communities too. In Sheffield we said, 'For God's sake, this revolution came in order to avoid these divisions. Let's come to our senses, why should we be divided when so many of our people have sacrificed their lives for unity?' In all the cam-paigns we worked together – in education, welfare, housing, in the com-pensation issue – in every concrete struggle we organized together, so we thought, why on earth should we be divided in this way? It didn't make sense. So as soon as the ideological issue was sorted out in Yemen through the unity talks, it was also sorted out here. As soon as it was decided that having two countries in one single land wasn't a good idea, then we moved to ensure that we wouldn't have two separate Yemeni communities in one city here. So we had our unity talks too. We now have one overall steering committee that guides our work, even though we have still retained the infrastructures of our original organizations, as it is these that continue to mobilize our people for all the community activities. But, as Salim Kasheem, the chairman of the Yemeni IG Union, the other community organization, declared at our joint celebration of Yemen's unity last month, we're drinking from the same pot now! [. . .]

CS: What is your hope now for the future, following the establishment of a unified Yemen?

AS: The new country faces a huge challenge. All the political groupings and social and economic forces that support unity are exercising their democratic right to enter the political arena. That democratic opportunity needs to be consolidated and developed. Of course, the same unity and growth in democracy is also happening in miniature in our community here in Sheffield, as in other Yemeni communities in Britain. It is, of course, much easier for us, because, on most things, we have always been united and now our political differences have gone. We shall never return to those old, artificial and nonsensical divisions again – neither here nor in the Yemen. We have always said that the progressive laws and develop-ments that have taken place in the Yemen, both in the north and south, will be consolidated and not lost. These are the fruits of the revolution and the population wants them preserved.

But, having said that, we also understand the truth that there are reac-tionary forces in the Yemen which will try to cause obstacles to progress and try to turn back these reforms – and there are, of course, also powerful and hostile external forces in the Arab world and elsewhere who don't like the idea of a united Yemen, and who know we have rich reserves of oil and have their designs on it. So, strategically, there are enemies of the revolution and our unity who work both politically and economically, and who will not accept the truth that there are certain resources that will need to be controlled by the state, that we're not a capitalized, industrial-ized country where the market can play a role. We're still a backward country economically, with limited technology, and the state has to ensure that the economy operates for the benefit of all our people, not for this or that group of rich men. If we allow the fruits of our economy to dictate the path of our development, we will live as the slaves, and not the controllers, of our material wealth.

It's a common fact in the Arab world that the remittances of Yemeni emigrants like us in Sheffield form over 50 per cent of the budget. It's one of the dynamos of the economy, and one of the strongest links which binds us back to the Yemen. There's a whole ministry of state, a very important ministry, devoted to issues related to emigrants. [...] That's how much importance is given to Yemeni communities outside Yemen – enormous time and energy is devoted to this work.

Emotionally, this unity for us is a dream come true. It's been a dream for centuries. No Yemeni will make a speech without mentioning or celebrating the nation's unity. Yemenis as far apart as Tanzania and Indonesia – where there are substantial numbers of our people – always yearned for this. It's made us whole again as a people. We can now feel more confident wherever we live – in Sheffield, too, of course – to struggle for better things for our people. And for others too. We are now a united people on the world stage. We understand and struggle with other divided peoples. We understand and support the Palestinians in their efforts to win back their land from the Zionists, like we are beside the South African people in their struggle against the apartheid system. Yet we also stand side by side with other black and working-class people in Britain and, with our nation *one* again, we feel deeply inside ourselves that our contribution will be stronger, more determined, and with greater purpose and meaning.

Since this interview was conducted, the Yemeni community in Sheffield has experienced turbulent times. During the run-up to the Gulf War the community became the target of increased anti-Arab racism. Their community centre was daubed with racist slogans and individual Yemenis were frequently insulted and received threatening telephone calls. A few days after the outbreak of war in January 1991, the minibus bringing Yemeni children to their evening Arabic language school was attacked and stoned.

In Yemen too, the war has caused dire problems. Over one million Yemeni migrant workers in Saudi Arabia were expelled and returned to Yemen as a vindictive measure against the Yemen government's position of neutrality in the war. The sudden arrival of these large numbers of unemployed workers and the loss of substantial remittances to the national economy have created serious setbacks for the new government of national unity.

NOTES

1 Abdulgalil Shaif was awarded a Ph.D. from Sheffield University in 1990.
2 In April 1990, Tebbit, then Tory Party chairman, suggested that loyalty to Britain was indicated by 'which side' in cricket Asians would 'cheer for'.

Chapter 17

Adult education, community development and older people

Christopher Pilley

Source: This is an edited extract of the report by the author, London, Cassell, 1990.

[. . .] Over the last twenty years or so, there have been spectacular changes in the situation of Europe's older people, changes which are not only profound, but which are likely to be long-lasting. The most pronounced change is the ageing of Europe. The trend [. . .] is common to all the industrial countries, will be extremely rapid and will bring long-term consequences. In OECD countries, the proportion of over-65s will grow by over 50 per cent – from 11.5 per cent to nearly 18 per cent between 1980 and 2025. In the EEC countries, the number of over-65s will grow from 43 million in 1985 to 51 million in 2000.

Though the trend is common throughout all industrial countries, there are differences between countries within Europe. Unless fertility recovers, the proportion of over-65s in what was West Germany will rise from 14.5 per cent of the population in 1985 to no less than 23 per cent by 2025. In Spain, Portugal and Ireland, on the other hand, the effect is less pronounced. In all countries, older people are living longer and the percentage of the oldest groups – the over-75s and over-85s – will increase most rapidly. Within these oldest groups, the proportion of widowed women increases rapidly with age.

[. . .] Not only are people in Western Europe living longer, but the working population is also ageing. Faced with a declining number of young people under 20, and a very large population between 20 and 59, we can expect a big increase in the proportion of over-60s after the year 2000.

This increase in the proportion of 20- to 59-year-olds, together with the economic crises of the 1970s and 1980s, has resulted in major policy changes concerning both the retirement age, which has been reduced in many countries, and measures to encourage older workers to leave the labour force prematurely. These changes have, in many cases, profoundly affected both economic and social support ratios. The 'dependency ratio' – the ratio of the economically active to the rest of the population – is worsening in many countries. Social support ratios – the ratio of those able to provide direct personal support in the family and household to other people – will also worsen in the face of these same demographic changes and of changes in household structures.

At the same time, the prospects for the future have a more hopeful side. Tomorrow's 'young old' are likely to have very different attitudes from the 50- and 60-year-olds of twenty years ago. They are a richer, better-educated generation who grew up in a very different world from their parents. They are the new Europeans who grew up after the Second World War, post-war 'baby boomers' who were young in the 1960s. Furthermore, there are signs that the decline in the number of young people entering the labour market in the 1990s, particularly in northern Europe, will lead to older people's potential being given greater recognition and the importance of their remaining active and making a fuller contribution to Europe's prosperity being given a greater emphasis as a result. [...]

At a more personal level, the increase in the number of older people, and the recent reduction of employment opportunities available to them, has meant that more and more active pensioners, and many other people below pensionable age who in the past might have held a job for a further twenty years or so, have had to find a new role and purpose for their lives. The significance of the ending of working life has become more varied; once it was generally thought of as a bonus – for those who lived long enough to achieve it – a chance to put one's feet up. Now, for some, it has become the longest, most stable, period of their lives, lasting as long as forty years or more. The characteristics and needs of older people have also become more varied. The situation of the active, prematurely retired person with substantial financial resources differs greatly from the growing number of very old people – mostly women, many of them widows – living alone and in poverty.

As employment takes up a smaller part of life, however, the danger increases of [...] 'a slide into purposelessness'. Yet the availability of this great pool of people, with the skills and experience of a lifetime, is also an enormous opportunity. The increased proportion of older people, particularly the increasing numbers of more active, generally younger, people with time on their hands, represents an important community resource, which only needs to be drawn out for their own benefit, for the benefit of their peers, and for the benefit of the rest of the community.

How can this be done? The case studies which follow are intended to give a few pointers. They focus generally on younger, more active older people who are not in paid jobs, and on activities in which they are doers and initiators, rather than passive consumers. The case studies seek to show how the resources of adult education, together with the range of other agencies, can help older people become agents for change rather than victims of it, and thus improve their situation, that of other older people and that of the rest of the community. [. . .]

One major problem experienced by many older people is their marginalization, not only from paid labour, but also from household labour and voluntary work. Besides the feeling of disappointment that many people experience as a result, it also means that on retirement, often in their early 50s, knowledge and experience accumulated over the years is not made available to others, but is simply wasted. [. . .]

GILDE PROJECTS – THE NETHERLANDS

The Gilde projects go against the trend which sees voluntary work as the province of young people, by providing an opportunity for older people to gain a role again in society. They do this by acting as a mediator between offers by older people to make their skills and advice available and the demand for this from the population at large. They provide the opportunity for older people to act as a resource, using the skills and experience they have accumulated during a lifetime of work, and to make these available to a wider community. It has been done by rediscovering the old 'guilds' (*gilde* in Dutch), the older master craftsmen held in high esteem throughout history in many European countries.

The oldest Gilde project, in Amsterdam, was set up in 1984 and is now matched by other projects in nearly forty centres throughout the country. Although, when it was first set up, both the numbers of the elderly willing to pass on their knowledge and experience and the needs of potential users of their services were unknown factors, it became clear early on that many older people wanted to pass on their knowledge and experience and that there was a great interest in skills they had.

The Gilde acts as a mediator between older people offering skills and those needing them. Offers are published in a Gilde guide, which is published four times a year as an insert in a free weekly newspaper in Amsterdam. This reaches some 750,000 people in the city, as well as welfare centres and other agencies. The guide describes the aim of the project, as well as giving details of current offers – whether they be welding, plumbing, chess, language conversation or photography. The older people offering their skills are not supposed to compete with employed labour but to show people how to do jobs themselves and how to improve their own skills. They are mostly between the ages of 60 and 70, and while most are not in any form of employment there are a few who still do some part-time paid work. They meet their clients generally in their own homes, or those of their clients. People using the older people's services only pay the expenses involved. The Amsterdam Gilde is assisted by Amsterdam City Council and is unusual among the projects in that it is run by a professional who has a background in pre-retirement education.

The project has developed steadily and the numbers of offers in the Amsterdam Gilde Guides grew from fifty in the first edition (January 1985) to 138 in the fifth (October 1986). The project now has some 180 offers and has had over 4,000 responses.

The Amsterdam project was soon inundated with requests for information and assistance to set up similar projects in other areas. Consequently, the Study and Information Centre for Policy on Ageing (NFB) applied successfully for European Community money, under the Second Programme to Combat Poverty, which has made it possible, since 1985, to employ two consultants. [. . .]

The project consultants for NFB were initially concerned with monitoring the Amsterdam Gilde and with disseminating information and lessons learnt to promote and support the model in other parts of the country. Efforts were concentrated in areas of high unemployment.

Lessons learnt from the projects were disseminated through a Gilde newsletter [. . .] covering such subjects as preparing the ground, encouraging regional co-operation, involving older people in the initiative, funding, insurance, research reports on the Amsterdam Gilde and details of local activities. In addition, national and regional meetings of the Gilde projects have also been organized. Five Gilde in areas with different characteristics were also selected as pilot projects for particular study.

By closely observing these projects over a period of time, the consultants were able to get a more detailed picture of the factors influencing the success of Gilde projects. It is clear that setting up a Gilde project generally requires a lot of time and energy – often a year or more. The thirty-seven existing Gildes differ greatly in character and size, ranging from under ten members to over 150. The number of 'matches' in a year can vary from under fifty for the smaller projects to hundreds in the Gilde projects of the large cities. While these differences are partly due to the size of the cities and the percentage of elderly people living in them, many other factors must be considered and in some smaller towns and cities (35,000–40,000 inhabitants) some of the projects have a surprisingly large number of participants. Besides a well-run publicity campaign, good information material and the frequent appearance of the Gilde guide in local free magazines, active recruitment by the elderly themselves and the development and use of social networks in the smaller areas also seem to be important factors. Finance for projects also differs greatly; while one may operate with only a few hundred guilders, another may have many thousand guilders at its disposal.

Costs are obviously greater when a project has independent accommodation than when it shares accommodation with another organization. The costs of publicity also differ. Some projects succeed in getting a door-to-door newspaper published free of charge, while the others pay the commercial rate. [. . .]

Most older people offering skills in the Gilde guides come from the middle classes. Carel Tenhaeff of NFB believes that this reflects the essentially individualistic rather than community ethic of the projects, at least until recently. Lower-income groups often do not consider that they have any worthwhile skills, knowledge or experience to pass on, and certainly would not pass them to a total stranger. Furthermore, volunteering often requires money, and the attractions of Gilde, Carel Tenhaeff believes, would be increased for lower-income groups if they could earn some money by offering their skills. Not surprisingly, those on low incomes are more likely to be among the users of Gilde projects.

Several projects had problems in attracting volunteers willing to set up a new Gilde. In Almelo, for example, it took one full year to find eleven volunteers to get a project started, and all of them came from outside the area. A similar situation was found in Tilburg. Both these cities have an older population consisting of a large number of long-term unemployed people and a large number of unskilled labourers.

Given the right people, the use of older people themselves to promote Gildes has increased their credibility among potential participants. The Apeldoorn project was started up by a group of older people themselves who consciously avoided professional help and went to places used by other older people to recruit offers – making direct and personal approaches. Apeldoorn, however, has many highly qualified 'incomers' who moved to the city when they retired and found the Gilde to be a way to remain active and make new social contacts.

A Gilde in a rural area can encounter problems such as the small size of the population, the distances between villages, inadequate public transport, a high percentage of older people from the agricultural sector (which means they often continue to work for longer), and sometimes also a distrust for new and unfamiliar activities. [. . .]

Views about the importance of employing a professional vary. Large city projects, it is felt, generally need a professional to ensure the continuation of the project and to provide the required organizational and social skills. The vast majority of Gildes, however, are run on a voluntary basis. [. . .]

The Gilde Projects are now exploring new directions. The use of the Gilde model in 'old for young' projects to improve the situation of underprivileged youth has recently been developed. Senior volunteers have been involved in teaching practical skills to young people aged 12–18 in a school for children with learning difficulties near Amsterdam, and several young people have been helped to get real jobs – often through personal contacts of the Gilde volunteers in their former workplaces. Despite the successes, other schools have refused to pick up the idea, fearing volunteers as a threat to jobs. The approach is now being widened to include other groups, including young immigrants. Another new project is for Gilde members to act as unofficial tourist guides – using their special knowledge of their own localities to offer 'alternative tours' of their own neighbour-hoods.

There is also a move away from the rigorously individualistic ethic of the Gilde. This is reflected in the work with schoolchildren, and an initial resistance to the idea of the Gilde by Folk Universities and community centres is being broken down as Gilde volunteers are being used as leaders and *animateurs* of groups. As the projects face the end of the European Poverty Programme funding in 1989/90, attention is now being paid to making them self-sufficient. Closer links to other community agencies may well be one of the answers. [. . .]

VIBORG STUDY CIRCLE, DENMARK

Study circles for adults are an established feature of the Danish adult education scene and, under the Danish Leisure Time Education Act, groups can have the services of a group leader paid for out of public funds. The idea of study circles specifically for retired people, on the other hand, is of more recent origin, though there are now over fifty such circles up and down the country. [. . .]

The pioneer city in Denmark is Viborg, where the first study circle started over ten years ago. It is still led by the original leader, Ulla Brita Gregersen, and includes many of the circle's original participants. Four similar groups, of more recent origin, are now also led by her. The members are mostly farmers, craftsmen and housewives and few have had more than seven years' schooling.

Gregersen believes that study circles are particularly important for older people, providing companionship in the face of the inevitable losses associ-ated with growing old. She also feels that they play a valuable part in breaking down stereotypes – older people in the groups are seen to be doing things, rather than having things done for them. Participants confirm these points.

The groups have studied a wide and quite ambitious range of subjects over the years, including regional planning, nuclear power, pollution, body language and agriculture. Generally, however, all the activities have fol-lowed the same pattern. The first step is to find out about a topic. This is followed by practical action, and the third step is to disseminate the results of what they have found out and done by giving talks, making films or tape-slide presentations or producing reports and exhibitions.

One of the first topics ever tackled reflects this approach. Discussions about 'old schooldays' led to research into teaching methods then and now. The group contacted a number of schools to find out what today's children learned and how, and suggested that they could tell the children about schooldays long ago. They wrote a report about their findings, sending a copy to the school, and the pupils sent the group their essays. But they did not stop there; the group went on to visit a high school, an arts and crafts school, a training college for nursery school teachers and, in particular, nursing schools.

The nursing schools have started using the older people as 'resource people' within the regular curriculum, discussing with nursing students such topics as how it feels to grow old, the role of grandparents, views on death and dying and on sexuality in old age. [...]

The same three-stage approach has often involved foreign travel. Following a study circle on how Denmark was seen by foreigners, which resulted in a presentation of music and an exhibition, another study circle looked at the Second World War Normandy Landings of 1944. As part of a study visit to Bayeux – Viborg's twin town – to study the Landings, the group organized Danish afternoons for Bayeux's senior citizens. This involved a whole year's preparation – finding appropriate films on Denmark and getting donations of food and drink from Danish firms. The group made traditional Danish costumes and put together a folk song book. They wrote their own song – then translated it into French – on the senior citizens' new 'Viking Invasion' to France, which they sang to their French hosts. They also brought a puppet theatre.

Fifty-two people, average age 79, went on the nine-day visit and were accommodated in student hostels. On their return, they wrote a report, made a slide show and exhibition and organized a French evening for family and friends. Subsequently, they visited nursing homes and older people's groups with their presentation. Exchanges have also been organized within Denmark and one project Gregersen has tried to introduce is to use older people as tourist guides within Viborg.

The group's interest in health education follows the same pattern. Over the past few years the group has become heavily involved in promoting health education among their peers. The effectiveness of using older people in this way is now coming to be accepted by doctors and other professionals. Groups studied the work of the UN for a week at a folk high school and subsequently made a study tour to Geneva to meet people in the UN offices there, including the World Health Organization (WHO). They have also shown the film they made about this visit to groups in Denmark. From their visits to the WHO, the group became involved in WHO's campaign 'Health for All 2000' and decided to make its own contribution to the campaign in the form of a tape-slide presentation on 'preventing falls'. Members of the group took this presentation to over a hundred older people's groups (each of them often numbering several hundred). The group have also been working on material on healthy eating.

While Gregersen's salary is paid for out of public funds, much of the group's other funds are raised by the members themselves. They get donations from friends and relations when they hold 'evenings' to talk about what they have done. Sometimes they get fees from talks given outside, and for their work as 'resource people' in educational institutions. This money goes to a common fund which helps to subsidize some of the more expensive projects, especially travel. Gregersen is convinced that no one has ever been deterred from joining on a foreign visit on the grounds of cost.

She believes that the study circle for older people, with its emphasis on 'education by doing', provides a vital alternative to traditional activities for older people, often imposed upon them by professionals. She feels it is important for the group themselves to decide what they want to do and the leader should be regarded very much as part of the group. The older people have a great deal to draw on in terms of their life experience and interests and she sees the group very much as the locomotive force. Her job, as she sees it, is to act as the rails – the means of getting where they want to go – by acting as a facilitator and a resource person.

The group is also notable for its outward-looking approach – epitomized by its motto 'out to gather impressions – back to give expression to them'. The international dimension of their work has been particularly important [. . .]. The groups also show vividly how older people can promote information to other older people and how the group can act as a bridge in the transitions associated with later life. As a resource to the community, their contribution is considerable. [. . .]

PENSIONERS' ACTION GROUP EAST, GLASGOW, SCOTLAND

Pensioners' Action Group East (PAGE) covers one area in the East End of Glasgow which shares the deprivation of many inner-city areas. One aspect of this is the large number of older people – of a population of just over 50,000, over-60s make up nearly a quarter. [. . .] Most pensioners are poor, living on the old age pension and many are entitled to additional benefits, though not all claim them. There are a large number of pensioners' groups in the area, including social clubs, lunch clubs and handicapped clubs.

In such areas, social work services have a big role and, traditionally, work with older people in 'East 3' – the PAGE area – had adopted a casework approach, concentrating on the provision of direct services to the elderly. However, in November 1983, the Community Development Team in the Social Work Department started looking at how they could help older people organize themselves to further their own needs and interests, rather than provide direct services. Strategies identified included working with the large number of local community groups to increase participation by older people in community activities and to help older people to come together themselves in 'interest' groups campaigning on specific issues of concern to them.

The potential of this approach had been highlighted by the setting up, earlier that year, of a forum for the elderly in another area of Glasgow – the post-war housing scheme of Castlemilk, on the southern outskirts – which had organized meetings with regional and district officials and councillors and had come to provide a more general voice for pensioners in the area.

Val Dick, Community Development Worker in the Social Work Department, set about identifying key older people within the clubs and organizations in the East End area, with a view to setting up a similar pensioners' action group. By May 1984, a small group of pensioners had begun meeting and it was agreed that the way forward would be to set up a campaigning group which would both make older people more aware of their rights and provide a structure by which older people could organize to take action themselves. Issues identified at this early stage included fuel poverty (the inability to pay for proper heating), health, transport and Post Office closures (pensioners draw their benefits from local post offices).

Meanwhile, in response to interest in the idea of setting up Elderly Forums in other areas of Strathclyde, the Castlemilk group organized a one-day conference, aptly named 'The Sleeping Giant Conference', which aimed to get pensioners from all over Strathclyde together, to encourage them to work in their own areas on campaigns for better services and to form their own forums. This conference, which was attended by members of the group, provided the inspiration and motivation to move forward. In November 1984 a public meeting was called in the area and over one hundred local people turned up. A committee was elected, a name, 'Pensioners' Action Group East', adopted and immediate issues – benefits and post office closures – identified. PAGE was on the move.

During the next six months, the group presented a petition with 3,000 signatures to the local MP, organized a pensioners' day and a campaign against the way in which cold weather allowances were allocated. Since benefits had been identified as an issue, welfare rights training was organized for the committee and a subsequent take-up campaign proved very successful. Training in committee work was also provided for committee members.

It was at this time that the structures within which the group operates became established. A core committee of ten to twelve, undertaking the day-to-day work, meets with the overall membership of over one hundred at two-monthly public meetings, which take major decisions. Information about what the group is doing is sent to all the clubs in the area to keep them up to date on progress. Representatives are also sent to the region-wide Strathclyde Elderly Forum, which grew out of the first 'Sleeping

Giant Conference' in Castlemilk. This now brings together representatives from some thirty similar forums throughout Strathclyde region, and acts as a lobby at regional level.

By the middle of 1986, PAGE was reaching maturity. It had held successful campaigns on the proposed closure of the local washhouse, had successfully fought together with other forums for an extra heating allowance during cold weather, and had produced 2,000 copies of its newsletter. [...]

A great deal of work went into welfare benefits campaigns, in advance of changes in the rules which came into effect in April 1988 on single 'one-off' payments for items such as household furniture, which meant that many people would no longer be able to obtain such items after this date. Members of the group visited and leafleted houses in the area, providing information about when and where local advice workers and members of the group (who had undergone training) would be available. The group, together with local advice workers, also helped with appeals against decisions made by the then Department of Health and Social Security. Close liaison was established with the DHSS. Over 1,000 claims for single payments were made between November 1987 and April 1988.

But the real boost for the group came with the approval of PAGE's Urban Aid application for a full-time support worker, employed by PAGE, and for an Advice and Action Centre for pensioners, run by PAGE members themselves.

Suitable shopfront premises for the Advice and Action Centre opened some time later, conveniently situated next to the local post office. Besides providing a focal point for PAGE's campaigning activities, it also acts as an advice centre, running surgeries on welfare rights, housing and legal issues, for example. With PAGE now having a physical and public location, more and more older people come in, initially seeking help and advice, perhaps, but also developing skills and confidence to help others. Dick – the full-time support worker – hopes that the centre will become more and more involved in researching local issues, feeding reports to the PAGE committee which can pass them on to the Strathclyde Elderly Forum and thereby influence policies at regional level. These include housing and older people, the availability of houshold aids to help less mobile older people do such things as get in and out of the bath, and the needs of older people in residential homes.

Since PAGE started, a whole range of educational needs have been identified and met. Educational inputs have helped members to develop as a committee, enabling them to learn about how to set up a committee, the role of committee members, organization and campaigns, funding and publicity. They have also learnt in practical ways about welfare rights by accompanying welfare rights workers. To help them in their new roles as employers, training has been organized in such areas as management skills, interviewing techniques and the group's legal responsibilities as employer. [. . .]

But perhaps most importantly, the members of the group have developed confidence; they have learned how to believe in themselves – dealing on equal terms with 'authority' represented, for example, by the DHSS, council officials and councillors. Professional support has been important, but it has sought to enable, rather than direct, and has taken the form, for example, of helping the group break down major issues into achievable steps. It has also provided information, advice and training and has helped to identify appropriate resources. In her new role, Val Dick sees herself as continuing to provide advice and support to the group – helping to negotiate the various elements of 'the system', while being clear that it is the group's job actually to take on that work. [. . .]

CONCLUSIONS

The projects were studied on the basis of four particular themes: information projects; transition from working to non-working life and the role of self-help educational programmes; the interaction between older people and the rest of the community; and international exchange projects involving groups of older people.

Most of the projects, however, straddle a number of these themes and, in some cases, all of them. Indeed, in many of the projects, the different themes seem actively to feed off each other. The process of encouraging change is indeed a many-faceted one and the strength of the international dimension is a particulary strong feature.

The projects also highlight problems of definition at a time when the nature of retirement is changing rapidly. [. . .]

There is evidence of a widening and potentially dangerous gap between chronological age, on the one hand, and psychological and sociological age based on stereotypes of retirement on the other, as people withdraw earlier from working life. Many of the projects are attempting to get to grips with the fact that people who retire in their early 50s are in their early 50s not in their 60s.

Another problem of definition concerns adult education itself. Traditionally, education has maintained not only a separate identity, but also a distance between itself and other agencies in the community. However, reflecting the community development approach, the educational dimension in many projects puts the emphasis on learning, rather than teaching, and is often part and parcel of the process of creating agents for change. The Viborg case study, for example, describes a three-stage process – finding out about a topic, practical action, and spreading the results. In this process (which has its echoes in many of the other projects), practical action – whether a visit to another country or talking to schoolchildren about schooldays long ago or even some form of voluntary work – is itself an integral part of the educational process involved in creating change. The whole environment thus becomes a learning resource and the adult education role is to make learning needs explicit and to tailor resources to these needs.

Another issue is the context in which the case studies are situated. The extent to which (and the means by which) older people can be empowered to become the producers or agents of development within their communities is crucially dependent on factors in the wider environment outside. One of these is cost to participants and most of the projects have received public money or other support. In the case of poor older people adequate pensions and other benefits are crucial prerequisites for many processes of development, though – as the case of Pensioners' Action Group East in Glasgow shows – the very lack of them can be a starting point. Participation in some of the international travel and exchange projects described requires substantial financial resources.

Accessibility has other aspects too. Even involvement in projects like study circles depends not merely on financial and physical accessibility, but also on psychological accessibility. This last factor is crucial in translating a mere idea or possibility into action. [...] A favourable legislative, financial and cultural framework thus has a great bearing on the nature and success of the projects undertaken, and further research is required on appropriate forms of this framework.

Author index

Subject index

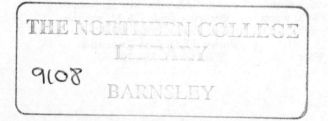